Opus Dei

An Investigation into the Powerful, Secretive Society within the Catholic Church

Michael Walsh

HarperSanFrancisco

A Division of HarperCollinsPublishers

Originally published in Great Britain by Grafton Books.

HarperCollins books may be purchased for educational, business, or sales promotional use. For information please write: Special Markets Department, HarperCollins Publishers, Inc., 10 East 53rd Street, New York, NY 10022.

HarperCollins Web site: http://www.harpercollins.com

HarperCollins®, 👑 ®, and HarperSanFrancisco™ are trademarks of Harper-Collins Publishers, Inc.

FIRST EDITION

Library of Congress Cataloging-in-Publication Data

Walsh, Michael J.
    Opus Dei : an investigation into the powerful, secretive society within the Catholic Church / Michael Walsh.
      p. cm.
    Reprint. Originally published: London : Grafton Books, 1989.
    Includes bibliographical references and index.
    ISBN 0-06-075068-5
    1. Opus Dei (Society)   2. Escrivá de Balaguer, José María, 1902-1975. I. Title.
BX819.3.068W34   1991
267'.182—dc20   88-45677
                                    CIP

04 05 06 07 08 RRD(H) 10 9 8 7 6 5 4 3 2

Contents

Acknowledgments   *v*

Introduction to the Paperback Edition   *vii*

1. In Search of Opus   *1*

2. The Origins of Opus   *21*

3. The Years of Expansion   *43*

4. A Change of Status   *67*

5. The Constitutions of 1982   *81*

6. The Spirit of Opus   *105*

7. Politics and Business   *131*

8. Sectarian Catholicism   *161*

9. The Apotheosis of the Founder   *189*

Notes   *201*

Bibliography   *209*

Index   *217*

Acknowledgments

This book was conceived in London in the autumn of 1983. It has been a long time in the making. My excuse for my dilatoriness was the need to travel to Latin America before I pressed a key of the word-processor, and that journey did not prove possible until the late summer of 1986. I am particularly grateful to all who helped me on my way, especially to Dennis Hackett who had ideas about the air ticket to Lima, and to those who so generously extended their hospitality while I was there: to the Society of St. James the Apostle in Peru, and in particular to John Devine who entertained me in his devastatingly beautiful parish of Huancarama, and who has since become superior of the Society in Peru; to the Columban fathers in Chile and to the Jesuits in Colombia. I should like to say a special word of thanks to Peter Hughes in Lima, to Tim Curtis S.J., then in Bogotá, and above all to Liam Houlihan of the Mill Hill Fathers in Santiago, in whose shanty-town parish I came to have some small inkling of what it was like to live beneath the brutal regime of General Pinochet.

The book would never have been written without the especial assistance of four former members of Opus Dei—Fr. Vladimir Felzmann, Dr. John Roche, María del Carmen Tapia, and Professor Raimundo Pannikar, whom I met in London, Oxford, New York, and Oxford in that order. In Pittsburgh I met Suzanne Rinni, who put me up at her house. Mrs. Roz Fishman and her husband Harry—who has alas since died—

were kind enough to let me use their delightful house in Fairfield, Connecticut, as a base during one of my forays into the United States.

In Washington I owe special thanks to Arthur Jones of the *National Catholic Reporter,* in Madrid to Pedro Lamet, lately of *Vida Nueva* as the text relates, and to John Hill in Sydney, Australia. In England many were kind enough to keep me supplied with information: John Wilkins of *The Tablet,* Nick Stuart-Jones of Thames Television, Robert Nowell of a variety of publications, Eduardo Crawley of *Latin American Newsletter,* Clifford Longley of *The Times,* and Peter Hebblethwaite, who might be said to have started the whole thing off nearly twenty years ago when he asked me to write an article. In addition the book owes a great deal to the diligence of Meryl Davies, once of the BBC, who kindly put into my hands fascinating material she had not been able to use in a program she produced. Ms. Elizabeth Lowe helped me with company reports.

A large number of people volunteered information when they heard about the enterprise on which I was embarked: some are named in the text, others—like the archbishop who is quoted, or the headmistress of a public school—have to remain anonymous. Opus Dei appears to have touched the lives of an extraordinary range of Roman Catholics for good or ill—usually for the latter. I am grateful to all who have spoken to me about their experiences, and I hope this book will go some way to setting the record straight.

Introduction to the Paperback Edition

On July 6, 2001, FBI agent Robert Hanssen pleaded guilty to more than a dozen counts of espionage. Inspired, apparently, by the shady career of the British double agent Kim Philby, for almost twenty years Hanssen had sold secrets to Russia. He had earned from his Russian masters some $1.4 million in cash and diamonds. Hanssen, who almost always dressed in black, thus earning the nickname "Doctor Death" among his FBI colleagues, was a most unlikely Russian spy. He was a regular, churchgoing, highly conservative Catholic. His wife and six children were avid participants in pro-life, anti-abortion rallies. The children attended private Catholic schools associated with the shadowy Catholic institute Opus Dei. Indeed, one of his wife's brothers is an Opus Dei priest, and one daughter a full, or numerary, member of the organization. The scandal of Hanssen's activities once again focused attention on Opus, attention they do not welcome.[1]

As this book that follows demonstrates, there have been other strange affairs involving Opus Dei members—though not, one has to say, involving Opus as an institution. But these incidents have served to put Opus in a lurid light, so much so that when Dan Brown was searching for a villainous Catholic organization for his novel *The Da Vinci Code* he looked to Opus. I also rather suspect that Opus Dei provided the model for the sinister-seeming religious order in Donna Leon's Venice-set detective novel *The Death of Faith*.

My book was written in the mid-1980s (the British edition appeared in 1989). At the time, Opus was little known outside Spain and parts of Latin America, except to those who took a quasi-professional interest in the doings of the Roman Catholic Church. Certainly it was little known in the United States outside a fairly small circle, as I discovered when I went to Washington, DC, in search of information. Now it is much more widely known, with some three thousand members in the United States, approximately a third of whom are full, or numerary, members, making promises of poverty, chastity, and obedience similar to the vows taken in religious orders. Those who are numeraries give all of their earnings to the institute, which helps to account for its apparent wealth (it has recently opened a new seventeen-story headquarters in Manhattan).

Partly because of the activities of some of its less reputable members, partly because of its wealth, partly because of its aggressively conservative stance in matters theological such as are recounted in this book, and partly because of its privileged status in the Church, with its members under the authority of the head ("Prelate") of Opus Dei in Rome, currently Javier Echeverria Rodriguez, Opus has incurred considerable hostility within the Church. It has, of course, its supporters—including Pope John Paul II himself—but its Catholic critics have been vociferous. It is little wonder, then, that Opus wanted to bring about as soon as possible the canonization of its founder, Josemaría Escrivá de Balaguer. There are many reasons for wanting someone canonized: the public, Vatican blessing on the life of an institute's founder and on his or her writings and form of spirituality is certainly one of them. After a canonization, critics can always be met with the response that the founder has the accolade of saint, and the full approval of the Holy See.

Escrivá de Balaguer was canonized on October 6, 2002. In the plethora of canonizations conducted by John Paul II, who has created more saints than all his predecessors put together, this event passed relatively unnoticed except by members of Opus. After Escrivá's beatification, the first step to canonization, sainthood seemed inevitable. The major controversy surrounded the beatification process, as some of Opus's opponents mounted a spirited campaign to prevent it.

The beatification of the founder of Opus Dei took place on May 17, 1992, as the American edition of this book was being finally prepared for publication. Italy, then in the grip of one of its recurrent political crises, was represented at the ceremony by its acting president. Former presidents of Venezuela and Colombia were there, as well as a number of members of Opus—Luis Valls and Laureano López Rodó, for example—who appear elsewhere in this book. In all it is estimated that 200,000 attended the service in St. Peter's Square. Some of those who came to Rome, admitted Joaquín Navarro Valls, the Opus Dei numerary who is the Vatican's chief spokesman, would take years to pay off the debts they incurred by making the journey.[2] Opus had determined that this beatification was to be an occasion to be remembered, the most remarkable ever. In all the furor, the fact that Pope John Paul II beatified at the same time a Sudanese nun who had once been sold into slavery was almost forgotten.[3]

But if the occasion was memorable for its splendor, it was no less remarkable for the debate surrounding it. No other similar event in living memory aroused so much controversy. According to *Newsweek* magazine, even an eighty-two-year-old Italian cardinal, Silvio Oddi, renowned as much for the conservatism of his views as for the bluntness with which he expressed them, voiced doubts about the wisdom of proceeding with the beatification. It would, he was quoted as saying, do Opus Dei more harm than good. The Opus press office in Rome promptly claimed that "Cardinal Oddi categorically denies having spoken to anyone from *Newsweek* and of making the statements attributed to him in the article." The Cardinal himself, however, later confirmed to a journalist from *The Catholic World Report* that he had indeed talked to someone from *Newsweek,* and that he continued to believe the beatification at that moment was ill-advised. He was, he added, personally convinced of the holiness of Mgr. Escrivá de Balaguer.[4]

Complaints about the beatification were nowhere more cogently put than by Kenneth Woodward in a press conference held in Rome on April 30. Woodward was religion editor at

Newsweek: more significantly in this context, he is the author of a major book about the process of determining to whom the title of saint should be accorded.[5] His criticisms were all the more telling because they came from someone with a detailed knowledge of procedures within the Congregation for the Causes of Saints.

Of the nine judges to whom it eventually fell to decide upon Escrivá's suitability for beatification, two were in favor at least of delaying the process, claimed Woodward, and this was an unusually high proportion. Clearly it was an embarrassment, a fact that Opus at first attempted to disguise. It was claimed, wrongly, that there had been unanimity. Finally, and on a technicality, only one "no" vote was recorded.

Second, argued Woodward, there had been so much haste that it was impossible within the time available to produce a rounded, mature portrait of Escrivá. Certainly in the weeks before the beatification some surprising charges were made, most particularly by Vladimir Felzmann, who claimed, from personal knowledge, that Escrivá was sympathetic to Hitler; that because of his distress at what had happened to the Roman Catholic Church since Vatican II he had considered joining the Greek Orthodox Church; and that he had a far from saintly bad temper (only one such loss of control was permitted to be recorded in the documents that went forward to the Congregation for the Causes of Saints).[6]

Felzmann himself was never interviewed by those looking into Escrivá's suitability for the title of "Blessed," granted to those who are beatified. Several other hostile witnesses were also not interviewed. Woodward claimed that attempts were made to discredit them. A note to explain why certain witnesses had not been heard was included in the documents, but when the journalist and Vatican expert Robert Moynihan asked to see it he was refused.[7] One person who *did* give evidence—great masses of it—was the late Mgr. Alvaro del Portillo, Escrivá de Balaguer's successor as head of Opus. His doing so, under present ecclesiastical legislation, was illegal, for he had regularly heard Escrivá's confession. His evidence was admitted, however, because he claimed to be able to distinguish what he learned in the confessional from what he had observed in daily encounters.[8]

A BBC television documentary broadcast the evening after the ceremony subjected the procedures of the Congregation for the Causes of Saints to close examination. There appeared in it Fr. Ambrose Eszer, an amiable Dominican and one of the Congregation's senior officials, or *relatores*. Fr. Eszer had been the person chiefly responsible within the Congregation for steering the cause of Mgr. Escrivá to a satisfactory conclusion. There also appeared the tall and elegant Mgr. Flavio Capucci, Opus Dei's own "postulator." It had been his task as postulator to ensure that the institution's founder found his way as a saint into the ranks of the officially holy.

The documentary's producers had wanted also to interview Peter Gumpel, a Jesuit priest of long experience in the Congregation who was described as the Congregation's "most distinguished, reliable, objective, and knowledgeable man." Gumpel had been, said the program, first advised, then warned, and finally instructed not to appear. The same prohibition clearly did not apply to avowed supporters of the cause.

So great was the volume of protest that the Vatican felt obliged to defend its handling of the case. The pope, said a statement released less than a week before the date set for the beatification, had asked a special commission to decide whether the ceremony should go ahead. The commission had come down in favor. During the service Pope John Paul II praised Escrivá as "an exemplary priest who succeeded in opening up new apostolic horizons of missionary and evangelizing activity."

The then head of Opus, Mgr. Alvaro del Portillo (some time later raised to the rank of bishop),[9] declared that "our founder's message and example are not just for a few but for millions of men and women until the end of time." Mgr. Flavio Capucci asserted that protesters against the beatification were ecclesiastical dissidents. We have their names and surnames, he claimed, and we have spoken to their bishops. Those who criticize the beatification are people who cause trouble to the Church in doctrinal matters as well.[10] The oft-repeated charge that Opus constitutes a "church within the Church" is mistaken. From the perspective of Mgr. Capucci, it would appear, Opus Dei and the Church are to be identified.

This is an extraordinary and arrogant claim. As readers of this book will discover, however, it was not an untypical example of the attitude of Opus Dei's members toward the Church. In 1986, at least in Britain, the institute asked that its members might be dispensed from the fast of Good Friday, that most solemn of days in the Church's calendar, because in that particular year it fell on the anniversary of Mgr. Escrivá's ordination to the priesthood. Members treat that day as a birthday, a spokesman explained. Their request was granted by the Vatican: a feast of the founder of Opus apparently took precedence over the fast to commemorate the death of the founder of Christianity.[11]

But that was back in the 1980s. Has the institute, now with a membership of about 85,000 (twice as many as the Jesuits), changed over the intervening years? Readers of the fictionalized portrayal in *The Da Vinci Code* and of the more sensationalized accounts of Robert Hanssen's shocking double life might well doubt it. But nonetheless, I believe there have been changes. In 1990, for instance, there was published *El itinerario jurídico del Opus Dei: historia y defensa de un carisma,* an account, albeit a defensive one, of its development as an institute within the Catholic Church. While there are schools and after-school programs for children associated with Opus Dei, its membership recruiting efforts focus on college students and pious adults.

As its amiable spokesman in London has admitted to me, in the past Opus's public relations were a disaster. Perhaps it is now trying to mend fences; it is perhaps becoming more open.

I was moved to write this book because as a (I would like to think) liberal-minded Catholic I was concerned to explore, and expose, an organization that was actively promoting a very conservative agenda, both socially and ecclesiastically. Opus is still promoting a conservative agenda, and, as time has gone on, it has become better placed to do so. There are at least half a dozen of its members at work within the Curia, the Vatican's bureaucracy. There are now two Opus Dei cardinals: Julián Herranz, who appears elsewhere in this book and is currently president of the Pontifical Council for the Interpretation of Legislative Texts (more or less the Church's attorney general), and Juan Luis Cipriani, the Archbishop of Lima. Neither of these is considered a likely choice for the papacy at the next conclave, whenever that may be, although Cardinal Tettamanzi—an outspoken admirer of Escrivá and Opus Dei—has been touted as a leading conservative papal candidate. Other possible candidates are thought to be sympathetic to Opus, but then, so too is Pope John Paul II. And while there are two Opus cardinals, there are nine Jesuit ones and rather more Jesuits in significant positions in the Curia—but no one thinks that at all sinister.

When I wrote this book I suggested that Opus was sectarian, an institute that, while claiming to be Catholic, was at odds with the Catholic Church. I no longer think that—at least, not quite in the same way. The present pope, in his quarter-of-a-century pontificate, has molded a Church that is, to my mind, on the way to becoming a sect. That is a point of view, but it is, I admit, beyond dispute that John Paul II's vision of the Church has much in common with that of St. Josemaría Escrivá de Balaguer.

There was an illuminating comment from the U.S. spokesman for Opus when questioned, in the aftermath of the Hanssen affair, about the secrecy of the institute. "We have just built a seventeen-story headquarters in New York," he said. "How can you operate a secret society from a skyscraper at 34th and Lexington?"[12] Fair point. It is just that many Catholics would think that a seventeen-story skyscraper on a prime site in downtown New York City is not what a Church, which has officially committed itself to the poor in our society, should be building. Opus, it would seem, has not after all departed far from the mind-set that is examined in the remainder of this book, which is presented here as I published it in 1992, except for the Afterword in that edition, which I have replaced with this new updating Introduction, and some minor editorial adjustments in the text.

Heythrop College,
University of London, 2004

1. See, for example, "Opus Dei in the Open: A Shadowy 'Church within the Church' Gets Its Saint," by Kenneth Woodward, *Newsweek International,* October 7, 2002; "A Question of Why: Contradictory Portrait Emerges of Spying Suspect," by Carol Morello and William Claiborne, *The Washington Post,* February 25, 2001.

2. Cf. the report in *The Tablet,* May 23, 1992, pp. 655–56.

3. Josephine Bakhita, beatified at the same time as Escrivá de Balaguer, was in the end canonized before him.

4. The journalist was Robert Moynihan. His account, "In search of 'the Father,'" appears in *The Catholic World Report,* May 1992, pp. 10–23.

5. *Making Saints,* (New York: Simon and Schuster, 1990, and London: Chatto and Windus, 1991.)

6. His bad temper is several times recorded in María del Carmen Tapia's *Beyond the Threshold: A Life in Opus Dei* (New York: Continuum, 1998), a memoir by his longtime secretary, who left Opus Dei.

7. Moynihan, "In Search of 'the Father,'" p. 15.

8. There is a summary, though only a summary, of Woodward's press conference in *The Tablet,* May 2, 1992, p. 556.

9. Alvaro del Portillo, 1914–94. He was ordained a bishop, by John Paul II himself, in January 1991. He is now a candidate for eventual canonization.

10. An interview with Miguel Angel Velasco in *Vida Nueva,* issue 1837/8, April 11–18, 1992, pp. 36–42. The words of Capucci to which reference is made occur on p. 36.

11. The English Catholic weekly *The Universe,* April 4, 1986.

12. Quoted by Ron Grossman in *The Chicago Tribune,* December 15, 2003.

1

In Search of Opus

It is only some 200 kilometers from Cuzco, Peru's second city and former capital of the Incas, to the town of Abancay, yet so bad was the road that my journey in a Toyota land cruiser took all of ten hours. Abancay itself is a frontier town, deep in the Andes. Soldiers guard the entrances. Its inhabitants prefer to drive jeep-type vehicles or pick-up trucks, if they can afford any vehicle at all. Only a handful of the streets are metaled roads; most are little more than dirt tracks.

The building I had come to visit was just off one of these tracks. The wall around it was broken by an imposing gateway. Inside the wall there were a swimming pool and elegant flower beds. Two fountains were playing, one into a basin containing goldfish. I visited one of the two chapels standing in the garden. Behind the altar, set in an elaborate gold frame, there was a picture of the Holy Family: Mary and Joseph teaching Jesus to walk. It was painted in the Cuzceña style derived from the art the Spanish conquistadores had brought to Peru in the sixteenth century. The contrast between the world I had entered when I passed under the gateway arch, and the world along the dirt track outside could hardly have been greater. This was like the hacienda of some wealthy landowner. It was, in fact, a seminary, a place for training Roman Catholic clergy.

I was visiting it at the suggestion of Ken Duncan, an aid and development consultant who had heard that I was interested in the Catholic organization Opus Dei. Duncan, not himself a Catholic, had been taken aback by the activities of Opus in Peru and wanted to tell his experiences to someone who might draw attention to what he saw as unacceptable behavior on the part of the Opus clergy.

Despite its isolation I was able to make my way to Abancay and call at the seminary, the luxury of which, when compared with the bitter poverty of the people outside its walls, Duncan had found scandalous. The seminary, run by a handful of Opus Dei clergy from Spain in well-cut soutanes—the long black gown which was once the everyday wear of Catholic priests in Europe—was just as Duncan had described it. Like him, I was startled by the contrast between the poverty and squalor outside the walls and the comfort within, and by the incongruity of finding such an institution in the depths of the Andes.

Ken Duncan had often worked with Catholic organizations. He had high praise for many of them. He was, however, alarmed at the growing influence of Opus in Peru. He was even more alarmed when I told him of the size and complexity of Opus around the world, at least three times the size of the Society of Jesus (the Jesuits) which has hitherto been considered the Roman Catholic Church's most influential religious order.

My own interest in Opus had first been aroused by an apologia for it which had appeared at the end of May 1971 in the color supplement of the *Sunday Times*. The paper had, apparently, published a hostile piece on the organization, which had demanded, and received, the right to reply. My attention was drawn to the pro-Opus article by Peter Hebblethwaite, then still, as I was, a member of the Society of Jesus and editor of *The Month*, the Jesuits' journal published from the Society's British headquarters in London's Mayfair. I wrote occasionally for Hebblethwaite, and he suggested I investigate the organization.

I had known little of Opus Dei before I started to research my piece. Its name gave little away. Opus Dei—the Work of God—had hitherto been most commonly used within the Roman Catholic Church to describe the prayers which monks sing in common at morning and night. Members of Opus regularly referred to it as "the Work," which sounded a somewhat provisional title. It has been suggested that its founder, Escrivá de Balaguer, had at one time thought of calling it the Sociedad de Cooperación Intelectual, or SOCOIN, though nothing came of the idea.[1]

In its early years in Spain in the 1930s it appears to have been little more than a group of Catholic lay men and women who continued in their own jobs, but frequently lived in small communities and were bound together by solemn promises if not by the formal vows taken by members of religious orders. The chief cement of their Christian fellowship was the form of spiritual guidance provided by their founder, Escrivá. This was best encapsulated in a little book of 999 maxims called *Camino (The Way)*. It all seemed fairly harmless.

I swiftly learned, however, that its alleged political role in Franco's Spain, its secrecy, its apparent success, its methods of operation, had all aroused great interest—and considerable hostility—both from within the Roman Catholic Church and outside it. *The Economist* referred to it fairly often in the 1960s and 1970s, and insisted on calling its members "Opusdeistas" as if they constituted a political party, something they bitterly resented. Even *The Times Literary Supplement,* a sober journal hardly given to polemics on Church affairs, had carried a hostile article on one of its center pages in April 1971 under the title "The Power of the Party: Opus Dei in Spain."

My interest was caught, partly because I was a Hispanophil and Spain was clearly the country which had the greatest concentration of members of Opus and where its influence was greatest; and partly because I was at that time a Jesuit and Opus was frequently being compared, and comparing itself, to the Society of Jesus. Not since the Society had been founded by Ignatius Loyola in the mid-sixteenth century had a religious organization within the Roman Catholic Church aroused such controversy, or risen so swiftly (so it appeared) to influence in both Church and State. And Opus had, consciously it seemed at the time, copied the Society in the work it was trying to do within the Church, in particular the education of the Roman Catholic élite. This time, however, the élite was not distinguished by birth but, more in keeping with the spirit of the twentieth century perhaps, selected mainly by wealth gained through commerce.

When my first article about Opus Dei was published in *The Month* in August 1971, I called it "Being Fair to Opus Dei." I felt it was fair because, for the most part, I had avoided what had been said about them by their detractors and limited myself to Opus's own productions—particularly the 1950 Constitution and the 999 maxims of Escrivá de Balaguer as contained in *Camino.*

Not surprisingly, perhaps, Opus did not think it fair. A few months after the piece appeared I arranged an interview with the Opus spokesman in Madrid. The meeting was to take place in the private flat of some friends. The Opus spokesman arrived just after lunch. He would not have a coffee. He would not sit down. He simply berated me for the injustice which he believed I had perpetrated against Opus, then stormed out.

Reaction in England was rather more subdued. Several

people I did not know solicited a visit. I managed to avoid meeting them. Then a gentle antique dealer from Norfolk found his way to my office on the grounds that he was a close friend of a friend of mine. He too took me to task, but more in sorrow than in anger. I had, he told me, totally failed to capture the spirit of Opus Dei. I was not unwilling to be corrected on points where I had gone astray. He mentioned one purely technical matter which was not of great importance. I asked him about the spirituality: had I got it right? He told me I had not, so I asked for examples. He was lost, and I suspected that the conversation was not going according to his brief. I tried to help him. I had worked from documents, I remarked, and I was aware that they could be misleading: one had only to think of an examination syllabus which, in the abstract, always looks so daunting but can usually be reduced to a reasonable size. Opus Dei's spiritual syllabus looked daunting but, I said, I suspected that living with it was a good deal easier than at first appeared. He eagerly agreed with the analogy. But when I asked him to give some examples of where the syllabus and the practice diverged, he was again at a loss. I tried to help him out of his embarrassed silence. "For instance," I said, "the Constitution states that you must all sprinkle your beds with holy water before you lie down to sleep at nights. I am sure you don't do that?" Again the embarrassment. "Yes we do," he replied. "After all, chastity is a very difficult virtue."

More than a decade later, a former member of the organization, Dr. John Roche of Linacre College, Oxford, told me that "Being Fair to Opus Dei" was the first thing he had read without previously asking permission since he had joined. It struck him, he said, as being as close to the spirit of Opus as it was possible to be without having been a member.

In the early 1970s little seems to have been available in English about the organization and aims of Opus. Hence my article found its way into libraries of cuttings. When an Opus story broke I was rung up by newspapers, television producers, radio researchers, and I therefore was able to keep in touch with events concerning the institution. When I began, years later, to do the research for this book, I quickly discovered that some distinguished Roman Catholics thought that Opus Dei was one of the major issues within the Catholic Church at the present time. José Comblin, a well-known Belgian priest who has spent most of his working life in Latin America, wrote to me from Brazil to say exactly that. In the cloisters of St. George's Chapel, Windsor Castle, on a wet April evening in 1986 the Swiss-born theologian Hans Küng talked to me at length and gave me a string of names of people to contact.

More recently I heard from a friend in Australia of the extraordinary events surrounding the publication of two pieces about Opus in the daily newspaper *The Australian;* he told me stories of computer codes being broken and Opus knowing about the articles even before the (supposedly secret) articles had appeared. Rather more sadly, in November 1987 Pedro Miguel Lamet was sacked from his post as editor of the Spanish religious weekly *Vida Nueva*. Under the editorship of Pedro, an old friend from my Jesuit days, this journal had become possibly the best of its kind in Europe, if not the world. As well as citing the hostility to *Vida Nueva* of the papal nuncio (the Pope's ambassador) in Madrid, Pedro blamed the antagonism and the power of Opus for his dismissal by the company which owned the paper.[2]

Lamet's fate is indicative of the power which Opus wields in the higher echelons of the Church. There is an increasing number of Opus bishops—though their percentage of the overall figure, well over 2,000 worldwide, is quite small. There are, perhaps, less than a dozen. More important is the influence they have in the papal curia, the Pope's Rome-based civil service. "Vatican-ologists," that small group of journalists who understand the convoluted inner workings of the curia, note with care the rise and fall—usually the rise—of ecclesiastical bureaucrats who, with their traditionally conservative outlook, are friendly toward Opus. They note, too, the more direct influence of the organization through its members' service as consultors to congregations (Vatican-speak for advisers to papal ministries), such as that for the Causes of Saints (they are very eager to have their founder declared a saint) or the Congregation of Bishops. Pope John Paul II also seems to be in sympathy with Opus, and in

1982 granted the organization a new legal status which made it unique within the Roman Catholic Church and, for all practical purposes, an autonomous entity.

When I told Catholic friends that I was engaged on this study, they humorously advised I increase my life insurance. But, joking aside, I have been astonished by the range and the reach of Opus. More than a dozen years after "Being Fair to Opus Dei" appeared, a friend in the United States arranged a meeting for me with his uncle, a member of Opus. The meeting could take place only after the uncle had asked permission of a certain Fr. Kennedy, a priest of Opus. "We know about him," Kennedy was reported to have said, "he is hostile, but you had better see him." Later, in Washington I went to see Russell Shaw, then spokesman for the American Catholic Bishops, and a member of Opus. He had also spoken to Fr. Kennedy. When I eventually met Kennedy himself he did not appear to think such behavior on the part of grown men as in any way strange. I found it exceedingly strange that an organization which claims to concern itself solely with the things of the spirit should so interfere in the personal lives of its members that they had to seek advice before they could see me. Indeed, I find it sinister.

But this is all part of the secrecy—Opus would prefer to call it discretion—which surrounds the organization. Its members do not wear any special dress or badge. Even during Church occasions they are required not to present themselves as a group. A member will admit to belonging, but will not say who else belongs. Their numbers likewise are not to be revealed, though a document prepared before Opus's most recent (1982) change of status in the Church then admitted to some 70,000 worldwide, about two percent of whom are priests. In the UK there are thought to be 300 to 400 members, and some 2,500 in the United States, with what Russell Shaw describes as "a corporate existence" in about a dozen cities.[3] Not all these are full members. Roughly 30 percent are full members or "numeraries," another 20 percent being "oblates" with similar commitments to numeraries but living outside Opus residences. The other half, "supernumeraries," have a rather more tenuous connection, though they are still governed by Opus's Constitution.

The obligation of secrecy extends in particular to the Constitution: in normal circumstances not even members used to be allowed to see it. María del Carmen Tapia, who was for ten years in charge of the women's section in Venezuela, did not have a copy of her own.[4] When on more than one occasion she needed to consult the Constitution she was lent it under strict conditions that she should return it promptly. In Washington I took the opportunity of asking Russell Shaw whether he had seen the Constitution. He said he had not. Then I asked him whether he was accustomed to joining organizations of which he had not read the rules. He did not, however, find this odd. He added later that he finds such documents dull reading.

The Constitution, then, was not on the library shelf of every Opus center. It was not even—as are, for instance, the constitutions of the Jesuits—a subject of study to the members of the organization as one might have expected. The new Constitution of 1982 was, however, made available to every diocesan bishop within whose territory Opus Dei was operating. Indeed, in some places at least, the local Opus director made a formal occasion of handing the document over to the bishop.

Knowing this, I inquired of a number of friendly bishops whether they could let me have sight of the document. The first thing I discovered was that the Constitution had been handed over to the diocesan bishop, and to him alone. Assistant bishops, who might have charge of an area of the diocese in which Opus had established centers, did not receive a copy. Then I discovered that the copy of the Constitution which I had most expectations of seeing had gone missing. It is not, admittedly, a very bulky volume.

Though I knew it had been reproduced in a Spanish periodical in mid-1986, I had begun to give up hope of laying hands easily on a copy, when one turned up in somewhat puzzling circumstances. I work in a college of the University of London. Entering my office one morning it was there—a photocopy of seventy-seven sheets representing twice that number of pages—sitting on a shelf. There was no note, no compliments slip. So many thanks now to my unknown benefactor.

After studying its two main Constitutions, there were very many more things about Opus that I found disturbing: these will be the subject of the rest of this book. But part of my own hostility toward Opus perhaps springs from a sense of disappointment.

At least since the end of the third century there has always been a form of "religious life" in the Catholic Church. That is to say, men and women have (usually) voluntarily chosen to live their lives in a way which seems to take the text of the Christian gospel rather more literally than is generally done. At first they led solitary lives as hermits in the desert. Then they came together to form groups, or communities, under the supervision of an abbot or abbess. Originally such communities dwelt in remote places, and there remain groups who have continued to do so, but gradually religious houses moved from the countryside into the towns, and monks mixed with lay people to some extent, while remaining for the most part tied to one place. Then came the friars who, like monks, said prayers together and met for daily mass, but who mingled much more freely with people and moved from place to place. After them came the "clerks regular," such as the Jesuits. They did not say prayers together or, generally, hear mass together. And, unlike monks, nuns, and friars, they did not wear any special dress, beyond that of the clergy. They therefore could mix with people much more easily. But they were still priests and bound by the vows of poverty, chastity, and obedience to their superior by which, traditionally, this stricter following of the gospel has been enshrined.

Opus, it seemed at first sight, was different. Religious life, whatever that may mean, has hitherto been limited to those prepared to take the vows: single people prepared to opt for celibacy for the rest of their lives. Though the catchment area, as it were, had broadened from those who spent their years as hermits in the desert to those who lived in town houses and identified closely with ordinary people, members of such groups or religious orders were very far from being themselves ordinary people. I understood it to be the special mark, or charism, of Opus that it provided a form of religious life in a broad sense for a much wider variety of person, whether married or single. In other words, I took it to be a natural extension of the development of religious life within the Church. I was soon disillusioned. Unlike many of the great religious orders within the Roman Catholic Church, it has become increasingly priest-dominated, narrow in outlook, and ultra-conservative.

Vladimir Felzmann, an Englishman of Czech origin, joined Opus in 1959 and was ordained a priest ten years later. He left the organization early in 1982 and now works as a priest in the diocese of Westminster, which covers London north of the Thames. Like many people who leave authoritarian religious movements or sects such as the Unification Church (the Moonies), Krishna Consciousness, or the Divine Light Mission,[5] Felzmann retains a strong affection for the founder of Opus Dei, Josemaría Escrivá de Balaguer, whom he knew well and worked with in Opus's Rome headquarters, while rejecting the organization he founded:

> The founder had outstanding qualities of leadership. He inspired. Like any great leader he was hard and he was soft. He had a dense intensity of what psychologists would call the masculine and the feminine, the *animus* and *anima*. He was marvelously human. He attracted by his strength and sense of direction—his faith—as much as by his vulnerability and warmth. He could be icy harsh and as soft as any mother. Impetuous, emotional, passionate, he counterbalanced these natural qualities with the abstract strength of ideals, discipline, will-power, order, dogma, and performance. He was wise enough to choose men with these latter qualities to be his closest coworkers in Rome. As he aged, their influence grew. When he died they tried to preserve what had just stopped breathing. The founder's "spirit" has become fossilized, cold.[6]

To members of Opus, Escrivá was a prophet with a direct, divine inspiration which continued "until his death or, as Opus Dei would prefer to call it, 'our father's transition to heaven' in 1975. . . . As he is a saint, the members are taught, his way is safe and his followers certain of heaven to the extent they identify themselves with him."[7]

Canonization is usually a lengthy process whereby a man or woman is officially recognized by the Roman Catholic Church as a saint. Thomas More, Lord Chancellor of England, who died for his faith in the reign of King Henry VIII, had to wait four centuries before his holiness was formally acknowledged by the Church. Those who are promoting the "cause" of the would-be saint have to be able to demonstrate that he or she is already prayed to, regarded as a saint, is asked for cures of sickness or help in difficulties, and that miracles have been worked through the potential saint's intercession.

For those who have been prominent in the Church through their teachings and writings, the scrutiny conducted first at local level and then by the central authorities of the Church in Rome (the Congregation for the Causes of Saints is the relevant department) is even more rigorous. All books and papers have to be inspected and reports studied. The least whiff of any teaching or belief which does not wholly square with the teaching of the Roman Catholic Church, and the candidate for canonization will be barred. Though there have been cases when the sanctity of an individual has been so manifest to all that the system can be short-circuited, the process is usually long drawn out. Opus does not intend to allow that to happen to the cause of their founder, and one can understand their concern.

Opus is not simply a new religious body, it is a new form of institution within the Roman Catholic Church, as the long search for an appropriate juridical status amply demonstrates. In order to be recognized as a legitimate institution, one which has the full approval of the Holy See and of the Church at large, it not only needs the formal approval of its legal position within the Church, it also requires recognition that the founder was a holy man, on a par with the great saints such as Francis, Dominic, or Ignatius of Loyola, the founder of the Society of Jesus.

All this is no doubt very laudable, but it makes for complications when trying to present a straightforward account of the life of Escrivá. Opus is in control of information about him. The books that it authorizes are, quite naturally, hagiographic in intent. The two most important are Salvador Bernal's *Msgr Josemaría Escrivá de Balaguer, Profile of the Founder of Opus Dei,* published in London and New York by Scepter in 1977 (just a year after it had first appeared in Spanish), and, more recently, a life by a former Spanish information attaché in London, Andrés Vázquez de Prada, *El Fundador del Opus Dei.* This was produced in Madrid by Ediciones Rialp in 1983. The publisher's blurb describes it as the "first extensive biography appearing in Spanish." Both Rialp and Scepter are, of course, Opus Dei-related publishing houses. Both authors are members of Opus, though in the biographies of neither reproduced in the books is this pertinent detail mentioned. Though there is at least one hostile—and satirical—little study,[8] there seem to be no works that attempt an unbiased assessment of Escrivá de Balaguer. It is not hard to discover why.

Opus is determined that as far as possible every portrait of its Founder will present him as a perfect candidate for the honor of official sainthood. He has to be seen as a person who was specially chosen by God for the supreme mission of founding Opus. He must be regarded as not only heroically holy, outstanding in all the virtues, but as wise and learned as well.

To take an example from Vázquez de Prada's book. Early on, he recalls talking to Escrivá de Balaguer during one of the latter's visits to London. Vázquez de Prada was about to write a biography of the English statesman and now saint, Thomas More. He asked Escrivá's advice. "You will have to enter into his personality," he was told, or, perhaps more accurately if somewhat freer, "You will have to get under his skin." Now this excellent advice is hardly original. However, my criticism is not of the banality of the advice but of what Vázquez then does with it. It becomes the opening sentence of this text. He treats it almost as if it were a remarkable revelation.

Vázquez then continues with his opening chapter of which he is clearly proud. He read it, Vladimir Felzmann recalls, to an expectant gathering of members of Opus in London. The chapter is a meditation upon the day on which Opus Dei was born, 2 October 1928. It was the day, he reveals, that Louis von Pastor, the great historian of the modern papacy, died in Paris. It was the eighty-first birthday of von Hindenburg, president of Germany, and the day that martial law was declared in Albania. It is a little difficult to account for this extraordinary performance, dragged out as it is at some length (Vázquez has even discovered what was showing at the cinemas in Madrid), unless it is to situate the event as if at some providential turning-point in the history of the world.

Opus began at a precise place and a precise time. It happened suddenly, "like a divine seed falling from heaven," says Vázquez. The founder was afterward to claim that it was entirely a thing of God's, that he was only a hindrance. A sign of his humility, urges Vázquez. Maybe so, but it also isolates Escrivá de Balaguer as a divinely chosen vehicle for divinely chosen purposes. Even Escrivá's refusal to talk about it all, recorded by Vázquez, sets him, and the foundation of Opus Dei, apart from normal life. The context in which his Opus biographers present him is not that of a mere mortal.

Bernal exemplifies the same style. Again at the very beginning of his book he tells a story of a priest who met Escrivá de Balaguer in November 1972. "I had to keep making acts of faith, to remind myself that I was in the presence of the Founder of Opus Dei," he is quoted as saying. Bernal is emphasizing his ordinariness, but the point of the story is that he was *expected* to be different. The image is being constructed of a man who is other—a saint. That is the background against which readers are expected to read his life. So when Vázquez insists that his task is to "trace the connection between [Escrivá's] public behavior and his deepest attitudes," that is just the task which the hagiographical approach to the Founder renders practically impossible.

Oddly enough, however, the first problem to face anyone writing this life is deciding upon the subject's name. Hitherto I have referred to him as Escrivá de Balaguer. According to the entry in the baptismal register of the church where he was christened, his surname was spelled "Escriba," but even during his school days José Maria adopted the rather more distinguished version spelled with a "v" rather than a "b," which, in Spanish, sounds exactly the same.

In June 1940 the family, which was then known as Escrivá y Albas, arguing that Escrivá was too common a name to distinguish it, petitioned that in future they should be known as Escrivá de Balaguer y Albas—though for the next twenty-odd years the "y Albas" was mostly ignored.

Up to this point, José Maria had been plain José Maria. In 1960 he began to sign himself Josemaría. Then, in 1968, he petitioned for, and was granted the title of Marques de Peralta. It was a curious thing to do, and his biographers claim that he pursued the title only after consulting with curial cardinals, Cardinal dell'Acqua, the Pope's Vicar for Rome and a close friend, and the Spanish Cardinal Larraona. He also told various other ecclesiastical dignitaries, including the papal Secretariat of State.

Some members believe the title had been solicited for the sake of his brother Santiago. Escrivá's own excuse, expressed in a letter to the Opus Dei councillor in Madrid, was that his family had suffered greatly in preparing him for his ministry, and this title was a form of recompense. Whatever the explanation, to petition for the revival, or grant, of a title of nobility would seem to be untypical of someone whose fundamental humility is among the virtues his supporters list as his case proceeds for canonization. Particularly so, in the light of Maxim 677 of his spiritual treatise *Camino:* "Honors, distinctions, titles, things of air, puffs of pride, lies, nothingness."

It is also a little strange, in the light of that maxim, that he should have collected a number of other Spanish decorations as well, such as the Grand Cross of St. Raymond of Peñafort, the Grand Cross of Alfonso X the Wise, the Grand Cross of Isabel the Catholic and others, as well as sundry gold medals.[9] It is, I suspect, totally unheard-of behavior in any other saint—at least after his or her conversion. It is a clear occasion of embarrassment to his biographers, perhaps even to himself. As he put it in the letter to the councillor, he had acted only after careful deliberation before God, and after taking advice. The petition for the title was "distasteful" (*antipatico*) to him, though anyone else would have enjoyed it, and acted without qualms.[10]

The Marquisate of Peralta, he claimed, was his by right, conferred upon his ancestor Tomás de Peralta, Secretary of State for War and Justice in the Kingdom of Naples, in 1718. Knowledge of the title, however, and certainly any claim to it, appears to have been absent from his immediate ancestors. It was a solid, deeply pious, middle-class family from Barbastro in north-east Spain, not far from the frontier with France. His father was a partner in a textile business in the town, "Juncosa and Escrivá." He had married Maria de los Dolores Albas y Blanc. There were six children, the eldest called Carmen, then José Maria born on 9 January 1902, three other daughters all called Maria, and the youngest, Santiago.

José was not a strong child. When he was only two years old he fell seriously ill. His life was despaired of. His mother Dolores took him to the small shrine of the Virgin Mary at Torreciudad, a local place of pilgrimage housing a statue of Mary possibly dating from the eleventh century. Her prayers were answered, and José recovered. Torreciudad has since become yet another monument to the founder.

Although the son was thus miraculously restored to health, unhappily for the family the three Marias all died in a period of just over three years between 1910 and 1913. José seems to have believed that he would be the next. He withdrew from the company of his friends and went into a massive depression from which he only slowly emerged—partly at least, it would seem, because of growing confidence that God had him under His particular care: it was at this time Dolores related to him the story of the cure at Torreciudad.

Perhaps the sickness in the family was linked to the progressive decline and ultimate collapse of Don José's business in Barbastro: it was put down to his too trusting nature, for which one might read lack of business acumen. Whatever the reason for the failure, the family was forced to dispense with servants, something unheard-of in middle-class Spain, and eventually to move to another town. In 1915 they all traveled to Logroño, still in the same region, but closer to Spain's northern coast line. There Don José went into partnership in a clothes shop grandly entitled "La Gran Ciudad de Londres" (The Great City of London). The family lived in a cramped flat with Doña Dolores having to do all the household chores —good practice, as it was to turn out, for her subsequent role in Opus.

While in Barbastro José Maria had been educated by members of a religious order, the Piarists; in later life he claimed the founder of the Piarists, St. Joseph Calasanctius, as a distant relative. In Logroño, however, he went to the state *instituto* in the mornings, and to a kind of tutorial college run by laymen, St. Anthony's, in the afternoon. As his Opus biographers recall in detail, his examination marks were good, his behavior beyond reproach. Though it appears to have come as a surprise at the time, in hindsight a decision to study for the priesthood seems inevitable.

In 1918, therefore, he began his ecclesiastical studies at the seminary in Logroño. He was not a fully-fledged member of the student body, his health was judged too delicate for that. He began his career in the Church as an external student, going into classes, but living at home where he also received private tuition. He completed an exemplary first year of theology, but then moved to Zaragoza as a full, internal, student at the seminary there.

The decision to go to Zaragoza has never been entirely satisfactorily explained. He had relations there, one of them a Canon of the cathedral, but he does not appear to have been very close to them. Or, if he had been, he very soon alienated them: the Canon did not even attend his ordination or first mass, traditionally major family celebrations within the Roman Catholic community. Possibly it was more important to him that there was a university in the town where he could begin his study of law alongside that of theology. In this way he could equip himself with a professional skill with which he might in later life support his family, a factor which would have weighed even more heavily after his father died very suddenly on 27 November 1924.

This news he took surprisingly calmly despite the additional responsibilities it placed upon him as the sole wage-earner. "My father was ruined," he said in later life, "and when Our Lord wished me to begin work at Opus Dei I had not a single resource, not a penny to my name."[11] His father's chief legacies to his elder son (Santiago was only five at the time) were good looks, and a distinct tidiness, not to say elegance, despite his straitened circumstances, in dress. In the seminary at Zaragoza his manner of dressing marked him out. The generality of seminarians, Vázquez remarks, were somewhat crude and uncultured. Escrivá de Balaguer was the exception. His clothes were always clean, his shoes always polished. It was apparently a matter of comment that he washed himself from head to toe every day.

A few months after his father's death, he was ordained priest on 28 March 1925. Two days later he was appointed as assistant priest in a country parish. Though the appointment might be seen as rather sudden, it was precipitated by the sickness of the priest in charge of the parish, and the need to provide for the Easter services—Holy Week had just begun. He was not there long, however. By the middle of May he was back in Zaragoza. He still had to finish his degree in law.

This he did by 1927. He was awarded his licentiate in March of that year, and he now asked permission from his bishop to go to Madrid to begin a doctorate. It was granted. In June 1923 the Cardinal of Zaragoza, Archbishop Soldevila, had been assassinated. His attention had been drawn to Escrivá de Balaguer by the latter's excellent record in the seminary where his rather solitary behavior marked him out from the rest of the students. Perhaps he was also struck by the poem composed by Escrivá de Balaguer for the president of the seminary, entitled *Obedientia tutior*. In it he praised the security provided by obedience to a superior's will.

Whatever the reason, Soldevila had singled out the student from Logroño for special treatment. He had personally conferred upon him the "tonsure," the ceremony by which a layman becomes a cleric. He had then appointed him to take charge of the rest of the students, ensuring that they kept the rules—a sort of prefect of discipline. Had Soldevila lived, Vázquez de Prada reflects, he might have served as Escrivá's patron, finding for him a post appropriate to his sensibilities and learning—and one that was financially rewarding. Escrivá's family was now in Zaragoza and relying upon him.

Without Soldevila, Escrivá de Balaguer had to find his own work. Even before his degree he began teaching Latin and Canon Law at a private college which prepared students for entry to higher institutions of learning, most notably the military academy in Zaragoza. Before they are ordained, seminarians must be able to show they are financially provided for. At one time a priest might be ordained "on his own patrimony"—in other words, he could show he was of independent means—and was therefore not attached to a particular bishop. But usually priests were, and are, "incardinated" into some diocese, and promise allegiance to the bishop of that diocese, who then takes responsibility for them. Technically Escrivá was incardinated into Zaragoza, though he worked there very little. Madrid was the diocese where he worked for most of the time from 1927 to 1942, yet he was not incardinated into Madrid until 1942 when he became a member of the diocesan clergy automatically, on taking up a benefice: one cannot help feeling he was avoiding the commitment required of most clergy. Though in Zaragoza he undoubtedly engaged in some pastoral work and was a member of that diocese, he had already in practice cut himself off, either because of his family's financial circumstances or his own personal preference, from the normal career of a priest.

Whatever the background to his request for leave from his diocese to study in Madrid, permission was granted for two years. In fact, he failed to qualify in the time available. His topic of research was the ordination to the priesthood of men of mixed race in the sixteenth and the seventeenth centuries. It was never completed. When he finally and successfully defended a thesis it was in December 1939, and it treated of the history, and more particularly the legal status, of the Monastery of Las Huelgas. Given Escrivá's apparent reluctance to tie himself down to a particular diocese, the subject of his thesis may be significant. The successive Lady Abbesses were powerful figures who ruled over their own territory, and were answerable only to the Pope.

The hold-up in his earlier studies may have been, once again, because of his need to earn money to support his family. He lodged in Madrid at a residence for priests and found a post once again teaching law, Roman and canonical, at a tutorial college, the Cicuéendez Academy.

During the late 1920s he was also serving as chaplain to the religious order, the Damas Apostólicas, who owned the house in which he was boarding. The Apostolic Ladies of the Sacred Heart of Jesus, as they were called in full, had only very recently been given formal approval by the Vatican of their way of life, but they had already developed a very diverse range of charitable works among the poor, and especially the sick poor, of Madrid. The sick they used to care for in their own homes, providing food and medicine and spiritual help.

That was where Escrivá de Balaguer came in. He ministered to the sick, bring them the sacraments and helping them to resolve personal problems. The work took him from the center of the Spanish capital into what were then its most distant suburbs. On Sundays he said mass at the church attached to the order's central residence.

This work with the Apostolic Ladies lasted until July 1931. It was during his time with them that he took the decision to found Opus Dei. From that date his own life was wholly intertwined with the organization he had created.

2

The Origins of Opus

One of the odd things about Opus Dei is its lack of a history. It has been going for sixty years and one might have expected some member somewhere to have set down an account of its development, how it grew and expanded, who went where and when, what were the problems and how they were overcome, what tensions existed and how they were resolved, how the various apostolic works came to be undertaken, how policy was decided, and so on. The obvious setting for such a treatment would have been the volume published in 1982[1] by the University of Navarra to commemorate, somewhat belatedly, the golden Jubilee of Opus Dei's foundation in 1928. There is indeed a section promisingly entitled "Opus Dei Fifty Years On," but it consists only of two pieces, a hitherto unpublished text of Escrivá's, and an uninformative—at least as far as the history of the organization is concerned—interview with the new man in charge, Monsignor Alvaro del Portillo. Not that some of the history cannot be unearthed from the many apologias for Opus which its supporters have produced over the years, but no directly historical study is mentioned in the bibliographical essay of Lucas F. Mateo-Seco written for the jubilee volume.[2] What is most remarkable about this bibliography is the paucity of serious works on any aspect of Opus—except that of its recently acquired juridical status as a personal prelature.

Nevertheless, of one particular event there is no shortage of accounts: the day and the manner of Escrivá's decision to found what eventually became Opus Dei. It happened, says

Vázquez with hyperbole understandable in one who is a devout member, "like a divine seed falling from heaven."[3] The idea came to Escrivá as he was making a retreat at a house in the outskirts of Madrid belonging to the Vincentians, a Catholic religious order. Escrivá was praying and, Bernal claims, he "saw" Opus Dei. At the same time he heard the bells ring out from the nearby church of Our Lady of the Angels to celebrate the patronal feast; 2 October is the day Roman Catholics commemorate the Feast of the Guardian Angels.[4]

What happened exactly, on the other hand, is not entirely clear. Some members of Opus seem to believe that Escrivá de Balaguer had a vision of God, but he himself does not claim as much. In fact, he claims very little. It is obvious enough that, as a young and ambitious priest in a country which then had far too many clergymen, he was looking for some particular role in life. And there is nothing wrong in that. It seems from the various accounts of the foundation that, during his meditations, he began to get an inkling about what his role in life might be. It was later, though not much later, that the notion became clearer and he could take steps to put it into operation. That was all that happened. But with Opus's proclivity for going to extremes, a plaque has been set into the façade of the new belfry of Our Lady of the Angels—and one of the old bells has been taken to Torreciudad as a memento of the founder. The Latin inscription reads, in rough translation: "While the bells of the Madrid church of Our Lady of the Angels sounded out, and raised their voices in praise to the heavens, on the second of October 1928 Josemaría Escrivá de Balaguer received into mind and heart the seeds of Opus Dei." Opus might more appropriately have put a plaque on the building where the founder received his first inspiration, but it is no longer standing.

What exactly was it that Escrivá had founded? There is little doubt about what Opus Dei has *become*. It has a precise legal structure, well-defined aims and clear-cut methods of achieving them. But it would be unusual for a founder of a religious organization within the Roman Catholic Church to foresee exactly what he or she wanted their foundation to become, down to the very last detail. The Franciscans, for instance, went through many traumas and decades, if not centuries, of internal conflict before they settled upon their structure, and then only at the cost of splitting the order. So it is fair to ask whether Escrivá's original vision is fulfilled in the form which his creation has now assumed.

Not that the problem is as simple as that. Escrivá saw Opus Dei develop the way it did, and encouraged it on its way. The turning-point may have come in the incident recounted below (see p. 47), when he returned from Rome in 1946 with his innocence or naivety shattered by his experience of the papal curia's manner of operation. It may be that his earlier notion of what it was he wanted to create was of something quite different.

Bernal, for example, describes Opus Dei as "an *unorganized organization,* alive with spontaneous responsibility."[5] That would be very far from the experience of recent members. Once the founder had died, comments Vladimir Felzmann:

> ... rules, regulations and restrictions burgeoned. Life became even more restrictive. . . . To protect and preserve his spirit—to avoid what happened to the Franciscans—the founder had ordered a comprehensive and meticulous codification of the work of Opus Dei and the lives of its members. But, as our Lord himself discovered, a spirit enshrined in a code tends to become dead, enslaving, pharisaical.[6]

But the "unorganized organization" of Bernal is close to what Raimundo Pannikar remembers of the early days. Pannikar was perhaps Opus's most distinguished academic theologian. Born in Barcelona of an Indian father and Catalan mother, he was technically a British subject and, as such, evacuated from Barcelona by a British warship during the Spanish Civil War (1936–39). He went to Germany to study, but returned to Barcelona in 1940 where he joined the small group of Escrivá's followers who were active in the city. He became a priest in 1946, one of only the second group of Opus members to be ordained. He left Opus in 1965. His memories of the early days bear out Bernal's description.

Opus, says Pannikar, when he first came across it was almost a "counter-cultural" movement.[7] People like himself joined it because it appeared to offer a way to overcome "routine" Roman Catholicism. They simply wanted to take their religion seriously, to follow the Gospel in the totality of the demands it makes upon someone who wants to be a disciple of Christ. There is an old ascetical tradition in the Church which likens the devout to the *militia Christi,* the soldiers of Christ—and that was the expression which Pannikar used of the early members of Opus. They were, apart from Escrivá himself, no more than a group of lay people who were trying to put the Gospel into action. There was no special kind of life, no fleeing the world. There was to be nothing distinctive about them except, perhaps, that for mutual support they lived together. That, then, was the ideal Escrivá de Balaguer offered those who came under his influence.

And people came rapidly under his influence. No sooner had he received his divine message[8] than he set about winning recruits to his cause. He talked about his ideas to friends from his student days in Logroño and Zaragoza. He sought support among the priests who shared his lodging house in Madrid. He wrote letters to people outside the Spanish capital. He asked his acquaintances, and those for whom he worked as a chaplain, if they knew of any suitable male candidates among the young, and especially among students. He told Fr. Sanchez Ruiz, the Jesuit who was his spiritual director, that he realized with increasing clarity that the Lord "wants me to hide myself and to disappear." He did not follow the Lord's advice. He was making influential friends both clerical and lay, he was developing Opus through his letters, he was cultivating the aristocracy, and he was making his first disciples.

There were some who joined him but did not stay. Others, such as Isidoro Zorzano Ledesma, who had studied with him in Logroño and whom he met by chance in Madrid (see below, p. 34), died young. Escrivá was introduced to Juan Jiménez Vargas, a medical student, by friends on the faculty of medicine in Madrid. Some he met through his work in the confessional, or through the Apostolic Ladies whom he served as chaplain. They linked up with Escrivá at a crucial moment in Spanish history, self-consciously, in Pannikar's words, a "counter-cultural movement."

From 1881, professors at Spanish universities had possessed the right to hold and to teach beliefs that were distinct from, or even opposed to, the Catholic faith.[9] The effects of this freedom of expression were slow to assert themselves, but by the 1920s many professors, including those with the most influence among university students, were propounding a doctrine which was at variance with received Catholic teaching. In a country such as Spain, where the relationship between Church and State had been so close, and the traditional manner of life of its people so imbued with Catholicism, this development in the university world could be seen as a threat not only to religious orthodoxy, but also to the very basis of "Spanishness," *Hispanidad*. As well as being a Catholic priest, Escrivá de Balaguer was a patriot. Maxim 525 of *Camino* begins: "To be 'Catholic' means to love your country and to be second to none in that love."

Not only was the teaching at the universities, and especially at Madrid, becoming increasingly secular, but other educational institutions were also encouraging this tendency. The Institución Libre de Enseñanza was founded in 1876 by a man who had left the Church because of its condemnation of liberalism in the *Syllabus of Errors,* a document listing the major—in papal eyes—aberrations of modern times, published by Pope Pius IX in 1864. Although not specifically anti-Catholic in its aim, the Institución was seen as such by many in Spain. A priest writing in 1906 for the Society of Jesus' most prestigious journal of the time, *Razón y Fe,* described it as "the mortal enemy of Catholic teaching." It was not a State-controlled organization, but nonetheless it had a profound effect upon the Spanish educational system. It established student residences at the universities, rather along the lines of Oxbridge colleges, and places in these houses were eagerly sought. More important, perhaps, was the influence it exercised over the Junta para Ampliación de Estudios e Investigaciones Científicas, which was founded in 1907 to establish research institutes throughout

Spain, and by this means to raise the general level of education throughout the country.

The spread of agnosticism among young Spanish intellectuals was encouraged by the freedom of expression enjoyed by the professors, and by the new institutes. Escrivá had good reason to be aware of the dangers, as well as the possibilities, inherent in education. "Books," he wrote in Maxim 339, "—don't buy them without advice from a Catholic who is learned or prudent. It is easy to buy something useless or harmful. How often a man thinks he is carrying a book under his arm, and it turns out to be a load of dirt!" The Spanish word here translated "dirt" is *basura,* which might equally, or perhaps even more appositely, be rendered as "garbage."

Opposition to the spread of agnosticism had begun long before Escrivá de Balaguer arrived in Madrid. In 1909 a Jesuit priest founded the Asociación Católica Nacional de Propagandistas, a continuation into business and professional life of the devotional societies called sodalities of Our Lady. The Sodality of Our Lady was—and is, though in many places its name has changed—an organization under the religious direction of the Society of Jesus which combines a modest form of ascetical practice with works of charity. Though they were typically to be found in Jesuit schools, sodalities were often also found in Jesuit-run parishes, or attached to Jesuit residences of other kinds. They could be seen as an attempt to adapt Jesuit spirituality and manner of life to lay people. Under the direction of the Society of Jesus, the Asociación Católica's aim was two-fold. It wanted to improve the social conditions of the poor in Spain, but also to do this without overthrowing the traditional values and way of life of the people. It was an élitist organization, drawing its recruits from among men of good social standing and education. Its method, like the communist cell movement of a later generation, was to work in small groups and, insofar as was possible, to work discreetly. This organization could not but have been well known to Escrivá. Indeed, in 1911 the Asociación purchased *El Debate,* a newspaper which was to become one of the most influential in

The Origins of Opus

the country. In 1923 *El Debate* welcomed the arrival to power of the dictator Primo de Rivera in the hope that he might be able to uphold the crumbling social order. Six years later it supported Primo de Rivera's Minister of Education in an attempt to give two privately-run colleges, one Jesuit and the other Augustinian, the right to grant degrees in certain faculties. This proposed interference in the State's monopoly of education caused so great an outcry that the plan had to be given up.[10]

Escrivá must have known of the Asociación. Indeed, after the Spanish Civil War he worked at the school of journalism attached to *El Debate,* though his lectures were on ethics and metaphysics rather than on the techniques of the journalist's trade. But he would not have needed that closeness of contact, or even the contact with his Jesuit spiritual directors, to have known of the work of the Society of Jesus in Spain. "The debt owed by Opus Dei to the Society of Jesus is immense," says Carandell, "so much so that one could say that if the Society had not existed, the birth of Opus would have been impossible."[11]

That Escrivá's vision for Opus might owe anything to anyone else is not a topic which the approved lives of the founder touch upon. Vázquez's book, for instance, has three references to a certain Don Pedro Poveda.[12] The first simply mentions that Escrivá had an interview with Don Pedro on 4 February 1931—the date was obviously important enough to be noted down—in the hope of getting some kind of ecclesiastical benefice; Escrivá turned down what was offered, according to Vázquez, because it gave no right of incardination. "Don Pedro's astonishment [at Escrivá's refusal] was extreme," Vázquez remarks. The second reference speaks of the friendly relationship between the two men. The third simply mentions Poveda's death by assassination in the course of the uprising against forces loyal to Franco in Madrid in July 1936 at the outbreak of the Civil War.

It is the second passage which is puzzling. The two men met: Poveda offered a preferment which Escrivá did not accept. Then, as far as the biography goes, the two men part. Except that, clearly, they did not. They were apparently quite friendly, even though Vázquez does not dwell upon it, and Bernal does not mention it at all. It may be that Poveda played a larger part in Escrivá's life than that for which he is given credit. He was the founder of an organization called the Teresians. It was well known, and its structure is similar to that of Opus. While it remains part of the Opus mythology that the idea for their organization was delivered by the Almighty direct to Escrivá de Balaguer on that day in October 1928, there is no room for any suggestion that the concept may have come from elsewhere, from the Society of Jesus, perhaps, or from Don Pedro Poveda. There were a number of other institutes similar to Opus which, though they did not gain papal approval before Escrivá's foundation, were certainly in existence before it.[13]

Escrivá chose to inaugurate his new society just as the dictatorship of Primo de Rivera came to an end. On 12 April 1931 elections were held in Spain. Two days later King Alphonso XIII abdicated and went into exile, and a Republic was proclaimed. Agnostic socialism had triumphed over the traditional alliance of Crown and Church. A month later there came the first burning of monasteries and churches. Less than a year after that the Society of Jesus was expelled from the country. Crosses were to be removed from schools and education entirely secularized. Ecclesiastical property was appropriated by the State, divorce was permitted, and the Concordat, which regulated relations between the Vatican and the government of Spain, was abrogated. When he was teaching at the Instituto Amado in Zaragoza Escrivá had demonstrated a particular interest in Church-State relations and the problems of ecclesiastical property.[14]

It is clear that it was not until after these disputes had arisen between the Spanish government and the Church that Opus Dei began to make any sort of headway as a movement; it can therefore be seen as one form of response to the basic "privatization" of Catholicism imposed by the new anti-clerical regime.

After his resignation from duties for the Damas Apostólicas in 1931, Escrivá was left without any fixed apostolic work, an unusual situation for a young and undoubtedly devout priest. Two months after surrendering one form of chaplaincy, however, he took up another, this time with an enclosed convent of Augustinian nuns. Santa Isabel was a royal benefice, though it seems Escrivá de Balaguer was unpaid for his labors, at least at first. Eventually he was appointed rector of the living, though not until the end of 1934. For that new role he had to ask the permission of his own bishop back in Zaragoza. He was given it. It is not recorded whether the bishop paused to wonder what had happened to the thesis he had been given two years' leave from the diocese to complete.

By this time his family, no doubt despairing of his return from Madrid, had themselves decided to move to the Spanish capital. From the end of 1932 Escrivá de Balaguer lived with his mother (who, it seems, took even more interest in finding a suitable benefice for her son than he did himself), brother, and sole surviving sister in a flat at 4 Martinez Campos. A year later, his financial situation presumably on the mend, he rented a flat at 33 Luchana, to serve as a meeting place for the group which was beginning to gather round him.

One of the earliest forms of Escrivá's new personal crusade was with the clergy of Madrid to whom he gave spiritual advice every Monday evening, showing them, says Vázquez "the loftiness [alteza] of the priestly dignity, and how the honor of a priest is much more delicate* than the honor of a woman."[15] He was also working with a group of young men and boys who began to meet for tea and conversation at his mother's flat. They talked, while Doña Dolores, Carmen, and, apparently under some protest, Escrivá's brother Santiago provided food and drink and generally waited upon the assembly. The numbers, and the frequency of the gatherings, increased. Escrivá determined on a more formal approach. In a room in a reformatory, lent him by the nuns who looked after the delinquents, he began to give spiritual direction—in the first

---

*The word is *delicado* which could also mean "exquisite" or "fine."

instance to three medical students, but this group, too, began to expand.

Escrivá then conceived the idea of an academy. He coined for it the slogan "God and Courage" (*Dios y Audacia*) and this in turn became the DYA Academy, which in turn was interpreted as the Academia de Derecho y Arquitectura (School of Law and Architecture). It occupied tiny quarters in the Calle Luchana which soon proved to be too small. Moreover, as an academy and nothing more it lacked the ministrations of his mother and sister. Escrivá therefore persuaded his mother to sink the inheritance she had received on the death of a relative into the acquisition of a property in Madrid, in the Calle de Ferraz. This was big enough to constitute a residence as well as an academy of law and architecture.

It was the first of many residences set up by Escrivá and his organization, and it set a pattern both for the style of accommodation and the manner of religious training conducted there. An oratory was erected, a refectory established. There was a room where the residents could meet to talk. There was, naturally, a bathroom. Despite constant washing, its walls were stained with blood from the flagellations Escrivá inflicted upon himself. He used a "discipline," a kind of cat-o'-nine-tails, to which he had attached bits of metal and pieces of razor blades. (Whether any other residents joined in is not related, though the use of the discipline [without the metal and blades] came into common usage in Opus.) The discipline and the spiked chain he would attach to his arm Escrivá de Balaguer kept in "Father's room." There, under a representation of the gospel story of the miraculous catch of fishes, confidential conversation was fostered and spiritual direction meted out.

Escrivá attempted to re-establish in the residence the intimacy of family life. He presided as the Father. Doña Dolores came to be known as the Grandmother, Carmen as Aunt. Others came to visit, and were won over to the life they found at the DYA: Alvaro del Portillo, the present Superior or "Prelate" of Opus, was one of them.

It was around this time Escrivá de Balaguer was composing what he first called his *Consideraciones espirituales,* a collection of spiritual maxims which eventually became *Camino, The Way* or, perhaps more correctly, *The Road*. (A Catalan humorist in the early 1970s produced *La Autopista, The Motorway*.) Escrivá's little booklet is hailed by his followers as "a classic work of spiritual literature,"[16] though this is a description of the later editions. Escrivá de Balaguer was not satisfied with what he had produced for the first version, published in Cuenca in Spain in 1934. When he was in Burgos in 1939 he put together his notes for a further edition, and this was published in September 1939. The book, with its new, and permanent, title was published in Valencia because, according to Vázquez, that was the only place where he could find paper. But all this is to jump ahead a little. Between the first and second editions of this booklet, Escrivá's life was to be turned upside down.

In May 1935 Escrivá led his residents at the DYA Academy on a pilgrimage to a shrine of the Virgin Mary in Avila. May is the month in which Catholics particularly celebrate Mary, and pilgrimages to Marian shrines in May have remained a feature of Opus life, in conscious imitation, it would seem, of Escrivá's first trip with his disciples through the Castilian countryside.

Despite the difficulties the Church was facing in Spain in the early 1930s, Escrivá's enterprise seemed to be a great success. Because of growing numbers in the residence, the Academy had to find other accommodation nearby. There was talk of acquiring more property in Madrid, and two of the Father's disciples were dispatched to Valencia to open a residence in that city. That was in 1936, the year civil war broke out. This did not entirely destroy what had been painstakingly built up, and some of the early followers remained loyal throughout. Despite the problems to which the battle for the soul of Spain gave rise, a house in Valencia was opened, though plans for a residence in Paris had to be deferred. It was. not until after the war that the definitive phase of Opus's development began.

What existed so far? There was the DYA Academy, though as an educational institution that seems to have been of decreasing interest to Escrivá. There was a residence attached, to which he devoted a good deal more attention. There was a group of admirers, and a rather smaller group which might have been called "members" had an organization of any kind existed, but at this time it did not. There was a name of sorts, though Opus Dei, "The Work of God" ("*La Obra de Dios*" in Spanish, or, more commonly, simply "*La Obra*") may have originally been intended as a working title until something more specific turned up. (It is noticeable, however, that whereas some religious bodies, such as the Friars Minor and Order of Preachers, have become known more familiarly by the names of their founders—Franciscans and Dominicans respectively—there seems to have been no suggestion that members of Opus Dei should be called "Escrivists" or "Balaguerians.") And though they had no specific form of spiritual direction other than that provided by "the Father," from 1934 members of Opus had at their disposal the thoughts of their Father in his *Consideraciones Espirituales,* published that year in Cuenca. And they also had, as has just been seen, a pattern of living based upon the *hogar,* the model of a family home, which Escrivá de Balaguer had developed with the help of his mother and sister in the residence in Calle de Ferraz—though the role of his immediate family seems to have been overplayed in Opus mythology of the early years.[17]

That is one side of it—the male branch of Opus. By 1936 the female branch was also in existence. It is not surprising, given the *macho* temperament of the Spaniards which Escrivá shared, that his initial inspiration was to begin an organization which catered for young men. They were the first targets of his zeal and, as we shall see, remained prime targets for his disciples. Despite the devoted support of his mother and sister, women were not at first regarded as suitable candidates for his new organization—and, in fact, neither Doña Dolores nor Señorita Carmen ever formally belonged to Escrivá's foundation.

All changed, however, one day in 1930, significantly 14 February, the feast day of St. Valentine. Escrivá de Balaguer was saying mass in the private oratory of the Marchioness of Onteiro, the eighty-year-old whose daughter had founded the Apostolic Ladies. After the communion of the mass "God made him see" that there should be a women's section in

Opus Dei. Whether women have ever attained the same status in Opus as their male counterparts is very doubtful, and is an issue which will be looked at a little later. But quite apart from his immediate female relations, who supplied funds, furniture, and domestic assistance for the residence he began in Madrid, women have always provided loyal and uncomplaining service.

At this time, before the Spanish Civil War, what was it these few men and women belonged to? There was, as yet, no legal structure, no "juridical personality." As far as one can tell, there was no specific way of life, certainly in the very early days, no book of spiritual maxims such as *Camino* to guide them. It was, as is often said as if it were something out of the ordinary, a "lay" organization as distinct from a "clerical" one. The law of the Roman Catholic Church distinguishes only between "lay" and "clerical." You are either one or the other, and the only people who fall into the clerical category are priests, or men who have progressed a considerable way in their preparation for the priesthood. Most people in religious orders in the world are nuns, women. Most people in religious orders, therefore, are lay people. Even many orders of men have a large complement of laymen among their members.

But it is perfectly plain that those men or women who belong to religious orders are not "lay" people in the technical, legal sense of that word, because they have, in some form or other, embraced the three traditional vows by promising, with a greater or lesser degree of solemnity, to observe poverty, chastity, and obedience to their religious superiors for the rest of their lives. Certain legal consequences, within the context of Roman Catholic canon law, flow from the degree of solemnity with which vows are taken, the chief differences depending upon whether the vows are taken privately or publicly. Members of religious orders take public, or solemn, vows; members of religious congregations do not take solemn vows. The distinction is a technical one, and for the most part of little significance. Even within the Catholic Church few are aware of it.

To suggest that Opus Dei saw itself as falling into either category, whether religious order or congregation, is to sin grievously against their self-image. There is, however, evidence, provided by Opus itself, in the case of Isidoro Zorzano Ledesma that Opus was headed at least toward the status of a congregation (a status rather less formal than that of a religious order) from its earliest years.

Clearly there is meant to be, in the mythology of Opus, something out of the ordinary about Zorzano. He had studied with Escrivá in Logroño, and then moved to the other end of the country to become a railway engineer in Malaga. Yet he and Escrivá met fortuitously in a Madrid street which, Vázquez is at pains to point out, Escrivá was not accustomed to traverse. Even the date of this meeting has been carefully recorded, so momentous was it taken to be: 24 August 1930. Rather oddly, Bernal and Vázquez relate this event in very similar words, almost as if there was an "oral tradition" to which they were both indebted. Bernal is much the earlier text, but textual critics would have little difficulty in showing that Vázquez was not dependent upon it. Zorzano was very close indeed to Escrivá—they were, of course, contemporaries—and was much involved in the very first Opus enterprise in Madrid, the establishment of the DYA Academy. He died in July 1943, before Opus was formally established by the Holy See.

At one time Zorzano was being actively promoted as a candidate for canonization, though his cause has quietly been dropped to prepare the way for Escrivá's: this happened long before Escrivá's death, and presumably was at his bidding. In 1964 a biography of God's Engineer, as another account of his life was entitled, was prepared for Rome's Sacred Congregation of Rites as it was then known, the official body in the papal curia responsible for the proclamation of new saints. This Roman biography states that Zorzano gave himself totally to the exercise of the evangelical counsels: poverty, chastity, and obedience.[18]

Those counsels, put into the form of vows, are, of course, the basis for life in a religious order or congregation. Escrivá de Balaguer probably did not have, at this stage, any clear idea of what form his organization was to take. There were, as has been seen, a number of models known to him. But it does seem clear that it was assumed that his organization would be based upon the traditional three vows which, in the way most people use the term, would have removed it from the realm of "lay" organizations.

Whatever Escrivá's hopes and expectations may have been for his institution, he had scarcely begun to consolidate its first undertakings when the Spanish Civil War appeared to bring them to a halt. Outside Madrid there was only Valencia—perhaps not formally an off-shoot of Opus, but the residence of Pedro Casciaro, one of Escrivá's first followers and a devout member. Certainly Valencia was the first city outside Madrid chosen by Escrivá after the war to establish a house for his group. Then came Valladolid.

On 19 July 1936 Madrid's Montaña Barracks were attacked and taken by the republican militia. The following morning Escrivá, who had spent the night in an Opus Dei residence, had to abandon his clerical dress and don a boiler-suit to make his way back to his mother's flat—no longer at Martinez Campos but in a street now called Rey Francisco. There he had to hide: it was dangerous to be a cleric in republican Spain where, in the course of the war, it has been calculated that well over 4,000 priests belonging to dioceses and nearly 2,400 belonging to religious orders met violent deaths.[19]

Escrivá had been in his mother's flat for just over a fortnight when he heard a rumor that the building was to be searched. He fled to the house of a friend. Only just in time, according to Vázquez: he was going down the service stairway as the militia entered the block. He disguised his tonsure, the clean-shaven patch on the crown of the head which used to be required of priests and which Escrivá wore rather larger than was customary. To hide his priesthood further he wore a wedding ring, cropped his hair, and grew a moustache.

During September he stayed with a family that had a relative degree of immunity because they were Argentinians. He spent some time on the run in Madrid. He was offered a flat, empty except for a maid who had been left there to care for it. He inquired her age: she was only twenty-three, so he declined the offer. He took refuge in a psychiatric hospital pretending to be mentally ill. From March to August 1937 he was safely housed inside the residence of the Honduran consul. He was eventually given accreditation as a legation employee so he could move about more freely. He was even able to rent a flat for which, risking capture, he went out to purchase a statue of the Virgin Mary. He acquired one for which, says Vázquez, he developed a strong affection because it reminded him of his mother.

But the situation in the city did not improve, and he, like other priests, was constantly in danger of arrest. He decided to leave his family in Madrid. In October 1937 he arrived in Valencia. From there he traveled by overnight train to Barcelona and, after a nail-biting delay, by bus toward the northern frontier. When the bus could go no further he and his companions tramped toward the border, hiding from the republican patrols and frontier guards. One night they camped in a wood called Rialp—the name was later taken by an Opus Dei publishing house. They had set out in the bus on 19 November. When by night the group finally climbed into the principality of Andorra it was 2 December.

His troubles were not yet quite over. After a few days in Andorra he made his way by lorry to France. The road had been broken by winter storms, however, and he had to travel the last few miles on foot. It had been a tough, uncomfortable, and extremely perilous journey. For the fastidious Escrivá de Balaguer it presented sufferings perhaps as acute as those he might have had to endure as a priest in hiding in republican Spain. The journey has entered the folklore of Opus Dei.

Escrivá, of course, had been fleeing from the socialist and communist militias of the republican government. He had not been fleeing from Spain itself. Once in France he made preparations to return to the nationalist side of the battle-lines. He paid a visit to the shrine of the Virgin at Lourdes, and then made his way, via the border crossing at Irun and the city of Pamplona, to Franco's headquarters in Burgos. In 1939 he was with the first column of nationalist troops to make their way into Madrid. There he found the property he had purchased for Opus lying in ruins. Though, as we shall see, some of those who had been with him before the civil war had remained loyal, he had to begin over again the task of building Opus.

This time his success was greater than in the years between 1928 and 1936. Opus's rapid expansion after the war is easy to explain. In Burgos, at the beginning of 1938, he had shared a room in the Hotel Sabadell with Pedro Casciaro, José María Albareda Herrera, and Francisco Botella. It is clear that by this time Escrivá de Balaguer had settled upon the establishment of Opus Dei as his life's work. While in Burgos he visited bishops within the nationalist zone, talking to them about his organization. It was becoming known and, rather more importantly, influential. Three things in particular were significant: first the ideology of "National Catholicism," secondly the educational needs of the new government, and thirdly the friendship between Opus member José María Albareda Herrera and José Ibáñez Martín, Franco's Minister of Education from 1939 to 1951.

Although National Catholicism is associated in particular with the post-Civil War years, it had in its essentials a long history.[20] Its fundamental tenet was the identification of being a Spaniard with being a Catholic. Love of country was to be associated with a rejection of all heterodoxy, Protestant or Jewish, liberal or socialist. Religious faith and political identity were as one: they were integral—hence the broad name for this kind of politico-religious stance not, of course, confined to Spain, "integrism," its proponents being the "integristes." Pope Pius XII sent Franco a telegram congratulating him on his "Catholic" victory. National Catholicism was an expressly illiberal doctrine, and it was one widespread among Catholics in Spain after the years of secular, anti-Catholic, government.

Escrivá de Balaguer was no exception to the general enthusiasm for this conservative Catholic ideology. On the contrary, it is clear from *Camino* that he embraced it whole-heartedly. Maxim 905 commends patriotic fervor—and compares it immediately with fervor for Christ. Indeed, the Introduction to the first edition appears to recommend the book as a means of saving the soul, not of the pious Christian, but of Spain: "If these maxims change your own life, you will be a perfect imitator of Jesus Christ, and a knight without spot. And with Christs such as you, Spain will return to its ancient grandeur of its saints, its sages and its heroes."

The victorious General Franco had led his rebellion (he called it a *cruzada,* crusade, a word which Escrivá used in *Camino*) against the republican government in an attempt to return to the supposedly Christian values espoused by the protagonists of National Catholicism. He had to reconstruct the traditional culture of the people through educational reform. Religious studies became compulsory even for all university students. Halls of residence were set up, where the strict discipline was to be under the control of members of religious orders. The Consejo Superior de Investigaciones Científicas (CSIC) was established in order to improve the educational standards of Spain not only by the creation of centers for research but also by the provision of residences, bursaries, traveling scholarships, and so on.

This time, however, the promotion of scientific research was not to be allowed to run counter to the ideal of *Hispanidad,* Spanishness. The preamble to the decree setting up the CSIC spoke of restoring "the classical and Christian unity of the sciences, destroyed in the eighteenth century." In overall charge of the CSIC as the Minister of Education from 1939 to 1951 was José Ibáñez Martín.

Ibáñez Martín himself was not a member of Opus, but in the course of the civil war he had spent some time as a political refugee in the Chilean embassy in Madrid. There he had met José María Albareda Herrera. The two became good friends, and Albareda, who was a member of Opus, was named vice-president of CSIC and put in charge of coordinating its activities. He effectively ran it until 1966, and used the research institute to advance, admittedly very able, members of Opus. Raimundo Pannikar, for example, became editor of CSIC's flagship journal *Arbor.*

The civil war had left a good many professorial chairs vacant in Spanish universities, which the government was eager to fill with ideologically safe candidates. In Spain, professors are chosen by means of a quasi-examination called an *oposición,* a tribunal consisting of several other members of the university staff. Ibáñez Martín was able to control the *oposiciones* and to ensure that candidates were appointed whose loyalty to Church and State—for practical purposes the two being more or less synonymous—was assured. It was hardly surprising, therefore, that Opus members were chosen in increasing numbers for professorial chairs. They were safe and reliable men, and known to the Ministry of Education as such. It must again be emphasized that the educational standards Opus Dei demands of its most committed members are very high, and would of themselves recommend Opus candidates for these posts.

In 1939, however, Opus Dei's steady infiltration of the Spanish university system lay in the future. Of more immediate concern to Escrivá, after he had successfully managed the publication of *Camino,* was the establishment of new centers and the recruitment of more members.

In Madrid the original DYA residence in the Calle de Ferraz had been destroyed. Accommodation was now found in some flats in the Calle Jenner, two on the fourth floor and one, for common services such as a dining-room, on the second. Toward the end of 1940 Escrivá acquired a small hotel in Calle Diego de Leon which, a year later, he opened as a residence for a score or more of students. He lived there himself.

Opus centers were also opened in 1939 in Valencia and Valladolid and in Barcelona, in a small flat in the Calle Balmes. Barcelona had, of course, been bitterly opposed to Franco throughout the civil war. The authorities in the city still felt they were on a knife-edge; the Opus group rapidly came under suspicion, perhaps denounced by members of the Jesuit-run sodalities of Our Lady. According to Vázquez it was in Barcelona that *Camino* was "condemned to the flames," that there was public preaching against the heretics, and a convent of nuns prayed for Escrivá's conversion,[21] despite the support given to the small group of a dozen or so by the assistant abbot of Monserrat, the great, remote Benedictine monastery and shrine of the Virgin which was, and is, the center of Catalan nationalism and Catholic devotion.

There was also opposition in Madrid. In Vázquez's description, this opposition was "directed and organized," though he does not say by whom. Rocca, however, makes a suggestion: Opus's opponents were again the sodalities of Our Lady, the Jesuit-run activist lay organizations, which may have resented a new body muscling in on their traditional territory, but which also may have been suspicious of the "secrecy" or "reserve" Opus Dei had already espoused. Certainly, at about this time, Escrivá seems no longer to have contact with his Jesuit confessor Sanchez Ruiz.

The accusation against Opus was quite specific: it was said to be a Jewish sect with links with the Freemasons. In the aftermath of the civil war that was a serious charge. There was a special tribunal in Madrid whose task it was to eradicate Freemasonry ("to guard the security of the State" says Vázquez).[22] Opus was hauled before this tribunal. Its members, the judge—a general—was told, live respectable, busy, and chaste lives. Do they really live chaste lives, asked the general, and when he was assured they did so, he dismissed the case. Never known a chaste mason yet, he said in explanation.

The Bishop of Madrid (more correctly, Madrid-Alcalá) explained some of the reasons for the hostility to Opus Dei in a letter he wrote on 24 May 1941 to the assistant abbot of Monserrat, in reply to the abbot's earlier letter about Opus. It is striking how little the charges against Opus have changed over the years. Dr. Escribá, said the bishop, giving the founder both his more plebeian spelling and his recently acquired title, has no other intention or desire except to prepare many professional, intelligent people so they may be useful to the fatherland and of service in defending the Church. Its detractors, he admitted, described it as a "secret association," but from the start it had the blessing of the diocesan authorities, and it did nothing without seeking that blessing.

The bishop then went on to speak specifically of the "reserve"—he denied it was secrecy—exercised by members of Opus. It was taught them by Escrivá, he said, as an antidote to pride, a defense of collective humility, and equally an instrument for the greater efficacy in their apostolate of good example and in the services that, on occasion, they might provide for the Church. He concluded by telling the abbot that, only the day before, he had read a letter from a Jesuit Superior saying it was to defame the Society of Jesus to assert that the Society was out to persecute Opus, or to seek its destruction.

The bishop, Mgr Leopoldo Eijo y Garay, was evidently much better informed than Cardinal Pedro Segura, Archbishop of Sevilla, or than Mgr (later Cardinal) Gaetano Cicognani, who was the papal nuncio in Madrid. Six weeks after the Bishop of Madrid's letter, Gaetano was writing to Segura for information about "the existence and functioning of the institution called Opus Dei" because there were very differing reports of it.

Replying at the end of July 1941, Segura confessed himself puzzled. First news of Opus was, he said, confused and alarming—and came from Fathers of the Society of Jesus. He ought to know more about it, he went on, because Sevilla was a university town, and students were "the preferred objective" of Opus. He had likewise achieved little by his investigations in Zaragoza, which only served to demonstrate the rigorously secret character of the organization. He had found it difficult to get hold of *Camino* which, he had been told, constituted Opus's rule, and though he now had it, he still had not had time to read it. He did not know, therefore, whether its work was political, social, or apostolic. No one he had been able to consult knew anything but generalities. He had little confidence in it for the good reason that it was adopting ways of proceeding that were alien to the tradition of the Church.

It is strange how soon opposition to Opus had arisen—and equally strange how the complaints that were then being made are still being re-echoed. Opus is secretive. Its rule is difficult if not impossible to get hold of. It is suspected of being politically active. It operates secretly among university students. It did not fit in well with the Church's traditional patterns of working. Its chief critics come from the Society of Jesus.

Perhaps because of this rising tide of hostility, Escrivá decided it was time for Opus Dei to lay claim to some modest, recognizable status within the Church. It had to go public. It became, with the approval of Bishop Eijo y Garay, a "pious union."

According to the Code of Canon Law of the time ("pious unions" do not merit a special mention in the new version of the Code) these were "associations of the faithful which have been formed to carry out some work of piety or of charity" (Canon 707, paragraph 1). They were the simplest form of ecclesiastical institution, requiring no more than the approval of the local bishop—which Eijo y Garay cheerfully gave at Escrivá's request. His letter of 19 March 1941 stated that, having read a number of Opus Dei's documents, he approved Opus as a pious union according to the sense of Canon 708—which simply gave bishops the authority to establish such organizations "capable of receiving spiritual graces and especially indulgences even though they are not juridical personalities." To assuage Escrivá's obsession with secrecy, Eijo y Garay had Opus Dei's documents placed in the diocese's secret archives.

For an organization that, at the time, had only some fifty members, male and female, and a few residences in Spain, the number of documents produced by Escrivá, consulted by the bishop, and then placed in the archives was considerable. They were, in their Spanish titles, the *Reglamento,* the *Régimen,* the *Orden,* the *Costumbres,* and the *Espíritu y Ceremonial.*

The group thus governed were all, technically at least, lay people, though with a priest at their head. So the fact that members of Opus Dei lived together in a form of common life rather like religious, did not alter their juridical position in the Church. From mid-March 1941 they were a recognizable, if little known, group of lay people with a canonically approved status.

Escrivá was, however, about to take a step which, ever since, has made Opus's position anomalous. The problem was the promotion of some of its members to the status of the priesthood.

3

The Years of Expansion

It was part of Escrivá de Balaguer's daily program that, each evening, he would join the members of his pious union in a lounge at the flat in Calle Diego de Leon and there develop for them the spiritual teaching summarized in *Camino*. But by the early 1940s there were several Opus Dei residences scattered throughout Spain. Clearly there was no way in which he could be in all places at once to instruct his neophytes in the manner he thought appropriate. Though there was by this time a small number of priests associated with Opus to whom he entrusted the formation of those members he could not meet personally on a regular basis, some of those clergy, remarks Vázquez, were a "crown of thorns."[1] Their lack of understanding of the spirit he wanted to inculcate caused him more problems than their assistance resolved. The only satisfactory answer, he concluded, was for Opus to have priests of its own.

While this may, at first sight, seem a reasonable solution, it betrays a fundamentally traditional, clerical attitude to roles in the Church—which, of course, Escrivá shared with the vast majority of Catholics of his time. He was himself a priest; the leadership and spiritual direction of his organization had to be in the hands of priests. There was no reason in theory why the lay pious union should not have remained just that: led by lay people, spiritually guided by lay people. Such organizations were beginning to emerge within the Catholic Church, but for Escrivá that was too great an innovation in the role of the laity, of whose ability he was in any case distrustful: "When a lay person sets himself up as a master in moral matters mistakes are frequently made: lay people can only be disciples" (Maxim 61). He decided to prepare some members of Opus for ordination, though apparently with considerable doubts in the first instance. "I love the lay condition of our Work* so much, that it really hurt me to make them clerics; yet, on the other hand, the need for priests was so clear that it had to be pleasing to God Our Lord that those sons of mine should be ordained priests."[2] For the record, the first three were Alvaro del Portillo, José María Hernández y Garníca, and José Luis Muzquiz. All three were civil engineers.

They began their studies in Madrid with a team of lecturers especially selected by Escrivá with the approval of the Bishop of Madrid. "They had the best teachers I could find," Escrivá said later, "because I have always been proud of the scientific preparation my children have had as a basis for their apostolic action. . . I thank you for having given me this holy pride— which in no way offends God—of being able to say that you have had a marvelous ecclesiastical training."[3] Escrivá spoke these words on the occasion of the silver jubilee of the first ordinations. The insight into the mind of God claimed by the founder in this and in the previous quotation is typical. So is the remarkably proprietorial attitude displayed toward the members of Opus.

Before the ordinations could take place, however, a problem had to be overcome. The Church requires that candidates for the priesthood be ordained to a "title": in other words, there has to be someone or some institution which will guarantee them a living. Normally they have to belong either to a diocese or to a religious congregation of some kind before the ecclesiastical authorities will sanction the administration of the sacrament. The pious union would not do: it was not an appropriately constituted institution.

The solution was found on 14 February 1943. On that morning Escrivá was saying mass in a house belonging to the

---

*Opus is, of course, Latin for "work," and although non-members in English-speaking countries refer to the organization under its Latin title, members themselves tend to call it "the Work" or, in Spanish, "la Obra."

women's section to celebrate the foundation of the section on the feast of St. Valentine, thirteen years previously. It came to him that he should create yet another section within Opus, one for priests, which would supply them with the "title" for ordination. And so was born the Sacerdotal Society of the Holy Cross.

The following day Escrivá went to see Alvaro del Portillo in the Escorial where he was preparing for his examinations. He told him of his decision, and of his desire to expand Opus Dei both to Portugal and to Italy—for which purpose an organization rather more high-powered than a pious union was necessary. But if there was to be a priestly society the Vatican had to approve. Obediently, Alvaro set off for Rome to solicit papal support. This was, of course, in the midst of World War II: during the flight to Rome Alvaro del Portillo witnessed the bombing of a ship in the Mediterranean. Otherwise the war seems to have impinged little on Opus, apart from the Allied landing in Sicily which, comments Vázquez, "got in the way of the negotiations begun by the President General of Opus in 1943."[4]

Much to the astonishment of the Italians, when Alvaro was granted an audience with Pius XII he went off to see the Pope in the full-dress uniform of a Spanish road engineer.[5] Afterward he returned to Madrid. The Sacerdotal Society of the Holy Cross received approval on 11 October 1943, though the news did not reach the Spanish capital for another week. It was greeted with rejoicing. On 8 December the Bishop of Madrid formally constituted the Sacerdotal Society in his diocese.

There were now, therefore, two organizations under Escrivá de Balaguer's command. Opus Dei, the "pious union," still existed, but a "clerical association" called the Sacerdotal Society of the Holy Cross had been created alongside it. The juridical problems which have since beset Opus have arisen from the difficulties of coping with two quite different institutions.

The opening words of the 1943 Constitution of the Sacerdotal Society highlight the issue: "'The Sacerdotal Society of the Holy Cross' is a society, preferably [*praeferenter*] clerical, of people living in common without vows." Whatever else might be said about membership of this group, it quite obviously ruled out women members, a fact made clearer by paragraph 8 of the Constitution, which declared the Society was made up of two sections, one of priests (there was, of course, only one priest, Escrivá de Balaguer himself, at the time of its foundation) and the other of laity who were en route to the priesthood and who were being prepared for ordination. The Church's law demanded that a clerical association should be run by clerics. There was no requirement, however, that only clerics might belong to it.

It was the special task of the Sacerdotal Society to look after Opus Dei (see paragraph 20).[6] Opus had its own statutes, appended to those of the Sacerdotal Society. There were, however, marked similarities: both had numeraries and supernumeraries, as the two ranks were called, roughly the equivalent of full-time and part-time members. Where the Society had "*electi*" ("the chosen ones") with a voice in the governance of the Institute, Opus had "inscribed ones" with rather more spiritual obligations than lesser members. The Sacerdotal Society had several houses for its members who lived in common. Opus was to have only one national residence (Article 11). One rather odd prescription was that no one could be received into the Sacerdotal Society who had been baptized as an adult. Nor could anyone be received who could not demonstrate that, at least on one side of the family, he had Catholic ancestors for three generations. With the exception of this last prescription, the outline of Opus and the Sacerdotal Society, as prepared for the Vatican's Sacred Congregation for Religious which looked after such matters, looked very much like a sketch for, and did not differ markedly from, the Constitution currently in force (see chapter 5)—at least to an outside observer.

Rather curiously, there was nothing in the statutes governing the Sacerdotal Society which laid down any specific requirement of secrecy. Article 12 of the statutes of Opus, on the other hand, was quite explicit: "Lest humility suffer harm,

(1) no papers or public books are to be published as belonging to Opus; (2) nor are members to wear any distinctive sign of membership; and (3) members should be persuaded against speaking to strangers about Opus."

So far Escrivá's foundation was a diocesan-based organization. By 1946 the Sacerdotal Society had about twelve clergy, some 250 numeraries, and as many as 400 "oblates," who lived similar lives to the numeraries, but did not live in Opus houses. The subordinate Opus Dei had in the region of 350 members. Its simple, practical, rather manly spirituality obviously had an appeal to the devout of Franco's Spain in their determination to revitalize the religious life of the country. There were houses of one kind or another in Madrid, Valencia, Barcelona, Zaragoza, Valladolid, Sevilla, Bilbao, Granada, and Santiago de Compostela. The year before, Escrivá had three times visited Portugal in the hope of spreading his work to that part of the Iberian peninsula. There were already members from other countries, some of them in Italy.[7] It was time, the founder felt, to rise a little higher in the ranks of Church organizations, to spread out from being a diocesan-based institution to one with status in the Catholic Church at large.

The loyal Alvaro del Portillo was once again dispatched Romeward to seek pontifical approval for a new status for Opus Dei. But that was something which the Roman curia was not willing to concede, only three years after Opus's erection as a diocesan institution. Alvaro found the going tougher than expected, and appealed to Escrivá for support. The founder left Madrid by car on 23 June 1945 in the company of an Italian-speaking member of Opus, José Orlandis, making his way to Barcelona, stopping off at Marian shrines along the road. From Barcelona he took a boat to Genoa, then traveled once again by car to Rome.

Raimundo Pannikar recalls Escrivá's return from Rome. "My children," he told them, "I have lost my innocence." According to Pannikar, he went to Rome a straightforward, honest, simple priest—in other words, naive. There he saw how the Church was run, the intrigue and the exercise of patronage within the papal court. If the cardinals and all the monsignori could behave that way, he reasoned, it must be perfectly proper, and therefore so too could he—all, of course, simply in order to further the Kingdom of God. In the interests of the Kingdom, the common rules of morality could be if not flouted, at least by-passed. Rome had certainly exercised upon Escrivá de Balaguer an immense fascination. He was back in Madrid by the end of August. Two months later he was again in the Italian capital, and Rome was to remain his chief place of residence for the rest of his life.

Meanwhile, the mission to the Vatican had not had great success. Alvaro del Portillo had to content himself with obtaining from the curia approval of a number of spiritual privileges. These were rather more important to Opus Dei than they might seem at first glance. It was typical of a religious institution that its members were privileged to receive, or its priest members entitled to dispense, a number of "indulgences" or blessings of one sort or another. It was a matter of pride. Lists of such privileges were made available to members of such institutes, and to those who came under their spiritual guidance. They played a far greater part in Catholic piety in the 1940s and 1950s than they do today. For Opus Dei to be granted its own privileges was a sign that it had arrived.

Alvaro collected a considerable number of such privileges. They make interesting reading, for they indicate the type of piety by which Opus members were expected to live.[8] The day a neophyte entered was marked by a "plenary" (or complete) indulgence, promising the remission of all punishment in Purgatory remaining after a sin had been forgiven, as was each further step up the ladder of membership. There was another plenary indulgence available to those who kissed the wood of a cross in an Opus chapel on the Feast of the Invention (Finding) of the Holy Cross (3 May), and a lesser remission of punishment for the same act performed on other occasions. There is no doubt that Opus Dei set, and continues to set, great store by this arcane piece of Roman Catholic lore.

With these concessions, Opus had for the moment to be content. But there were greater things in the pipeline. On 2 February 1947 an "Apostolic Constitution" issued by the

Roman curia and known, as is the custom, by its opening words as *Provida Mater Ecclesia,* set up a new juridical structure in the Catholic Church, the secular institute.

The distinctive features of a secular institute were well-suited to the form of life Opus promoted among its members. No one wore a special form of dress, or habit; no one took public vows, though they might take private ones. Those in secular institutes did not change their profession or trade because of their membership, nor did they change their ecclesiastical status: lay people still remained lay, priests did not cease to be clerics.

This new form of organization was greeted eagerly by Opus as the solution for which they had been looking. So eagerly, in fact, that the Sacred Congregation for Religious rushed through a decree constituting it the first secular institute: indeed, those were the very words with which the decree opened and therefore by which it is known: *Primum Institutum Seculare.* It was dated just three weeks after *Provida Mater Ecclesia,* 24 February 1947. That *Provida Mater Ecclesia* should have seemed to fit Opus so well was not surprising. Through his increasing involvement in the papal curia Alvaro had played a part in bringing the new structure into existence. The Constitution was welcomed whole-heartedly by members of Opus who gave every appearance of taking it over, rather as they have tried, with considerable success, to monopolize their latest status—they are still the only example of what is called a "personal prelature." In 1948 Escrivá delivered a lecture in praise of secular institutes. At that date the founder and his associates were eager that Opus should be recognized not just as a secular institute but as in law the first of them—the "in law" is important, for there were of course organizations older than Opus which either never took up the new status or received it later.

Rather curiously, in a bibliographical article published in 1981, the compiler, Mateo-Seco, omitted any mention of Escrivá's lecture, which had been published.[9] Four years later, however, in his contribution to *Mons. Josemaría Escrivá de Balaguer y el Opus Dei* (ed. Pedro Rodriguez et al.) he has repaired the omission—as an aside in a footnote and, as he admits, out of place. The passage which he quotes from Escrivá's own piece does not mention *Provida Mater Ecclesia,* the subject upon which he was writing. Instead he cites a section which lays stress upon those elements of Opus Dei life which, eventually, Escrivá decided did not fit into the pattern of a secular institute.

Mateo-Seco's quotation is therefore tendentious. But it draws attention to the problems which Opus Dei was to face, and which brought it to the point where it stopped attending meetings of representatives of secular institutes, and then rejected the status entirely. Not, it would seem, without reason. For *Provida Mater Ecclesia* put secular institutes under the control of the Sacred Congregation for Religious, and there was a definite tendency to make them increasingly like religious orders. Escrivá de Balaguer was opposed to such an assimilation.

Two months after the recognition of Opus as a secular institute, Escrivá was appointed to the rank of a "domestic prelate" to the Pope, which gave him the right to the title of Monsignor, and to wear purple as part of his clerical dress.

> He always tried to be properly dressed for each occasion [writes Bernal]. There was a time when he wore a skull-cap to make up for his youthful appearance. . . . Later by way of emphasizing the secularity of Opus Dei, he would sometimes wear the crimson-lined cassock and the other distinctive marks of his status as a Domestic Prelate. Years later he confessed that he found this harder than wearing a cilice.*[10]

Escrivá's successor, Alvaro del Portillo, also has the title of Monsignor, but as the head of the newly instituted Prelature he sports a bishop's ring and a cross hanging upon his chest in the manner of a bishop—which, until quite recently, he was not. Rather curiously for a formal Constitution, the document

---

*A cilice is the spiked bracelet occasionally worn by Opus members upon the arm or leg as a form of penance.

approved in 1950 made special mention that "titles of honor such as those customarily granted by either civil or ecclesiastical authority to clerics or lay people are not forbidden to members of Opus Dei"—though it was forbidden to intrigue for them (paragraph 14.5). Priests of Opus who became Superiors were also permitted to wear some sign indicating their rank (paragraph 14.6)—a concession of which the new Prelate obviously made much.

The new status of Opus required that its headquarters be in Rome, but at the beginning of 1947 it had no formal residence in the city. The problem was mentioned to an Italian duchess, Virginia Sforza Cesarini. She knew of a building in the Viale Bruno Buozzi which had once housed the Hungarian Embassy to the Holy See, and which the owner wanted to sell. It was acquired in July and was named by Escrivá the Villa Tevere (i.e., Tiber). Extensive improvements were undertaken to make it an elegant, imposing mansion untypical of other headquarters of religious institutes in Rome. Work was not completed on the refurbishment until early 1960.

Clearly, Opus was by now established in Italy. Outside Italy and, of course, Spain it had centers in Portugal (from 1945) and England (from 1946). In the year of its approval as a secular institute it expanded to France and to Ireland. Two years later it was also in Mexico and the USA. In 1950 it began in Chile.

It had begun to expand in other ways as well. No sooner had approval been given as a secular institute than Escrivá determined Opus was to have married members. Vázquez de Prada can quote long passages from the founder in praise of matrimony,[11] but a distinctly different attitude is to be found in *Camino*. Even the *approved* translation of Maxim 28 reads,

> Marriage is for the soldiers and not for the General Staff [i.e. officers] of Christ's army. For, whereas food is a necessity for each individual, procreation is a necessity for the species only, not for the individual.
> Longing for children? Children, many children, and a lasting trail of light we shall leave behind us if we sacrifice the selfishness [*egoismo*] of the flesh.

One has to remember that, for Catholics brought up in the traditional mold as was Escrivá, the procreation of children was the primary purpose of marriage. It was the begetting of children which a call to serve in the officer corps made impossible (though of course it also preserved one from "the burdens of the home"—Maxim 26). Quite apart from the disparagement of marriage, the objectionable feature of Escrivá's remark is the clear "class" distinction which he introduces. It may not, of course, have been at all uncommon for the clergy to think such thoughts or to put on paper the preeminence of the celibate life. It is odd only in a priest whose charism, one is urged to believe, was his appreciation of the lay, or secular, status within the Church.

Be that as it may, 1947 saw the addition of a married category to the ranks of Opus. From then on married people could, and do, enter as supernumerary members, without hope (or, no doubt, desire) of rising higher in the ranks.

By 1950 the men's branch of Opus had about 2,400 members, of whom a score or so were priests.[12] About two-thirds of these were in Spain. The next largest group was the Portuguese, with approximately 260 members. Mexico and Italy (in the latter country Escrivá himself had been particularly active in searching out recruits) numbered one hundred or so each. The countries mentioned above were the ones in which Opus Dei had been most successful. In addition, there were about 550 members of the women's branch.

The year 1950 is an important one, because this was the year in which Opus Dei was rewarded by formal approval as a secular institute by Pope Pius XII. The 1946 document had been a "decretum laudis," a generalized statement of approbation. On 16 June 1950 came the formal document, with approval of the new Constitution. Though another Constitution was issued in 1982, this fascinating document has not been superseded. Section 2 of the "Final Dispositions" of the 1982 version insists that the earlier rule remains in force, except where specifically abrogated. In particular it retains its interest because, in contrast to the latest version, it has a great deal to say about the institution's spirituality and method of operating. So much so, in fact, that even former high-ranking officials of Opus such as María del Carmen Tapia believed the version printed at the back of Jesús Ynfante's *La prodigiosa aventura del Opus Dei* (1970) was not the actual Constitution but a first draft of it. Opus officials have not denied it is the Constitution of the institute, however, though they have commented unfavorably both upon the translation and upon the editing.

The greatest change from past variations of the Opus rule in the 1950 version is the permission granted to diocesan priests to become members. They might, according to paragraph 72, become oblates or supernumerary members. They could not, however, become numeraries because that would withdraw them from their obedience to their diocesan bishop. Thus was solved a problem which had been vexing Escrivá: he had been thinking, so Vázquez de Prada relates, of leaving Opus to dedicate himself to the spiritual advancement of diocesan clergy; now he could do this within his original foundation.

Another innovation in the 1950 Constitution (paragraph 29) was the rank of "co-operators" to assist by their prayers and alms-giving, and by actively helping with projects commended to them by the superiors of the institute. In return they profit from the spiritual benefits of Opus. Co-operators can even include those "who do not profess the Catholic truth": they are, however, in danger of being proselytized. When one distinguished English Catholic journalist learned that, because of some service he had performed for Opus when it first came to London, he was regarded as a co-operator he was incensed.

There are a number of unusual features in the new Constitution as it was approved in 1950 by the Sacred Congregation for Religious.[13] The Congregation broke rules that it, or other departments of the papal curia, had long established for the better management of religious institutes. For example, the 1917 Code of Canon Law had insisted that, without the special approval of Rome which, in this instance, Escrivá de Balaguer had not sought, women's religious institutes were not to be dependent upon their male equivalents in terms of government: they had to have their own superiors even at the highest level. The women's branch of Opus, on the other hand, was totally dependent upon Escrivá at the highest level, and at the regional level upon the regional counselor.*

It had also been agreed by the Roman authorities that although "manifestation of conscience" *might be* beneficial as a spiritual exercise, it was so open to abuse that it was not to be obligatory upon members of religious institutes. The practice, which involved telling the superior everything about oneself, one's difficulties and imperfections, was made obligatory upon all members of Opus.

Finally, the Sacred Congregation for Religious had been eager to ensure that the divisions within an institute were as few as possible. Within Opus Dei, however, there were not only co-operators, supernumeraries, and numeraries or oblates: even within the ranks of the numeraries themselves there were class distinctions.

Overall, however, what is important here is the sort of organization that arose out of the granting of the decree of the Sacred Congregation for Religious on 16 June 1950, what one commentator calls the "physiognomy" of Opus.[14] According to Opus, it is, was, and has always been a distinctly lay organization (lay as opposed to "clerical," not run by "clerks" or priests). The 1950 Constitution, however, is, in anyone's estimation, distinctly clerical.

This can be seen on two levels. The first, and most obvious, is that the direction of Opus Dei was in the hands of priests. The numbers of the clergy in 1950 were few, around a score or so out of a total membership of some 3,000. Of these latter, about 550 were women and therefore not eligible for the priesthood. The remaining 2,400 men were divided into the two ranks of numeraries and supernumeraries, so those

---

*The pretense of being separate has been maintained. When asked what would have happened after Escrivá's death had the female section chosen as his successor somebody other than the priest chosen first by the men, a woman member of Opus was quite taken aback at the question. Apparently this possibility had never crossed her mind.

The Years of Expansion

available for ordination (the numeraries) numbered about a thousand.

The first two sections of the very first chapter of the 1950 Constitution state that the proper name of the organization is "The Priestly Society of the Holy Cross and Opus Dei," and that the whole of it is a "clerical" institute. However, a number of people who, in the estimation of the Father, are judged suitable for ordination to the priesthood, although they are not technically clerics, also belong to the Sacerdotal Society.

That is the first thing: Opus Dei is clerical in its command structure, and in the way that full membership appears to be reserved to those who are priests and to those who might be priests.

Secondly, it is clerical in the looser sense in which Catholics use the word to cover nuns as well as priests. This is a common-sense usage. "Lay" in English tends to mean "non-professional." But of course nuns as well as priests, and the numerous unordained members of religious orders, earn their keep by being "professional" or full-time, active members of the Church. Their common denominator is that they live in communities. They live, in other words, a "common life." Conventional family life is replaced by a form of family life based upon the life of the religious congregation to which they have committed themselves.

We have already seen that it was Escrivá de Balaguer's desire that the life within Opus Dei should be, as nearly as possible, a "family" life. This he went to great lengths to achieve, both in the style of life and in the language which he encouraged about himself and his own close relations. But the numeraries, the only full and proper members of the Sacerdotal Society, were required to follow the evangelical counsels of perfection, as, in the traditional understanding of the Catholic Church, members of religious orders were required to do. They were also required to live a "common" life in special Opus houses.

Though they were, in 1950, given the rank of "secular" institute—and boasted of the fact that they were the first of its kind—secularity did not mean "lay" in any ordinary sense of the word. To all intents and purposes the full members, the numeraries, were monks and nuns.

That impression is strengthened when the 1950 Constitution goes on to talk about the process by which people become members of Opus Dei. First there is a period of "probation," then a five-year-long "oblation," and finally the "fidelity," with its life-long commitment. For those joining as numeraries, the fidelity required that they take the traditional monastic vows of poverty, chastity, and obedience. (They were also, incidentally, required to take further vows which safeguarded the institution and, by insisting on consultation with superiors, increased the degree of control that superiors might exercise over members.)

Again like fully fledged monks or nuns, the spiritual life of members was rigorously controlled by the 1950 Constitution. Where members live together as a "family" there is to be set up a black cross without the figure of Christ upon it. Each evening they were to recite together—or individually if that were not possible—the rosary, the prayer to the Virgin Mary made up of fifteen decades of ten Hail Marys each, followed by a reflection upon the gospel which had been read at mass for that day. Each room was to have an image of the Virgin, to be greeted on entering and leaving.

Then there were the daily obligations upon individual members: naturally, mass had to be attended each day, and there was half an hour's mental prayer in the morning and another half hour in the evening. There was to be spiritual reading. Each month a whole day had to be dedicated to things of the spirit, and each year several days given over to "spiritual exercises" or a retreat.

Nothing of this would be at all odd, in any religious order, male or female, with the possible exception of the practice of the cross without the figure of the Crucified.* What was odd

---

* "When you see a poor wooden Cross, alone, uncared-for, and of no value . . . and without its Crucified, don't forget that that Cross is your Cross: the Cross of each day, the hidden Cross, without splendor or consolation . . . , the Cross which is wailing for the Crucified it lacks; and that Crucified must be you" *Camino*, Maxim 178.

was Escrivá's insistence that Opus Dei was not a religious order at all, but a lay organization. At that level it did not make sense. Nor did it make sense when the male and female branches are compared. Escrivá was unable to take women seriously as equal to the male members of his institute. Perhaps it was nothing out of the ordinary for his time (though one has to remember that it is Opus's boast that Escrivá de Balaguer was ahead of his time in the organization of his institute), but it was expressed in remarkably petty ways.

Take, for example, the prayer which Escrivá instructed was to close all formal gatherings of the male branch of Opus. It was an invocation to the Virgin Mary: "Holy Mary, Our Hope, Seat of Wisdom, pray for us." The prayer appointed for the women in similar circumstances was only slightly different, but the difference was significant: "Holy Mary, Our Hope, Handmaid of the Lord, pray for us." Though women numeraries as well as men were expected either to have, or to be able to earn, doctorates, they were, apparently, not expected to invoke Mary as "Seat of Wisdom." Wisdom was not for them. That invocation was replaced by one which reminded the female branch of Opus at the end of each meeting that their role-model was that of a servant, in a position of subordination.

But hierarchy is part of the Opus mentality. The 1950 Constitution appears to have enshrined no less than four classes of members. There were the numeraries; there were the numeraries who had taken further vows (or "fidelities"); there were those numeraries known as "inscribed" members who were basically in charge of Opus Dei's activities, directing houses and so on, and who had a vote, when it came to a vote, in the institute's affairs; and finally there were those numeraries, the "elect," who could be voted *for*. Movement up these grades depended on the whim of Escrivá and his consultors.

Just at the time that Opus was legislating for these class distinctions, other religious bodies in the Catholic Church were doing exactly the opposite, trying to curtail the rigid distinctions which had hitherto existed between, for example, "lay sisters" and "choir nuns"—the former doing all the manual labor and the latter (rejoicing in the title "mother"), playing all the leading roles. By 1950 such distinctions were already seen to be disruptive of good community life, yet Escrivá de Balaguer insisted upon them. Far from being in the forefront of the development of religious life, Opus Dei was harking back to old models which were being abandoned by others just as Escrivá was imposing them.

This, then, was the Constitution under which Opus Dei continued to exist for more than thirty years, although with an increasing conviction that it was not a suitable juridical form for what Escrivá had in mind when he founded the organization. That, at least, is how the story of the institute's legal development is presented by Opus itself.

All of this makes it odd that Opus Dei should be the first organization to receive the status of a secular institute. One would have expected the first Constitution approved to have been a model for others, rather than one that transgressed the Sacred Congregation's own norms by harking back to practices the Congregation was eager to phase out. Yet Salvador Canals, in his *Secular Institutes and the State of Perfection* dated, from Rome, 26 October 1952 can recommend the structure of Opus Dei as approved in 1950 as an "ideal solution" to a canonical puzzle he has set himself.[15] His book then devotes a whole chapter to "some 'juridical notes' on the first of the Secular Institutes, the *Sacerdotal Society of the Holy Cross and Opus Dei*."[16] This is not surprising for, of course, Dr. Canals is a priest of Opus. He was also a member of the Sacred Congregation for Religious, and in charge of the special office set up to handle secular institutes. Perhaps the curious provisions allowed in Opus's Constitution in contradiction to usual Congregation practice owed a great deal to the influence of Opus Dei within the Congregation itself.

There was a somewhat bizarre coda to the story of the granting of Opus's Constitution as a secular institute. In the summer of 1947, at a time of the year when professional Vatican-watchers were either escaping from the heat of Rome, or at least, not at their sharpest, Alvaro del Portillo on behalf of

Opus Dei asked whether bishops or other religious superiors, who had to know details about secular institutes which regarded themselves as to some extent secret, were also obliged to observe that secrecy about these institutes in their dealings with others. The Sacred Congregation for Religious decided they had so to act.

Two years later almost to the day, Alvaro again put a question about secrecy to the Sacred Congregation. Would it be necessary, or indeed expedient, to show to a local bishop in whose diocese Opus wished to open a center, or to engage corporately in apostolic work therein, the full text of the Constitution of the institute? If the Congregation should determine that it was not necessary to hand over the full Constitution, then how much should be made available, Opus wanted to know. The Congregation decided that it was neither necessary nor expedient to hand over the full Constitution. The only documents Opus, or any other similar institute, would be required to reveal were the decree of approbation, a summary of the Constitution, and a list of those privileges enjoyed by the institute which might in some way involve the local bishop.

At almost exactly the same time as the second request was being made of the Congregation, Alvaro also wanted to know whether the local bishop absolutely *had* to be told about each and every Opus residence—or only about the most public ones. Again he got the reply which he no doubt wanted: only the existence of full-scale centers (and formal apostolic activity of a corporate nature) had to be revealed to the bishop within whose jurisdiction these activities were being carried on.

These three remarkable documents from the Sacred Congregation of Religious were originally published, with a very sympathetic commentary, in a technical canon law journal, the *Commentarium pro Religiosis* that same year, 1949 (vol. 28, pp. 303–4).[17] They resurfaced in the same periodical on the occasion of the granting to Opus of its new status as a personal prelature nearly a quarter of a century later (vol. 64, 1983, pp. 351–53). The sympathetic commentary was still in place. The commentator pointed out that Alvaro was apparently not asking these provisions solely for the benefit of Opus Dei, but for all the new secular institutes.

These further exercises in secrecy, or furtiveness, took place, of course, between the approval of Opus as a secular institute and the definitive approval of its Constitution. Just what Opus felt it had to fear from the Constitutions falling into the hands of a bishop—and not just any bishop, but one who was sympathetic enough to have allowed the institute to come to work in his diocese—is far from clear. The 1950 Constitution proclaimed the organization regarded it as a distinctive mark that it should show "absolute and total adhesion and submission to the hierarchy and to authority in the Church" (paragraph 208). That, apparently, did not mean it was prepared to trust members of the hierarchy with copies of the Constitution.

It is difficult to reconcile these documents so eagerly sought between 1947 and 1949 with Escrivá's own assertion:

> It is easy to get to know Opus Dei. It works in broad daylight in all countries, with the full juridical recognition of the civil and ecclesiastical authorities. The names of its directors and of its apostolic undertakings are well known. Anyone who wants information can obtain it without difficulty.[18]

The charge of secrecy will not go away, despite constant denials by Escrivá and lesser members that it is a secret organization. Here it is remarked upon simply to bring home yet again the problem of sorting out the history of the institute. Such official or semi-official accounts that there are dwell upon the apparently miraculous spread of the organization. We have seen above how far it had got by 1950. The following year, according to Vázquez de Prada, it had reached Colombia and Venezuela. Then during the next two decades it established itself in Germany, Peru, and Guatemala (1953), Ecuador (1954), Uruguay (1956), Brazil and Austria (1957). There were by the end of the 1960s centers in Japan (from 1959), in the Philippines (from 1964), and elsewhere.[19]

Opus also went to Africa, specifically to Kenya though it soon afterward expanded to Nigeria, in 1958. Three years later two schools, Strathmore College and Kianda School, were set up in Nairobi. With some justification, Opus claims these as the African continent's first multi-racial schools.

In 1957, four years after arriving in Peru and at the direct request of the Holy See, Opus members were sent to work in the Prelature of Yauyos. This type of activity, in which Opus took charge of a whole area of the country the Church was unable to supply with clergy, was a new departure for the institute, but it was one which was to have a major impact, particularly in Peru (see chapter 6).

Opus's role in Australia has been particularly controversial. The organization first established itself there in 1963, and in 1971 it set up, at the request of Cardinal Gilroy, the Archbishop of Sydney, a college at the University of New South Wales. Called Warrane College and, as is usual in such cases, without any outward sign of its affiliation, it is the only Catholic college at the university and seems to attract in particular students from country areas who know little of Opus before they arrive. Only three years after it had been established, the university itself set up a committee of inquiry into the management of Warrane in response to campus unrest. Though the report of the committee in general terms exonerated Opus, it expressed surprise at the degree of pressure put upon students to join Opus, and at some of the college rules—students have complained, for instance, at the censorship of both newspapers and television. Great numbers, far greater than in other residential colleges of the university, find alternative accommodation as soon as they possibly can. In 1985 his priest advisers recommended to the Archbishop of Melbourne that Opus be refused permission to open a house in that diocese.[20]

Perhaps Opus's most important, certainly its most prestigious, educational institution began life in 1952. In that year the University of Navarra was established at Pamplona, Spain, under the direction of one of Opus's most distinguished members, Sanchez Bella, who was brought back from Argentina specifically for this purpose. In 1960, when it had some 1,500 students, it was formally recognized as a university by the Holy See, and Escrivá de Balaguer was appointed Grand Chancellor.

On the face of it there was nothing unusual in all this: Spain already possessed pontifical, or papal, universities, and the concordat between Spain and the Holy See allowed such institutions to be created. But what Opus managed to set up at Pamplona, with the support of the papal nuncio in Madrid, Mgr Antoniutti, a loyal friend of Opus Dei, and Cardinal Ottaviani, one of the most conservative of Roman prelates, was something quite out of the ordinary. Of the five faculties thus formally established, only one, that of Canon Law, was directly related to the Church; the others were secular. Opus, in other words, had provided an alternative to State institutions—and they saw to it that some of its faculties and schools were second to none in Spain.

But matters were not quite so straightforward. The Jesuits ran two venerable universities in the north of Spain, those of Comillas then near Santander but now in Madrid, and Deusto in Bilbao. They were looking for a similar sort of status for one or other of these institutions—preferably for Deusto, then seventy-five years old. Rome's choice of the upstart University of Navarra was a severe blow to the Jesuits' hopes, and to their prestige. It did nothing to improve relations between them and Opus.

There was another issue. Navarra was a private university, and supposedly supported by private funds. When Vázquez lists its sources of income he gives them as local businesses and corporations, cultural institutions, and grant-making foundations, both Spanish and foreign.[21] This is not quite the whole story. The provincial government of Navarra supplied considerable funds and the fact that it is now, under a socialist regime, in the process of withdrawing its support is causing considerable problems for the university administration. Central government likewise has provided subventions in "important quantities."[22] Given these facts, it seems a trifle unfair, not to say ungenerous, of Escrivá to say when interviewed by Peter Forbarth:

> In very few places have we had fewer facilities than in Spain. . . . The situation in Spain with respect to our corporate apostolates has not been particularly favorable either. The

governments of countries where Catholics are in a minority have helped the educational and welfare activities founded by Opus Dei members far more generously than the Spanish government.[23]

Though other Opus Dei universities were to open else-where in the world, the University of Navarra remains the organization's showpiece, with particularly strong departments of journalism and business studies, two typically Opus enter-prises. It has recently opened an off-shoot in Rome, in an attempt to establish its own school of theology at the head-quarters of Roman Catholicism. Opus no doubt wishes to emulate the Jesuits, with their prestigious Gregorian Univer-sity, or the Dominicans with the Angelicum, or other religious orders with their own institutions, drawing students—mainly church students and nuns but including some lay people—from around the world.

Opus's attempted entry into this area has been given a decidedly chilly reception by the established Roman colleges. Part of the hostility is to its distinctly conservative doctrine, discussed elsewhere in this book, and part is due to the general hostility to Opus felt by many Roman Catholic clerics. But in part also it is a simple matter of survival, especially for the rather more traditionally minded colleges such as the Lateran and Angelicum which fear they could lose their clientele to Opus. As an academic administrator of one of the older pontif-ical universities commented, it is becoming increasingly diffi-cult to recruit from round the world—most nuns or students for the priesthood would rather study where they will eventu-ally have to work. The last thing Rome needs is another eccle-siastical faculty.

Despite the opposition, it opened in a house next to the church of St. Jerome. In this house, at the end of the sixteenth century, St. Philip Neri had lived out his last days. Neri had founded a society of secular priests, the Congregation of the Oratory, and the Oratorians regarded the building as their mother house. They did not own it but were its custodians and served the church beside it. There had been moves even dur-ing the pontificate of Paul VI to get them out and to hand the buildings over to Opus—though in its account of the events the Oratorian journal does not name Opus, simply calling it "another very powerful entity which operated through doubtful but effective channels." The Oratorians went to court and lost. Only the personal intervention of Paul VI prevented them from being dislodged.

After Paul's death in August 1978 the Vicariate of Rome (the body which looks after the diocese of Rome in the name of the Pope who is, of course, technically Rome's bishop) appointed a priest of Opus to the church of St. Jerome. Civil measures followed that gave the house adjacent to the church to Opus Dei. It was gutted and restored to house Opus's center of studies.

Universities, however, were and are as such a very small part of the Opus apostolate. Much more typical is the establishment of university halls of residence, both for men and for women. Netherhall House in Hampstead, London, is one such for men. It is situated in one of the pleasanter, and notably more expensive, parts of London.

Members of Opus first came to England in 1946 to further their studies. By 1948 they had established themselves in a flat in Rutland Court, Knightsbridge, a particularly fashionable part of town, and had begun to contact undergraduates and give them spiritual guidance. At first they met with little success, at least by Opus standards: Vázquez de Prada remarks that by 1950 only one Englishman, named Michael Richards, had asked to join. Such a paucity of candidates was clearly an unexpected occurrence.[24] The situation was very different in Ireland, and Irish recruits were used to bolster the spirit of the slender intake in England. There were still scarcely half a dozen English members when Escrivá determined to open a university residence in London.

The permission of the Cardinal Archbishop of Westminster had already been obtained to open a center of some kind. A hotel in Netherhall Gardens was swiftly found and promptly purchased. It opened for business in mid-1952, with members of the women's section being brought in to look after the domestic arrangements. Two years later a formal trust deed was drawn up with Michael Richards and Juan Antonio Galarraga named as trustees. The purpose of the trust was declared to be the advancement of the Roman Catholic faith.

Other residences were later founded, both in London and elsewhere, such as Greygarth in Manchester and, in 1958, Grandpont in Oxford. Vázquez's account of this latter event is careful. He is also careful to emphasize the part played by ecclesiastical authority in the form of an auxiliary bishop of Westminster, Bishop Craven, and the administrator of Westminster Cathedral, Mgr Gordon Wheeler, later to be Bishop of Leeds.[25]

It was natural enough that Opus, with its heavy concentration on the university apostolate, would have wished to establish a center at Oxford. Its natural approach was to open a residence for students as it had done in London. But it was ill-advised and had insufficient knowledge of the Oxford system. The colleges of the university are precisely halls of residence—or so they began. Opus's desire to open a hall seemed at the time to be tantamount to opening a college. The plans for such a college had been prepared—Fr. Michael Hollings, Roman Catholic chaplain to the university in the late 1950s and 1960s, recalls seeing them displayed in Opus's Roman headquarters. The university authorities were not having it. Hollings recalls his predecessor telling him that the Archbishop of Birmingham, Joseph Grimshaw, in whose diocese Oxford lay, was unhappy with the idea that Opus should be in his territory. Luckily for Opus a house came on the market—Grandpont—which was just across the river, still in Oxford, but in the much more compliant diocese of Portsmouth. It was acquired and opened as a kind of lodging house catering to post-graduate students of the university. It has proved an excellent recruiting ground for candidates for Opus Dei.

Rather oddly, perhaps, Escrivá seems to have been particularly fond of England. Vázquez has calculated that, apart from Italy and Spain, he spent more time in the United Kingdom than in any other country of the world.[26] He first came to London in 1958, and then each summer until 1962 he escaped the heat of Rome or Madrid by taking a house to the north of

Hampstead Heath or in West Heath Road. He came because he was eager to promote Opus Dei in the "Anglo-Saxon" world, but he also came because he saw England, and especially London, as a crossroads, a place from which his organization could reach out to people in many different parts of the world—or where they could come to Opus. On a personal level he seems to have been especially impressed by the two ancient university towns of Oxford and Cambridge, by the old churches—in which he said rosaries, knelt before high altars, and uttered ejaculatory prayers quite unmoved by Protestant sensibilities. This is perhaps not surprising: he had never before been exposed to a non-Catholic culture, certainly not for any length of time.

4

A Change of Status

It is part of Opus Dei mythology that Escrivá de Balaguer pre-empted the conclusions of the Second Vatican Council (Vatican II). The Council, summoned by Pope John XXIII, brought together the world's two thousand and more Roman Catholic bishops. The documents it drew up and published between 1962 and 1965 marked a major liberalization (Pope John preferred the word *aggiornamento*, "bringing up to date") on issues such as religious toleration, the relation between the Church and the world, the structures of the Church, and so on. In particular the Council emphasized the important role to be played by the lay Christian, and this is the reason why it is suggested that Escrivá was a precursor of Vatican II's vision of the Church's future. The truth of the matter, however, is quite otherwise.

Far from welcoming the outcome of the Council, Escrivá worked hard to oppose it. His biographers do not attempt to hide the distress which the Council caused him, and they take pride in his efforts to see that its unwelcome conclusions did not affect members of Opus. The Council was inspired by Pope John XXIII, but it was carried to its completion, and its decisions put into practice, by Pope Paul VI. María del Carmen Tapia served for ten years as head of the women's section in Venezuela, but before that had worked for Opus's Rome headquarters. She came into close contact with Escrivá. She told me that she had once heard him say of Paul VI that "God in his infinite wisdom should take this man away."

Nothing upset Escrivá more—and this was also true of many of the older clergy in the Catholic Church at large who found it hard to change the habits of a lifetime—than the new regulations about the way in which mass was to be said.

The purpose of the "misa normativa" (or "standard mass"), as it was called, was to make the celebration of the eucharist each Sunday more intelligible to the congregation in the pews. Hitherto, Roman Catholic priests had said the mass with their backs to the people. This rather odd position had its defenders. It was claimed that this stance better exemplified the structure of the Church: a priest at its head, addressing the Almighty on behalf of the people. It was hierarchical, and it certainly meant that for the most part a congregation had no idea what was happening at the altar, being effectively barred from seeing it by the heavily vestmented body of the priest. One of the first things to change, therefore, was the position of the altar. Where possible it was brought away from the back wall of the church and located nearer the congregation. The priest was to stand behind it, facing the people and associating them with him in prayer. It was a rather more democratic understanding of the liturgical celebration.

At Opus's London residence for students, Netherhall House, Vladimir Felzmann, the director, was much taken by the reforms in the liturgy and determined to re-align the altar with the priest facing the people. This he did, with full approval at the time of the Opus authorities. The work was undertaken in the best possible taste and very expensively. It looked attractive. Then a message came from Rome: there were to be no altars facing the people. Felzmann's work was dismantled, again at great expense, and the old, back-to-the-congregation position restored.

But it was not just a question of the position of the altar. The "misa normativa" had a variety of possible structures to allow one priest a considerable degree of freedom in suiting the liturgy to his congregation. The form to be used in Opus Dei houses was rigorously controlled, even down to which of the four acclamations might be used after the elevation of the sacred elements. One of the major changes, of course, was in the language that could now be used. Masses might be said in the vernacular—except in Opus Dei houses where Latin was to remain the rule. Escrivá de Balaguer studied the new regulations about the mass with care. He sent detailed guidelines to the members of Opus Dei about how they were to apply them, warning them at the same time of the dangers they were facing by the disruption in the life of the Church. Vázquez records that Escrivá de Balaguer also insisted on lectures being given to members to help them "discover the truth." He laid down precise instructions about their content.

Later he was to spend a good deal of time in Latin America, warning his faithful about the dangers that had come in the wake of the Council. He went to Mexico for a month in 1970, to Brazil, Argentina, Chile, Peru, Ecuador, Venezuela for three months in 1974, the following year he was back in Venezuela and went on to Guatemala. Latin America, of course, was the home of Liberation Theology with its central theme of seeing the world and the Church through the eyes of the poor. Escrivá de Balaguer would have none of this departure from the traditional theology of the Roman Catholic Church. Commenting upon those clerics of the 1970s who had "filled their heads with psychology and had been contaminated by a social propaganda of a Marxist hue," Vázquez remarks they built up the idea that in the past the Church had been the Church of the rich. To balance the extremes, he says, many gave their support to "suspect movements in the community, or went over to the sector 'of the poor.' (The Founder, open to the universal call of Christ, used to prefer to speak of the 'Church of souls' because filiation with the divine has nothing to do with any socio-political affiliation)." Priests who did get involved in such "socio-political movements," Vázquez adds, were going down a blind alley.[1]

Meanwhile, things were not going well for Opus as a secular institute. On 1 October 1958 Escrivá wrote a somewhat pompous letter to the members of his institute. Its existence was unknown (except, presumably, to those in Opus who had received it) until it was printed as part of the documentation included in the volume of the new Constitutions of 1982. It is the letter *Non Ignoratis* ("You cannot be unaware"), and it contains the remarkable statement: "In fact we are neither a secular institute, nor can we any longer be called by that title." It was for the time an extraordinary thing to say, given that the formal Constitution of Opus Dei as a secular institute had been granted only eight years before, and that the whole idea of secular institutes had been embraced and carried forward by Opus just a decade earlier. It is even odder that, if such was Opus's official attitude, it still continued to attend gatherings of secular institutes, and its members still continued to describe themselves as such, at least up to 1962. What had made Escrivá change his mind?

The answer is clear from the letter itself. Although they were part of a secular institute, he alleged, Opus members were being forced more and more into a pattern of life which was the equivalent of that of members of a religious order. The Opus canon lawyer Julián Herranz wrote in 1964 that all other secular institutes had deviated from the model originally proposed for their manner of life: only Opus Dei had remained faithful to the original insight. There was perhaps some foundation to this criticism that secular institutes had been steadily assimilated to the model of religious orders, though Opus's strong influence in the Sacred Congregation for Religious should have been able to prevent it from happening. In his conversation with Peter Forbarth referred to in chapter 3, Escrivá himself put it like this:

> A powerful organization I prefer not to name and have always esteemed spent its energies over many years falsifying what it did not understand. They insisted on considering us monks or friars, and asked, "Why don't they all think the same way? And why don't they wear a religious habit or at least a badge?"

According to one former Opus member, the organization thus blamed for traducing the true spirit of the Opus Dei was the Society of Jesus. I was myself a member of the Society of some seven years standing by that time. I cannot recall that Opus figured on any Jesuit agenda.

Whatever the reason, in January 1962 Escrivá de Balaguer took the first steps along the road to a change in status for his organization in a letter addressed to Cardinal Amleto

Cicognani, then the papal Secretary of State—the Pope's chief minister. He was requested to pass the contents on to Pope John XXIII.

At this point Escrivá was asking that Opus Dei be established as a "prelatura nullius." This curious little anachronism, left over from the Middle Ages when powerful abbots controlled the land around their abbeys and had the right to hold courts, had recently proved useful. In essence, an abbot or a prelate had a tiny enclave which gave him a status roughly equivalent to that of a bishop. Priests could be associated with the enclave, and be governed according to its particular laws even though they operated elsewhere. In 1954 the ancient Cistercian abbey of Pontigny became the legal base for the Mission de France, an organization of over 175 priests working for the reconversion of their countrymen. When he was a chaplain in Madrid, Escrivá had been associated with a prelatura nullius. His doctoral studies on the Abadesa de Huelgas would have made him even better informed about such structures and their possibilities. This was the solution he wanted for Opus. He was turned down. His proposals contained, said Pope John, insuperable, and unspecified, difficulties.

Two years later Pope John was dead, and Escrivá tried again. Again he was turned down. Paul VI told him that the matter would have to be resolved in accordance with the decisions of the Second Vatican Council, then in full flow. In practice all the main religious organizations were put in a state of suspended animation. If for any reason they had to call a general meeting of the organization during this period—as the Jesuits did when their Father General died—the meeting had to be adjourned until the Council had completed its business. When reconvened, the structure of the organization was to be brought by the gathering into line with the conclusions of Vatican II. Escrivá called a General Congress of Opus for June 1969. Its chief purpose was to decide whether the new structures which had been emerging in the Church since Vatican II held out any greater possibility than had the prelatura nullius for a new legal basis to the institute. Four years later Escrivá formally notified Paul VI about the progress of the Congress, but two years after that, almost to the day, on 26 June 1975, Escrivá de Balaguer died.

He died quite suddenly, about midday, in the Villa Tevere. That evening, his successor, Alvaro del Portillo, said mass and preached a homily about him. "Ever since the Father died," he said, "I have been saying that now we have been left orphans. But it is not true. It is not true! Because, in addition to having God our Father who is in heaven, we have our own Father who is in heaven, and from there he concerns himself with all his children." The play upon "Our father who is in heaven" was to become a common one among members of Opus. The expression elevated Escrivá to an almost god-like status in people's consciousness. At the very least he was a saint.

Saint or not, he had still not delivered the documents of the 1969 Congress to the Holy See. Early in March 1976 Alvaro del Portillo, now in charge of the organization, went to see Paul VI. Paul told him that the question of Opus's juridical status still remained an open one, but a solution was in sight. At this point the new President General suggested that, so soon after Escrivá's death, the moment might not be opportune. Paul agreed, but he indicated then, as he did in June 1978 when Alvaro del Portillo went to see him again, that Opus had only to ask . . .

In November that same year the new Pope, the conservative John Paul II, wrote a letter of congratulation to Opus on the fiftieth anniversary of its creation. The Cardinal Secretary of State, when he handed over the Pope's personal message, added that John Paul wanted the matter of Opus's status to be resolved. It was still answerable to the Congregation for Religious and Secular Institutes, but steps would be authorized so that it might cease to be a secular institute. In January 1979 Opus had its first official contact with the Sacred Congregation for Bishops. It was an exchange of views, little more, but the hope was expressed that Opus might soon be transformed into a personal prelature (for this structure, see below, pp. 81–85) dependent upon the Sacred Congregation for Bishops.

The following month Alvaro del Portillo went again to see John Paul. He told the Pope of all that had so far been done, but as only the Pope himself could formally initiate the process to create Opus as a personal prelature, Opus's President General asked that this might be done. Not only did the Pope agree, but he acted promptly. At the next working session of the Sacred Congregation for Bishops, the Prefect in charge of the Congregation, Cardinal Sebastiano Baggio, a close friend of Opus, received from the Pope the task of undertaking the necessary studies. Less than a week later Baggio wrote to Alvaro del Portillo requesting that he produce a full study of the matter: this was 7 March. By 23 April a full report was on Baggio's desk. Though it had been updated both factually and juridically, the report was basically the one originally prepared for Paul VI, as the accompanying letter made clear.

The first part of this document ran through the history and status of Opus Dei, revealing in passing that there were at that time 72,375 members in eighty-seven different countries, and that roughly two percent of the members were priests. The report stressed the unique nature of Opus, and the problems which had arisen because hitherto the Catholic Church had not had an appropriate legal structure available for it; this fact, said the report, had occasioned the founder grave suffering and had impeded its work. It then went on to discuss the other juridical forms it had been obliged to adopt, and finally to point out that Opus Dei fulfilled the requirements for a personal prelature. There would be advantages for the Church if it were to be granted this status, the report concluded, for it would strengthen the service which Opus could offer the local Church and would put at the disposal of the Holy See a "mobile corps" (an expression, incidentally, more commonly used of the Jesuits) who could go where most needed. Members of Opus would thereby be freed from some of the problems they faced when working (and here again useful statistical details appeared) in 479 universities and high schools in all five continents, in 604 publications, in 52 broadcasting stations, both radio and television, in 38 press and publicity agencies, in 12 film production and distribution operations. Many other religious institutes of varying juridical status had managed, and continue to manage, to get along quite satisfactorily without benefit of being a personal prelature. Opus found it difficult.

At the beginning of June, Alvaro del Portillo wrote to Baggio once again, just to tidy up a few possible misunderstandings. It was planned that this letter, or part of it, would be read by Spaniards in a long article published by the Catholic weekly magazine *Vida Nueva* from which, in fact, a good deal of the above has been taken. But shortly before publication, two members of Opus Dei turned up bearing a letter from authorities in Rome forbidding the appearance of the piece, called "The Transformation of Opus Dei." It is not clear what the objections were: the article is admirably factual for the most part, despite *Vida Nueva*'s long hostility to Opus. It stuck closely to the documents except for a final section of comment. There it was surmised that the opposition to Opus Dei's advance in Paul VI's time had arisen in particular because of secret reports sent to Rome by "personalities of the Spanish Church." There was opposition, says the anonymous author of the article, even from the "most elevated" sectors. That he had the Cardinal of Madrid in mind can hardly be doubted. The editor at first rejected the Opus members' request, but *Vida Nueva* is a Church-run journal. The article did not appear.

Despite such opposition from Spain, a "technical committee" was set up by the Sacred Congregation for Bishops. Between February 1980 and February 1981 it met in twenty-five working sessions. There was also a special commission of cardinals, appointed by the Pope himself, to look into the affair. It reported on 26 September 1981. Next were solicited the views of more than 2,000 diocesan bishops. This information comes from a letter of Cardinal Baggio, printed in the Vatican's own newspaper *L'Osservatore Romano* on 28 November 1982, written to accompany the declaration that Opus had achieved its goal of the status of a personal prelature. The detail about the consultation of the bishops is very curious indeed: not the fact that they were consulted, of course, but the silence about their response. Had the response been eager, or even favorable, Baggio would certainly have said so. The fact that he did not comment on episcopal reaction can only be taken to mean that it was negative. Indeed, the Spanish reaction was particularly hostile.

Not long after the report of the cardinatial commission, the new status was agreed upon. Alvaro del Portillo informed his members of the fact in an excited letter of 8 December 1981: the letter, however, had to remain a secret for the moment, to be shared only with the General Councils (male and female) of the institute. They had to wait quite a time before they could pass it on to other members. Pope John Paul II granted an audience to the Prefect of the Sacred Congregation for Bishops on 5 August 1982, in the course of which he "approved, confirmed, and ordered" the publication of a declaration announcing the erection of the prelature. The Vatican press office announced on 23 August that the Pope had decided to create Opus Dei a personal prelature. The documents had been held up "for technical reasons," but were to follow shortly. This news was reported by the press the world over, except in the Vatican itself. L'Osservatore Romano did not carry the story.

When the formal declaration came, it bore the date of the Vatican's announcement, 23 August. Quite suddenly, it became available in an Italian text, and was reported by Catholic news services. It was officially made public only on 28 November, on which date the Constitutions were approved. That is also the date of the Apostolic Constitution, signed by the Pope, which formally created the new personal prelature. That document, however, was not released until March the following year when yet another step had to be taken. The church of San Eugenio is one of the two Roman parishes under Opus control. The apostolic nuncio (or papal ambassador) to Italy handed over Opus's new title deeds to the President General. It was 19 March 1983.

Rather oddly, the declaration establishing the personal prelature was published with a commentary written by a member of the Sacred Congregation for Bishops, Mgr Marcelo Costalunga. It is he who reports that the idea of a personal prelature was commended to Mgr Escrivá de Balaguer by Paul VI as far back as 1969. It was the decree of Vatican II on the Ministry and Life of Priests that had floated the idea of personal prelatures. When talking of the need to redistribute clergy to areas of greatest need, the Vatican II document adds:

> To these ends, therefore, there can usefully be established certain international seminaries, special dioceses, or personal prelatures and other agencies of this sort. In a manner to be decreed for each individual undertaking, and without prejudice to the rights of local ordinaries [i.e. diocesan bishops], priests can thereby be assigned or incardinated for the general good of the whole Church. (Decree on Priestly Life and Ministry, paragraph 10)

What this might mean more precisely was determined by Paul VI in a document dated 6 August 1966 and known as *Ecclesiae Sanctae.*

This new structure, however, was not originally intended as a means of setting up a quasi-religious order but as a means not only "for the appropriate distribution of priests, but for special pastoral objectives on behalf of diverse social groups, whether these goals are to be achieved in a given area, a nation, or anywhere on earth." These "diverse social groups" were identifiable categories of people who could not easily be accommodated within traditional structures either because of their particular manner of life, or their mobility—gypsies, for example, or soldiers. Personal prelatures, in other words, were not designed for the likes of Opus Dei members.

It is, then, far from obvious that this new structure will prove any more satisfactory to Opus than its former incarnation as a secular institute. There will be no problem as far as priests are concerned. They will be incardinated into the prelature in much the same way as other clergy are incardinated into dioceses. Difficulties arise with the lay members. Pope Paul's *Ecclesiae Sanctae* foresaw that lay people, whether married or single, might wish to associate themselves with the work of a prelature. But it is clear that the laity are, for the most part, viewed as the recipients of a prelature's ministry not as a major—in Opus's case *the* major—element of that ministry.

The Declaration of the Sacred Congregation for Bishops stated that lay members of Opus Dei "dedicate themselves to the fulfillment of the apostolic aims proper to the prelature by assuming serious, specific commitments. They do this by means of a contractual bond and not by virtue of particular vows." *Particular Churches and Personal Prelatures* is a translation of a Spanish work published by the University of Navarra in 1985.[2] The author, Pedro Rodriguez, is, of course, a member of Opus, though this fact is not stated in the English-language edition, and Opus is scarcely mentioned, certainly not discussed. Rodriguez argues a technical point that the bond tying lay people to Opus falls under the canon of the new Code of Canon Law governing contracts. Since the content of the contracts is very similar indeed to the content of vows taken by monks and nuns, it is unclear what the significance of this legal distinction might be.

What implications does the new status of Opus Dei have for the future? Pope Paul's document stressed there were to be close links between the personal prelatures and local ordinaries (bishops). None of the provisions of the declaration, however, gives an ordinary much control over the lay members of Opus who live within the borders of his diocese even though they should technically be subject to his authority. He might refuse permission to open an Opus center—but once one had opened it would be very difficult indeed to close it. He might refuse Opus clergy permission to minister to the lay people under his jurisdiction. He could not refuse them permission to minister to other members of Opus. In fact, there seems no reason why a member of Opus should not receive his or her entire education in the faith, from catechism classes through first confession and communion to confirmation and beyond, within centers belonging to Opus. Though any such person would theoretically be subject to diocesan authority, diocesan priests might never have occasion to come into contact with that person.

An even more anomalous situation could arise from the new status of Opus Dei clergy. They supposedly remain "secular" priests, and as such enjoy "active and passive voice" in the councils of the clergy. Yet, provided a center has been properly constituted, a bishop does not have any say about their presence in his diocese among his clergy. Some members of his own diocesan clergy could be recruited into Opus's auxiliary wing or "Third Order." They would not be required to reveal their adherence to it unless expressly asked to do so. Against such a background it is possible to conceive of a senate of priests dominated by members of Opus.

The situations outlined above may seem far-fetched—but are they? In January 1985 there was a curious incident in the Spanish diocese of La Rioja. In the course of an assembly of the clergy to discuss pastoral strategy, the Rector of the seminary of Logroño, where Escrivá de Balaguer himself had been a student from 1918 to 1920, produced a report on morale in his college. Opus Dei, said the Rector, had been well established in the seminary long before he had himself been appointed. Between its members and their sympathizers (some of them, he added, less than fifteen years old) and the other diocesan clergy there was, if no longer open conflict, at least a constant cold war, giving rise to division not only in the college itself, but throughout the whole of the diocese.

He accused Opus of putting the interests of the prelature before the good of the diocese and, through the spiritual guidance they were giving seminarians associated with them, destroying the unity of spirit that should prevail in the diocese. When asked for an explanation none had been supplied. "Are they really diocesan clergy," asked the report, "or do they belong to the personal prelature?"

It is in the liturgy, says the report, that people should show unity of purpose. Opus members, however, cling closely to the letter of the liturgical law, and there is no active participation in the spirit of the liturgy. The Rector then bitterly attacked the standard of teaching by Opus Dei lecturers in the seminary, and accused them of heresy-hunting. His was not the only seminary thus suffering, he concluded: others in Spain were similarly divided. He wanted the situation examined by the Spanish bishops' committee on seminaries and universities, and if they could not resolve the conflict between the personal prelature and the dioceses, then the case should go to Rome.[3]

The situation had become worse, said the Rector, since the creation of the personal prelature. That event had given Opus sympathizers "a certain air of victory, and of being right about everything." It clearly had not instilled in them the sense of co-operation between diocese and prelature which the legislation establishing prelatures as a new form of government within the Catholic Church expected and required.

The experience of the diocese of La Rioja does not inspire confidence. It is difficult not to think of Opus as a church within the Church, which is exactly what the Spanish bishops were afraid of when they lobbied Rome unsuccessfully against granting Opus the status it now, quite clearly, enjoys.

5

The Constitutions of 1982

Escrivá de Balaguer's ambition had at last been achieved after his death. Though Pope Paul VI had refused the request for a *prelatura nullius,* the more sympathetic—to Opus, that is—John Paul II had granted to Escrivá's successor the status of a *prelatura personalis* for the organization. It was no longer a secular institute. Whether the outcome was quite what had been intended either by the Vatican or by Opus is another matter.

Since Opus was granted its present status there have been occasions when the establishment of another personal prelature would seem to have been appropriate, at least in the context of the decree which opened up the possibility of this structure within the Roman Catholic Church. But they have not been taken up. It may be that the papal curia has begun to treat seriously the anxieties of bishops at having a separate jurisdiction within the boundaries of their dioceses. Or they may have heard of more problems such as those suffered by the diocesan seminary of La Rioja. Cynics, on the other hand, have seen in this the results of further machinations by Opus Dei. Opus was happy enough to be the first secular institute, but was not at all pleased when other organizations joined them in that status and began to bend the understanding of secular institute to suit their own model a little more. While Opus Dei remains the only personal prelature it can determine, within the boundaries of Canon Law of course, just what a personal prelature is. It can hardly be a coincidence that almost every article appearing in Catholic journals about personal prelatures turns out to have been written by a member of Opus. Not that they tell you that in the article itself; they do not feel it necessary to declare an interest.

From the point of view of Opus, the real difficulty with the prelature solution is that it does not cope adequately with full members of the institute who are lay. The law of the Church recognizes a system by which priests become members of a diocese (or a religious order if they are Jesuits, Franciscans, Passionists, and so on) through a process called incardination. Though eight canons in the Church's new code of law—canons 265 to 272—discuss incardination, and the term is occasionally mentioned elsewhere, it is not defined. Its meaning is nonetheless clear enough: it is the process through which a priest becomes a member of a diocese, religious order, or personal prelature (this is expressly mentioned). The institution undertakes to look after his needs in return for his service to the diocese, order, or prelature.

It is evident from the code that this process refers only to clerics—it occurs in a section entitled "Sacred Ministers or Clerics." Lay people do not figure. They can collaborate with the prelature, bind themselves to it by a form of contract or convention if they so wish. But they cannot, be they numeraries or not, claim to be incardinated into the prelature, and consequently full members of Opus. They are not even full members in the way they were when Opus was a secular institute.[1] For an organization which claims to be thoroughly lay, that is a paradox. It has become a more clerical body than ever. Hence the question raised above, whether the leaders of Opus will, in the long term, be satisfied with the legal position they have now negotiated for themselves.

It may be that the leadership believed its lay members of whatever rank, whether men or women, would be subject to the priests of the prelature rather as ordinary Catholics are subject to their bishop within their diocese. But that is not the case. Though the laity may attend all religious services within Opus Dei centers, going there for mass, confession, instruction in religion for their children, spiritual guidance for themselves, they are technically members of the local diocese. Though *in fact* they may be treated as if members of a diocese which is the prelature, they are *in law* still subject to the local bishop. This may not have been the intention of the document setting up the personal prelature, but it is the consequence of the legislation contained in the new Code of Canon Law.

The code is unequivocal. There are four canons governing personal prelatures. Of these the first, no. 294, says: "Personal prelatures may be established by the Apostolic See after consultation with the Episcopal Conferences concerned. They are composed of *deacons and priests* of the secular clergy. Their purpose is to promote an appropriate distribution of *priests*" (italics added).

Similarly, on lay involvement, all the code says is that "Lay people can dedicate themselves to the apostolic work of a personal prelature by way of agreements made with the prelature" (Canon 296).

In contrast, those clergy who are incardinated into Opus are certainly outside the jurisdiction of the local bishop. All the Opus authorities need to do is to get a bishop's permission to set up a center in his diocese. After that his authority within that center is limited to ensuring that the chapel, the tabernacle in which the sacred hosts are kept, and the place where confessions are heard, are all in good order.

That does not, of course, prevent Opus members treating the local bishop with considerable, sometimes exaggerated, respect, at least superficially. One bishop reporting on his "visitation" of an Opus center said that to his astonishment he had been met at the door by "bugia," a candle carried by an altar server before a bishop as a sign of his rank. This archaic practice had died out years before and had never once been performed for this particular bishop in his fifteen years of office. But despite such ceremonious treatment, his actual authority over the clergy of Opus, once the center had been established and the prelature initiated, was minimal.

All this might seem a touch pedantic, were it not for the fact that Opus Dei itself sets so much store by the niceties of Canon Law. Canon Law, indeed, is the faculty of which the University of Navarra, Opus's intellectual flagship, is most proud. As they stand, the Church's regulations insist that only priests or deacons can be members of personal prelatures. Therefore, despite Opus's claims to have some 80,000 members, it can with confidence be said that Opus is not a lay but a clerical organization, and that its numbers, as given in the latest edition of the Vatican's almanac, the *Annuario Pontificio,* are only 1,273 priests (of whom fifty-six are denominated "sacerdoti novelli" or new priests) plus 352 "major" seminarians, or students for the priesthood. The *Annuario,* which rather oddly places personal prelatures (Opus being the only one) not after the list of dioceses, nor after the list of religious orders and congregations, but after the "Rites" of the Roman Catholic Church thereby giving it a wholly spurious appearance of independence, mentions the existence of only one Opus Dei church.[2]

The printed version of the Constitutions, then, opens with the Apostolic Letter *Ut sit.* It is dated 28 November 1982 and begins with praise for the work of Opus (begun, says Pope John Paul II, by Escrivá de Balaguer led by a divine inspiration, on 2 October 1928 in Madrid) among the laity not only in the Church, but in society at large, for the sanctification of its members through their work and in their work.

The Pope then goes on to stress (effectively in contradiction to the Constitutions which follow) the "organic and indivisible" unity of Opus, in its priests and its laity, both men and women. In 1962, says the letter, Escrivá set out to try to find an appropriate judicial form for his organization. With the reference to the Second Vatican Council and its decree *Presbyterorum Ordinis* which follows, the Pope gives the impression that Escrivá first solicited a personal prelature. As has been seen, that was not the case: he first wanted a prelatura nullius. The letter glides over the problems which arose, and moves swiftly on to 1969, when Pope Paul VI granted Escrivá de Balaguer's wish to call a special general Congregation to study the transformation of Opus Dei in line with the guidelines laid down by Vatican II. (In fact, all religious orders and congregations were expected to call general Congregations for this purpose.) Ten years later, the Pope goes on, he handed the whole matter over to the appropriate Congregation, that of Bishops, which, after considering the matter in detail, recommended turning Opus Dei into a personal prelature. The Pope then spells out, in seven numbered sections, the terms of the creation of the new personal prelature.

This is followed by a *Declaratio* from the Congregation for Bishops which has already been discussed (see pp. 75–76), and a short decree from the apostolic nuncio to Italy declaring that the papal letter has now been implemented. This document is dated 19 March 1983.

Then there comes "The letter *Non Ignoratis* of our dearly beloved Founder." It is called *Non Ignoratis* ("You cannot be unaware") after the manner of Roman curial documents, though of course it was not one. This letter, of fourteen numbered sections, is dated 2 October 1958 and is signed "Iosephmaria." A footnote explains that on 14 February 1964 when the founder formally began the move to change the status of Opus Dei from that proper to secular institutes, he sent a copy of this letter, together with the statutes then in force, to Pope Paul VI. Now that what the founder so eagerly wanted has been achieved, the note goes on, it is a great joy to include it in the edition of the statutes.

It is indeed an important letter (see pp. 69–70), for it reveals Escrivá's depth of feeling against the status of secular institute which Opus Dei had worked to obtain in the late 1940s. "In fact," he says, "we neither are, nor wish any longer to be called, a Secular Institute" (paragraph 9). He had earlier insisted (paragraph 2): "We are not religious, nor can we be called religious or missionaries." He used the same letter to address two other issues, the accusations that members were manipulated for Opus's own ends, and that Opus was a secret organization.

Important though it is in Opus's history, it is a little odd to find the letter given such prominence in the Constitutions, particularly since events had clearly overtaken the main point of the letter—Escrivá no longer wanted Opus Dei to be considered a secular institute. The style of the letter, on the other hand, gives the impression that it was written for posterity, and in that sense it is only proper that Escrivá's words should be enshrined in the Constitutions.

This letter of the founder is followed by another, slightly longer, missive from Alvaro del Portillo, signed "Alvarus." It is dated 8 December 1981, almost a year, in other words, before the letter of John Paul II formally establishing Opus Dei as a personal prelature, and a good deal longer before the other necessary steps had been gone through. Again, like the letter of Escrivá's, it is given a curial-type title: *Nuper Nuntiatum*— "Lately announced." What has been "lately announced" is the transformation of Opus Dei into a personal prelature. This news, says the man shortly afterward destined to become the Prelate, cannot yet be proclaimed to the world at large, or to members of Opus, because the Pope wants to let those bishops hear it first who have Opus Dei operative in their dioceses. Nonetheless, Alvaro is writing the letter in preparation for the moment when he can make the news known: even in the stylized Latin, his excitement is palpable. He naturally speaks of this outcome as the one for which Escrivá de Balaguer had worked and, he appears to say, given up his life.

The prelate-to-be then goes on, in section 3 of his letter, to claim that this new form had long been wanted by the founder and that it was the "definitive legal configuration for our vocation," that which God had inspired in the founder on 2 October 1928. Given the vicissitudes of the legal form Opus Dei has taken down the years, to declare this latest to be "definitive" was a bold statement indeed. The implied claim that Escrivá had all along been working for just this outcome seems a little at variance with the facts.

In the next few sections, Alvaro addresses himself to the problem which had exercised Escrivá in his *Non ignoratis* letter, the "lay" nature of Opus Dei. The vocation of a member of Opus, he stresses, in no way changes an individual's personal situation. In a sentence of Latin so unusual that the editor has seen fit to put at the foot of the page the original Spanish version, they do not differ even by as much as (the thickness of?) a cigarette paper. As a sign of this lack of difference between Opus members and the rest of the laity, he instances the devotion of Opus Dei members to the directives and advice of the Roman Pontiff and diocesan bishops. They have had battles, he says, before they arrived at this status. People have accused them of wanting to be outside the control of the hierarchy. But none of this was true because both the "fully secular clergy and the ordinary faithful . . . happily remain dependent on the local bishop for normal pastoral care." What distinguishes Opus members, Alvaro asserts, is the degree of devotion they show to the bishop—they are the most faithful of his flock, praying for him and mortifying themselves for him at least once a day.

He concedes that some bishops—"almost exclusively from dioceses in which we do not yet work, or some newly appointed bishops in dioceses where we have already worked for many years"—do not like Opus Dei. This he puts down to a lack of understanding: they think of Opus, he says, as if it were a religious order, or a pious association or an ecclesial movement ever active both in Church structures and in those of the State. When the differences are explained, he asserts, all is well.

For the remainder of the letter, the only point which Alvaro picks up and comments upon at length is the status of priests who associate themselves with Opus through the Sacerdotal Society of the Holy Cross. Should they wish to join, he says, they should tell the local bishop, talk it over with him. There is, he stresses, to be no division of authority between Opus and the bishop, no conflict of obediences. The only obedience a member of the Sacerdotal Society owes, Alvaro insists, is to his bishop. Except, presumably, the obedience owed to the new statutes, which came into effect on 8 December 1982. "All those incorporated into Opus Dei, both priests and laity, and also oblate priests and supernumeraries" were to keep the same "oaths" which they had sworn under the previous regime, unless the new statutes expressly legislated otherwise, said the "Final dispositions" of the new Constitution.

These new Constitutions, the *Codex Iuris Particularis Operis Dei* (the Code of Law Proper to Opus Dei), consist of five "titles" or major sections, which are then sub-divided further into chapters. The chapters consist of a group of regulations, many of them again with subsections, which are numbered consecutively from the beginning to the end. The model for this is quite clearly the Catholic Church's official *Code of Canon Law* organized in exactly the same pattern.

Though they might question the tenor of some of its provisions, few Catholics would deny that an institution as vast and as complex as the Church requires a body of rules such as the Code of Canon Law. They would, however, regard the necessity for such a code as unfortunate. As St. Ignatius Loyola remarked in the preamble to his own Constitutions for the Society of Jesus, he would have been much happier had there been no need for them at all, if his Jesuits had been ruled solely "by the interior law of charity and love which the Holy Spirit writes and engraves upon hearts."[3] He recognized that this was impracticable, but the approach which is manifest in the preamble, and which recurs throughout the Jesuit Constitutions, makes of them a spiritual rather than a juridical document.

Opus Dei's Constitutions, on the other hand, are strictly juridical—and seem to revel in it. This is further evidence of the degree to which Opus is out of touch with the mood of the Church which, in the period during and subsequent to the Second Vatican Council, has placed considerably more emphasis upon the work of the spirit and a good deal less upon minute observance of rules.

The first chapter of the first title is concerned with "The nature of the prelature and its purpose." The prelature embraces people both clerical and lay, says the opening section, but it promptly goes on to make clear that while the priests may be incardinated into it, those laity who "have been moved by a divine calling" are incorporated "in a special manner" by a "legal bond." It is a worldwide organization, with its headquarters in Rome (it is odd how much emphasis is put on this geographical detail), and is regulated by the norms proper to personal prelatures and other particular statutes laid down by the Holy See.

The aim of Opus Dei is defined as the sanctification of its members through the exercise of Christian virtues appropriate to their state in life. It is open to all states and conditions of people—though especially "those who are called intellectuals." The apostolate for which members are prepared in this manner is to be lived out within society at large.

The Constitutions then go on to list the means by which sanctification is to be achieved. These are basically the traditional Christian means—prayer and sacrifice, theological study ("solidly linked to the Magisterium")—as appropriate to each one's ability, and the imitation of the hidden life of Jesus in Nazareth. "Magisterium" simply translated means teaching, but its overtones are rather less neutral than that, especially when the term is spelled, as it is here, with a capital letter. In this usage it means the teaching, not of the Church at large but of the bishops, and more particularly of the Pope and his curia in Rome: what is known to theologians as the "ordinary magisterium." No one suggests that such teaching is, in the full Catholic sense of the word, "infallible," but many Catholics regard it as authoritative even though, used in this way, it is untraditional, a creation of nineteenth-century, ultra-papal sentiment.

The Opus faithful are obliged to fulfill the duties of their professional life, because that is the way they achieve sanctity and carry out their apostolate. They are expected to fulfill the duties appropriate to their state in life—"but always with the greatest reverence for the legitimate laws of civil society." They also have to carry out the apostolic task committed to them by the Prelate. The remainder of the first chapter stresses the unity and complementarity of clerical and lay members, and lists its patron saints.

Chapter 2 of "title I" concerns itself with the "faithful" of the prelature. All members are to be "disponible"—at the disposition of the prelature—whether men or women, whether numeraries, oblates, or supernumeraries, though each according to his or her personal circumstances. The text then goes on to discuss the different ranks.

The first among them are the (male) numeraries who observe celibacy, give themselves entirely to the apostolate of the prelature, and would normally live in Opus Dei centers. The female numeraries, on the other hand, have in particular the "administration or domestic upkeep" of the male Opus Dei centers, though they are strictly segregated. The difference in expectation between men and women is stark. This is all the more strange because the Constitutions then go on to insist that all numeraries, male or female, should normally either have, or be able to obtain, a degree or some equivalent professional qualification. There is, however, a class of women numeraries called "auxiliaries" who dedicate themselves to manual work—cooking and cleaning in other words—in the Opus Dei centers.

The next rank are the "*aggregati*" or oblates, as they have been called in this book. They take on the same obligations as the numeraries, including celibacy, and the same ascetical practices, they even carry out many of the same apostolic works, but for personal reasons they do not reside in Opus centers, perhaps living with their parents or other relatives instead.

The supernumeraries also live with their families. Unlike the ranks above them, they may be married, though as far as the regulations go, the openness to marriage appears to be the only feature which distinguishes them from the oblates. It is, on the other hand, quite clear that it is an inferior rank in Opus since paragraph 14, section 2 and paragraph 15 make it clear that one goes upward rather than sideways into the ranks of oblate or numerary.

The final rank is that of co-operator. These are people who help Opus Dei by their prayers, their alms, and by working for Opus causes. They need not be Catholics—though members of the prelature are in that case required to pray for their conversion.

The Constitutions then go on to speak of the admission of members. There are three stages: a simple "Admission," which can be done by the regional vicar; a year later there is the "Oblation" or temporary membership which lasts for a minimum of five years and has to be renewed annually; finally there is the "Fidelity."

Naturally there are strict rules governing who may be admitted. Candidates are expected to show signs of concern for their spiritual development, and to have "the other personal qualities" expected of a member of Opus. These are not defined—though it is clear from elsewhere in the Constitutions that they include the ability to earn a doctorate if members do not already have one. More importantly, because it is one of the most controversial issues surrounding Opus, candidates have to be at least seventeen years old.

But that is not quite the whole story. In paragraph 20, section 4 the Constitutions lay down that a candidate must spend at least half a year working in the Opus apostolate "under competent authority," before admission, which brings the age of effective entry down to sixteen. There is a further comment that the work must be done even if the candidate has been wanting to join Opus for some time. It is clearly envisaged that teenagers much younger than the official age of entry will be already closely allied with Opus, if not formally members.

There are, of course, some people who may not be admitted, quite apart from those who do not display the requisite qualities. It is commonly the case that religious institutions theoretically refuse membership to those who have been members of some other similar body—though in practice this rule is frequently waived. Opus, however, takes it further. It not only forbids admission to anyone who took the very first steps to enter such an organization; it even rejects candidates who have been in "apostolic schools"—forms of junior seminaries sometimes run by dioceses or religious orders. These colleges function mainly as educational establishments, and nowadays few of their students progress to formal clerical training. Nonetheless, those who have been through them may not enter Opus.

Much less, of course, may those in the major seminaries, or priests already ordained, be admitted. Paragraph 20, section 3 says this is in case dioceses are deprived of clergy. As has been seen, however, a more likely reason is the Opus attitude to spiritual training as given by others. Even schoolboys who might have come under the formal guidance of an order or diocese in an "apostolic school" are considered unsuitable. This prohibition does not extend to boys who have been at an ordinary school, even if that was run by a religious order.

When a candidature has been approved, the new member-to-be is instructed in the spirit of Opus, and advised that he has got to provide for himself by his own professional activity. He has also to provide where necessary for his family and he (or she) must contribute generously to the upkeep of apostolic works.

At this point in the Constitutions the candidates are, rather oddly, advised to make full use of the social security system provided by the civil law in case they are out of work, taken ill, or become pensionable and so on. In a somewhat parsimonious fashion the prelature undertakes to look after needy numeraries and oblates—and also, though insisting there is no legal obligation to do so, their parents. The final section of this first "title" is concerned with dismissal from the prelature. The rules are straightforward enough. It should be said, however, that according to Rule 31 dismissal has to be done "with the greatest charity," not something that ex-members have experienced, and that no one who leaves has any call on the prelature for what they gave to it either by way of their work for it, or their professional activity. The emphasis is entirely on dismissal. That people might wish to leave of their own accord is acknowledged, but not dwelt upon.

The next "title" is devoted to the clergy of Opus. They are to be drawn from the ranks of the numeraries or oblates and their main purpose in life is to take care of the spiritual needs of the other members of Opus. They may also have a role in the local church and join the senate of priests and other diocesan bodies. They are urged to be linked by bonds of charity with the other clergy of the dioceses in which they operate. Mention is also made of "co-operators" among the diocesan clergy who, like the lay co-operators, assist by their prayers, their aims and, where possible, by their priestly ministry as well, though how this might happen is not spelled out.

Promotion to the priesthood is at the will of the Prelate, and so are the tasks which are to be assigned to the clergy of the prelature. Insofar as tasks are mentioned in the Constitutions, there is clear emphasis laid upon the hearing of confessions and, rather oddly, on the obligation of the clergy to look after the funeral arrangements of fellow members. The need to foster a "fervid spirit of communion" with the clergy of the local church is again stressed.

What has been said about Opus priests so far, apart from the mention of co-operators, concerns those who become incardinated into the prelature. There are, however, those priests (and deacons) who are incardinated into a diocese who wish to follow the spiritual life and practices of Opus. They can become oblate or supernumerary members (seminarians must wait for ordination before they can join, though they are allowed to become "aspirants"). The Constitutions stress that this in no way sets up a "split" obedience—they have no superiors other than the local bishop, and their only duties as far as Opus goes arise from the fulfillment of its rules "as in any society."

The difference between oblate and supernumerary priests is a little difficult to grasp. What is required of a cleric who is an oblate, according to Rule 61, is

1) above all an eagerness to fulfill perfectly the pastoral task given him by his bishop, each one realizing that it is to the bishop alone that he is answerable for the fulfillment of this role;

2) the determination to dedicate all his time and labor to the apostolate, especially to helping his brother clergy of the diocese.

The same requirements are made of a supernumerary priest, except that, "for personal, family or similar reasons," he cannot totally and immediately give himself to apostolic work.

This last provision seems to presume that diocesan clergy might be engaged in other than "apostolic" activities, may be earning a living to provide for their families. This sort of situation may have prevailed in a very few countries, Malta, for example, or Spain, where there were more priests than posts for them in the Church. It always was, however, a somewhat untypical situation, and especially so nowadays.

It is a constant theme in this section of the Constitutions that Opus members who are diocesan priests must be distinguished by their devotion to their local bishop, and encourage all other priests of the diocese equally to follow the directions laid down by the bishop. There is not to be, says Rule 73, the slightest sign that Opus provides an alternative hierarchy—though the regional vicar will appoint a spiritual director for such priests, and they should come together periodically for study and to increase their fervor. They are grouped together, and attached to a particular Opus center for spiritual direction and other training: the regional vicar also appoints an "admonitor" to deal with the bishop about these clergy. Spiritual directors and admonitors both serve for a period of five years.

The third "title" looks at the life, training, and apostolate of members of the prelature. They are urged to keep before their minds the example of the fruitfulness of Jesus' working life in Nazareth, about which, of course, absolutely nothing is known. Daily celebration of, or attendance at, mass is required; they are reminded that it is the bloodless renewal of the passion and death of Christ—no mention is made of the resurrection. The Constitutions then descend to particulars.

1) there is to be half an hour of mental prayer each morning, and another each evening; the New Testament is also to be read daily, together with another spiritual book; the common prayers of Opus are to be said;

2) there is to be a day of spiritual retreat each month;

3) each year there is to be a retreat of several days;

4) members are to keep themselves in the presence of God, make "spiritual communions," ejaculatory prayers, and so on).

The faithful are warned against the pride which may arise from learning, social status, or professional activity. They are particularly warned against an assault on their chastity. They are to combat it by "an assiduous, childlike recourse" to the Virgin Mary, by frequent reception of the Eucharist, by fleeing occasions of sin, and by chastising their bodies. Mention of

Mary turns the attention of the compilers of the Constitutions toward her. Members are to say all fifteen mysteries of the rosary each day, at least five of them out loud.

But, say the Constitutions, the particular character of Opus is that its members are to achieve sanctity through their professional lives. Although earlier on members had been advised to join social security schemes in case they were ever out of work, an unemployed member of Opus Dei would seem to have little standing in the organization. Rule 86, section 1, says:

> Work is the outstanding human value, necessary for safeguarding the dignity of the human person and the progress of society; it is also the special opportunity for, and means of, personal union with Christ, imitating his busy hidden life of generous service to others, and thus lovingly co-operating in the work of the creation and redemption of the world.

The prelature, the Constitutions go on, is wholly devoted to the service of the Church. For that members are to be ready to give up honors (remember the Marquis of Peralta?), goods, even their souls. They are to show sincere love for, veneration of, meekness toward, and adherence to the Roman Pontiff and all other bishops in communion with the apostolic see. Opus is to make a special point of fostering obedience to, and service of, the Pope and the bishops. And insofar as it affects the ends of the prelature, they are equally to obey the prelate and other authorities in all things—though the obedience is, apparently, "voluntary."

Rule 88, section 3 deals with the highly controversial matter of political or social bias within the prelature. The organization is often accused of being right-wing. In fact, the rule legislates very strictly against any advice or instruction being given on political issues, and stresses that "within the limits of catholic teaching on faith and morals, each member of the prelature is to have the same liberty as every other catholic citizen."

After the question of political attitudes in the prelature comes the other vexed topic, that of secrecy. It is presented, in Rule 89, within the context of humility: "It is to be the highest glory of Opus Dei that it lives without human glory." For that reason members of Opus are not to act collectively, or to have a collective name (like, presumably, Jesuits or Dominicans). They are not even to take part in religious processions as a group. Nevertheless, they are not to hide the fact that they belong to the prelature, and they are entirely to shun secrecy.

To avoid the appearance of secrecy, the names of the vicars of the prelacy are to be made known to all, and also the names of those who make up their council. Any bishops who ask may also be told the names, not only of the priests of the prelature who work in their dioceses, but even the names of the directors of Opus centers. It has to be said that this level of disclosure is very modest indeed. The tone of the rule sounds grudging, but it would be a very odd situation in which a bishop did not know the names of clergy working within the geographical area of his jurisdiction even if, as would often be the case, Opus clergy operated outside the bishop's mandate, namely in houses of the prelature.

A final prescription of Rule 89, section 3 insists that no publications are to be put out in the name of Opus.

The next rule urges the cultivation of *natural* virtues, those highly thought of in society at large. They are listed: fellowship, optimism, courage (*audaciam*—it might just be audacity), a "holy intransigence" in what is good and right, happiness, simplicity, nobility, sincerity, and loyalty. They are believed to help in the apostolate.

"Fraternal correction" is ordered in Rule 91, no doubt to ensure that members keep their natural virtues up to scratch.

Rule 94, section 1, while advising members to throw all the cares of this world upon God, and behave as pilgrims seeking the city which is to come, allows each member to live "according to their own state or condition." Rule 94, section 2 again imposes the duty upon those engaged in professional work of providing for his or her personal needs and those of the family and, as far as possible, of helping to maintain the apostolate of the prelature.

The next chapter of "title III" turns its attention to the religious education of members, to deepen members' "knowledge of the Catholic faith and of the Magisterium." For that purpose, regional or inter-regional centers of studies for philosophy and theology—separate ones for men and women—are to be established.

Numeraries and, as far as possible, oblates are to attend the equivalent of a two-year course in philosophy and a four-year course in theology, modeled on Roman pontifical universities. The women auxiliary numeraries are to have courses accommodated to their, presumably more modest, requirements, and other members of Opus Dei are also to have appropriate courses arranged for them. The full six-year education should technically be enough to equip a member for ordination to the priesthood. But they are nevertheless expected to go through a further year's training in a center especially set aside for them, and are required to undertake doctoral studies "in some ecclesiastical discipline." Courses are also to be provided for cooperators.

As for the courses to be followed, there seems to be something of a contradiction. Rule 103 ties the prelature to the "argument, teaching, and principles of the Angelic Doctor"—St. Thomas Aquinas in other words, a towering talent of the thirteenth century—though always according to the norms "handed down and to be handed down by the Magisterium of Councils and the Holy See."

That is fine as far as it goes, but the final rule of this section, Rule 109, insists that Opus Dei does not have any opinion of its own on philosophical or theological issues where members of the Church in general are free to choose as they wish: "Within the limits laid down by the Church hierarchy, which guards the deposit of faith, members of the prelature enjoy the same liberty as all other Catholics."

The Constitutions then move on to consider Opus Dei's apostolate. This is summed up in Rule 111, section 1 as "zeal . . . with Peter [i.e. the Pope] to lead everyone, as if by the hand, to Jesus through Mary." No one is outside their concern: they are to be the leaven in the mass of human society. That said, however, they are to have a particular pastoral solicitude toward the other members of their own chosen profession.

The first means of leading others to Christ is to be the living of an exemplary life, both religiously and professionally.

But members are also to speak openly of God, "spreading the truth with charity, in a constant doctrinal and catechetical apostolate which should be suited to the particular needs of those among whom they live and work" (Rule 114).

Though it is piously said (Rule 115) that the apostolate is directed to all without distinction of race, nationality, or social standing, members are advised in the next rule to have especial concern for intellectuals, those of high office or status, because of the great weight they carry in civil society. The way to do this, they are then advised (Rule 117), is to build up friendship and mutual trust, "friendship is the particular means of the Prelature's apostolate." Friendship in the understanding of Opus cannot be for its own sake, it is a means to an end.

Apart from this personal apostolate, Opus Dei as such offers to help in a more general way, especially in educational projects. It will, for instance, supply specially chosen chaplains and teachers of religion both for schools promoted by Opus Dei and for those begun by members of the prelature, together with others, in a private capacity. Such assistance is to be very carefully chosen, and the Prelate himself is warned not to fail to consult his advisers on the appointments.

The fourth "title" discusses government. The prelature is divided into regions, with a "regional councillor" over each. The office of Prelate is for life, all others are only temporary. Only the prelate or his delegate can represent the whole prelature in legal matters, and both the prelature and its various regions have a legal personality so that they can properly acquire, own, administer, and dispose of property (Rule 129, section 1). The regions are individually responsible for the obligations they incur, not the prelature as a whole, and they must observe the civil law prevailing in the countries in which they operate.

The Constitutions then go on to legislate for the central government of Opus Dei, beginning with the prelate. He is to be chosen by a specially summoned congress, and his election confirmed by the Pope. The congress itself is made up of both priests and laymen, at least thirty-two years old and with nine years' standing as full members. The position of "elector" is a status to which a member is appointed for life. He is chosen by the Prelate on the advice of his council.

The requirements for Prelate are exacting. He must be:

1) a priest member of the General Congress, a member of the prelature for at least 10 years and five years ordained, the son of a legitimate marriage, in good repute and at least 40 years old;
2) outstanding for his prudence and piety, showing exemplary love and obedience toward the Church and its Magisterium, outstanding for his great devotion toward Opus Dei, for his charity toward members of the prelature, and for his zeal for his neighbors;
3) adorned with a high level of merely secular learning, but also with a doctorate in some ecclesiastical discipline and with the other qualities necessary for the task. (Rule 131)

The rule then goes on to describe his role within Opus, fundamentally one of supervision. But he, too, is to be supervised—by two "Guardians" or admonitors, selected by him from a short-list of nine drawn up by the general council, of which they may not be members. They are to live in the same "family" as the Prelate and are to look after his health, both spiritual and bodily.

Apart from the congress to elect a new Prelate, there has to be one every eight years to undertake a general survey on the state of Opus. There may also be "extraordinary" congresses if the need arises.

After a discussion of the appointment and possible role of the vicar auxiliary, a sort of deputy to the Prelate, the rule goes on to the general council which is made up of "consultors": the vicar auxiliary, secretary general, vicar for the women's section (known as the priest central secretary), three vice-secretaries, a delegate from each region, the prefect of studies, and general administrator. There is a permanent commission of the general council made up of the Prelate, vicar auxiliary, priest central secretary and one of the vice-secretaries, the prefect of studies, and the general administrator. Some of the members of the permanent commission may be laymen, though most of the posts must be, and all of them might be, held by priests.

Governance of the women's section is necessarily different. They do not have a congress to elect the Prelate, though they have all the others, presided over by the Prelate and his chief (male) assistants. In place of the general council there is the "central assessory." This body is made up of offices equivalent to those of the men, some with slightly different titles, with the addition of the prefect of the auxiliaries. The whole thing is ruled over by the Prelate, together with the vicar auxiliary, secretary general, and priest central secretary.

For the whole organization there are two further important posts, though they are not to be held by members of the general council. The first is that of the procurator, who represents the interests of Opus to the Holy See on a regular basis. The other is the spiritual prefect, who has charge of spiritual guidance throughout the prelature, and also has particular concern for the spiritual lives of the oblates and supernumeraries.

Opus is divided into regions, and the governance of these is the subject of chapter 3 of this "title." Over each region there is a regional "councillor," nominated by the Prelate with the approval of his own council. The regional councillor can himself have a commission of up to twelve people to advise him, one of whom, called "the Defender," has the task of making sure the rules are kept. (The women's section, Rule 157 makes clear, again mirrors the structure of the male section.) Rule 155 points out, yet again, that the regions (or other lesser geographical unities) have their own legal identity. At a more local level, government is in the hands of directors (of centers), with their own advisory group or council.

Every ten years, the next chapter lays down, there has to be a gathering in each of the regions to examine how things have gone. To this all present and past office-holders are summoned, as well as all who are of the rank of "elector." Everyone is expected to send reports or comments, even the non-Catholic co-operators should they so wish. The conclusions of these gatherings do not have any force until they have been approved by the Prelate.

Chapter 5 of "title IV", is headed "On relations with diocesan bishops." It starts off, however, by pointing out that Opus Dei is "immediately and directly" subject to the Holy See and not to diocesan bishops: "All members of the Prelature must humbly obey the Roman Pontiff in all things: this obligation of obedience ties members with a strong and sweet bond" (Rule 172, section 1). Otherwise they are subject to the local bishop in the same way as are all other Catholics.

The Constitutions dwell upon the Holy See, saying that it is the Prelate's task to see all its decrees and so on, insofar as they affect Opus Dei, are made known to members. "It is the spirit of Opus Dei," says Rule 173, section 2, "to foster with the greatest love, filial union with the Rome Pontiff."

As for the local bishop, someone has to talk to him frequently, and the appropriate authorities in the prelature have to ensure that members know, carry out, and cooperate with all rules and regulations laid down either by the episcopal conference or the local ordinary. The ordinary has to be informed, because his approval is of course necessary before an Opus center is opened in his diocese. The opening of a center implies the establishment of two domiciles; each approval implies that a center for women may be opened at the same time: "by right and in fact there are two centers in each residence of Opus Dei" (Rule 178, section 1). Secondly, there is to be a chapel, with exposition on the night of the first Friday of each month. The particular celebration of the first Friday of each month is a common Catholic practice. What the Constitutions imply here is that the sacred elements be removed from the tabernacle, placed in a "monstrance" or showcase, and exhibited in the chapel for worshipers to pray before. The bishop is then expected to grant to Opus Dei clergy that they may say mass twice a day, and possibly three times on Sundays and holy days. It is now actively discouraged in the Catholic Church that clergy should say more than one mass a day—though on Sundays that frequently proves impractical. Building into the Constitutions the expectation that Opus Dei priests should do so, however, is going very much against the tide of reform within the Church.

The limitations on a bishop's right of visitation are spelled out in Rule 179. He may visit only the church, the tabernacle, and the confessionals. The situation is, of course, different where Opus Dei priests take over an already existing church on behalf of the diocese. In that case, Rule 180 insists on a form of contract being agreed beforehand.

The final "title" discusses the "stability and force of this Code": "This Code is the foundation of the Prelature. Its norms are to be held to be holy, inviolable, perpetual and changing any of them, or introducing new ones, is reserved to the Holy See" (Rule 181, paragraph 1).

The Code then goes on, however, to lay down a strict mechanism for bringing about changes.

Next it looks at the binding force of the Code. Those regulations which stem from either divine or ecclesiastical laws have the force of those laws; those to do with government oblige in conscience, "according to the seriousness of the matter" (Rule 183, section 2). The next section of the same rule adds that, although merely disciplinary, rules do not oblige in precisely the same way. It is, however, a sin to transgress against even the smallest of these rules if this is done out of formal contempt.

Except for the brief "final dispositions" mentioned earlier (see p. 52) the Code ends with Rule 185:

> Whatever is laid down in this Code for men, expressed in male language, is equally legally applicable to women except where the context of what is said or the nature of the case make it clear there is a difference, or special provision is explicitly made.

In Rule 182, section 1 the authorities of the prelature are warned that they must foster the observance of the norms of the Code because it is "the sure means of holiness for members of the Prelature." As a spiritual document it leaves a great deal to be desired. It will have been clear from the summary above that it is highly juridical; that it displays excessive concern for the observance of the letter of the law and subservience to those in authority in the Church—and, for that matter, in the

State. On the other hand, it says very little about the practices of Opus Dei, or about the apostolates it or its members adopt.

As the book proceeds, readers will be able to judge for themselves whether the practice of Opus stands four-square with its theory.

6

The Spirit of Opus

Constitutions provide the letter but not necessarily the spirit of an organization. The most recent Constitutions of Opus Dei do not enter into the details of a member's spiritual life and penitential practices, perhaps because it had become obvious that the rule could not remain secret or perhaps simply because a constitutional document was not the appropriate place for such information. The 1950 Constitution did so, however, and still remains the best description of what goes on in Opus Dei. (Apart, perhaps, from *Praxis,* a book which lays down in the most minute detail how members are to lead their lives. According to one former member it even regulated the number of handkerchiefs and pairs of underpants someone might possess. Unhappily, it remains a most elusive volume.)

The 1950 Constitution might provide the structures, lay down the obligations which bound members, and tell them what to do but it could not provide their motivation or tell them why they should do it, except in very general terms. These external practices require some internal back-up that has to come from elsewhere. Its most obvious source, of course, is *Camino* which contains 999 Maxims or pieces of advice, though why there are that number, unless it be the number of the Beast of the Apocalypse (666) upside down, is unclear. In addition there are also the publicly available writings of the founder, and the devotional lives of Escrivá de Balaguer which are beginning to appear.

Camino apart, the main source of enlightenment for those who had not the privilege of meeting and hearing Escrivá personally is *Cronica*. This is a journal which is circulated privately within Opus. It consists of sayings and reflections of the founder and advice, sometimes very detailed, on how members should regulate their spiritual lives. "The formation which is given us in the Work tends to simplify our interior life, make us simple. . . . Let ourselves be led like little children, becoming like children through fortitude, violently rejecting the tendency to manage ourselves," advised Escrivá in the pages of *Cronica*. Perhaps this may account for the extraordinary naivety that strikes one in many of Opus's members.

Precisely fifty of the maxims in *Camino* are entered under the headings of "Spiritual childhood" and "Life of childhood." "The Father" was the title by which Escrivá de Balaguer, as President of Opus Dei, preferred to be known, and it is clear how he preferred his children: "Who are you to pass judgment on the decisions of a superior? Don't you see that he is better fitted to judge than you? He has more experience; he has more capable, impartial and trustworthy advisers; and, above all, he has more grace" (Maxim 457). Father knows best.

Yet despite this, in his apostolate the Opus member is exhorted "*Esto vir:* Be a man" (Maxim 4), a man of will-power, energy, example (Maxim 11) whose motto is "God and daring" (Maxim 401). He is ambitious—for knowledge, for leadership, for great adventures (Maxim 24). He remembers that his heart is a traitor (Maxim 188), and that it is beautiful to be a victim (Maxim 175). He is uncompromising, for to compromise is a sure sign of not possessing the truth (Maxim 394). He is in no way effeminate (Maxim 888): "Tender, soft, flabby . . . that's not the way I want you" (Maxim 193). On the contrary, he needs to be strong, for "The plan of sanctity that God asks of us is determined by these three points: holy intransigence, holy coercion, and holy shamelessness" (Maxim 387). One cannot but reflect that, the epithet "holy" apart, there were a good number of men in Europe of the 1930s looking for just those qualities in their recruits. It is hardly surprising that the words used for "leader" and "leadership" in his little book of maxims are *caudillo* and *caudillaje*: General Franco was, of course, Spain's *caudillo*.

At times *Camino* reads like a manual of how to win friends and influence people, or how to succeed in business by trying very hard indeed. The sections on penance and mortification seem to be a collection of hints on the training of the will, rather than a treatise on Christian asceticism. It sounds very much like Pelagianism—the doctrine named after the British monk Pelagius who taught in Rome toward the end of the fourth and at the beginning of the fifth centuries. Pelagians believe that Christians can take the first steps to their own salvation of their own accord. It was condemned as a heresy. No doubt Escrivá would not want to go that far, but the stress on religious practices and self-reliance at times sounds like it.

In fact, the passages of a more spiritual nature do not impress by their depth of understanding. The words "Opus Dei" are, of course, a traditional expression for the formal worship of God in the liturgy of the Church—especially the blend of prayers, psalms, and other passages from the scriptures and selections from early Christian writers which is recited by monks, nuns, and priests of the Roman Catholic Church, and is more commonly called "the Divine Office." When Mgr Escrivá de Balaguer recommends liturgical prayer to readers of *Camino* he does not understand it as an act of communal devotion: though "I would like to see you reciting the psalms and prayers from the missal rather than private prayers of your own choice" (Maxim 86), the prayers are still to be said by the individual alone.

The rosary, novenas, holy water, the Christmas crib—these form a larger part of the spirituality of *Camino* than does formal liturgical worship as such. As, in particular, does devotion to guardian angels, whether one's own, or the guardian angels of tabernacles on the altars of churches, or the guardian angels of those one wants to influence ("Win over the guardian angel of that person whom you wish to draw to your apostolate. He is always a great 'accomplice,'" advises Maxim 563).

One pious practice urged upon readers of *Camino* is the very impressive, if somewhat morbid and theologically doubtful, suggestion that they are to put before themselves a plain wooden cross and to imagine themselves upon it (see p. 56).

The first requirement of the section of the 1950 Constitution devoted to "The observance of pious customs" requires that: "Where three or more members live together as a family there should be set up in an appropriate place a black cross without the figure of the crucified. On the feast days of the Invention and the Exaltation of the Cross it should be adorned with crowns of flowers from morning to night" (paragraph 234). "From morning to night" should more strictly be translated "from Prime to Vespers," the first and next to last "hours" or divisions of the divine office. The feasts of the "Invention" (commemorating the finding by St. Helena, mother of the Emperor Constantine, of the cross) and the "Exaltation," on 3 May and 14 September, respectively, are major feasts in the Opus calendar.

While neither *Camino* nor the 1950 Constitution of Opus Dei give much evidence of any deep spiritual understanding on the part of their author, they set up a style of spirituality reduced to external practices in which it is easy to find security. The practices are, for the most part, designed to be relatively simple to observe in the midst of a busy professional life. It is Mgr Escrivá's genius to have concocted a manner of life especially suited to the bourgeoisie, the growing middle-class of Spain from the mid-1940s onward.

As well as hints on leadership and self-discipline, *Camino* contains a good deal of spiritual advice which would console any businessman trying to stay a good Christian while making his way in the world. "Charity," for example, "does not consist so much in 'giving' as in 'understanding'" (Maxim 463). Even the giving of wedding presents to members of one's family was not encouraged, nor the direct giving of alms to the poor. They were, however, encouraged to make friends with the rich to solicit donations. John Roche recalls that members were encouraged in this "apostolate of not giving":

> It's human nature to have little respect for what costs but little. That is why I recommend to you the "apostolate of not giving." Never fail to claim what is fairly and justly due to you from the practice of your profession, since your profession is the instrument of your apostolate. (Maxim 979)

Profits from the profession of members, of course, go into Opus Dei's coffers. Former members recall that there was rarely a gathering in an Opus house that was not followed by a collection.

The apostolate is the yardstick. To businessmen who linger too long over a business lunch he brings consolation: he recommends the dinner-table apostolate (Maxim 974). But they will be spared the possible embarrassment of mixing with unsuitable guests. Members of Opus are expected to exercise their apostolate principally among their equals (1950 Constitution, paragraph 186). They will, moreover, be expected to maintain a standard of living consonant with their professional status: in the matter of poverty there is to be no uniformity among members. Even the shops at which the various ranks can buy their clothes are graded according to status within Opus, claims Vladimir Felzmann: the higher ranks can purchase from the top-class shops, the lower ones, especially the women auxiliaries, from cheap chain stores.

Women get a raw deal from Escrivá: there is a strongly anti-feminist streak in *Camino*. "Women needn't be scholars: it's enough for them to be prudent," says Maxim 946, rather hinting that they will find prudence a hard enough virtue to attain. A separate part of the 1950 Constitution was devoted to the women's section (a practice abandoned in the new Constitution), where it is not envisaged that women will rise to high eminence. The tasks which Escrivá listed in paragraph 444 were firmly traditional. Women Opus Dei members were expected to take on such tasks as running retreat houses, producing Catholic "propaganda" ("written with the help of publishers"), working in book shops or libraries, instructing other women and "encouraging them in Christian modesty," promoting the education of girls—though apparently only in single-sex schools—teaching women farm-workers "both the appropriate skills and the Christian precepts," and preparing servants for domestic work, a major undertaking for Opus women members, and a significant source of recruits. And they were also to look after chapels (paragraph 445).

Most important for the well-ordering of the whole organization, women were to look after the running of all the institute's houses. However, they were to live in places "radically" set apart in such a way that there were effectively two houses in the same residence (paragraph 444.7). Female members of Opus were not, and are not, allowed to associate with the more privileged males. Escrivá's fear of promiscuity was such that the most rigorous rules were laid down to safeguard the prohibition against mixing. At Netherhall House, the London University residence in Hampstead, double doors separate the two houses and are ritually locked each night.

Both sections of Opus Dei follow more or less the same practices as far as their spiritual lives are concerned. The bare cross has already been mentioned. In addition, each member of the organization is to have in his or her room an image of the Virgin Mary—Escrivá de Balaguer, it will be remembered, was so eager to lay hold of one for himself that he risked coming out of hiding in republican-held Madrid. Even an annual pilgrimage to a shrine of the Virgin is laid down among the devotional practices, and a collection is to be taken each Saturday in the houses for flowers to decorate the statue of Mary.

All members wear the Carmelite scapular—a cloak worn as part of the habit of a religious order and usually distinctive. It has also become in a much reduced form a kind of Roman Catholic devotion through which the wearer associates him- or herself with the spiritual privileges of a particular order. Normally, to qualify for such privileges the scapular has to be bestowed by a member of the order whose dress it recalls, or by someone specifically designated for that purpose. The practice of investing members with the Carmelite scapular goes back to the early days of Opus, but in 1946 Alvaro del Portillo had formally asked the Vatican for permission to do so without making them members of the Carmelite confraternity which, he said, would be a burden to them. Permission was granted.

Penitential practices fall under paragraph 260 of the 1950 Constitution:

> The pious custom of chastising the body and reducing it to servitude by wearing a small cilice for at least two hours a day, by taking the discipline at least once a week, and by

sleeping on the ground, will be faithfully maintained, taking into account only a person's health.

The "instruments of mortification" are given to members in little brown sacks. One former member alleged they had been given to children only fifteen years of age. The same young man was told that the amount of mortification he undertook could be increased with the approval of his spiritual director. He was also told how Escrivá's blood spattered the walls of the bathroom from the ferocity with which he beat himself.

A report in the Liverpool Catholic newspaper, the *Catholic Pictorial,* for 29 November 1981 described the induction of young girls into the organization. They were introduced gradually to "the 'mortifications' practiced by Opus Dei members. They were encouraged to kiss the floor upon rising instantly to the morning door knock." They had "cold showers and long periods of silence." They wore the "cilis" (*sic*)—a spiked chain—around the thigh for a two-hour period each day (not on Sundays and Feast days) "and applied a rope whip to their buttocks once a week."

Some of these practices still exist within Opus. They are an integral part of the spiritual formation of its members. The way Escrivá beat himself with the discipline is obviously a matter of pride to the members. And it is also the case that, with the increasing understanding of the unhealthy psychology of these basically masochistic acts, they have quietly been dropped from the customary behavior of other religious orders.

Nonetheless, weekly or more frequent beatings of oneself with a discipline, and the wearing of a spiked chain, kissing the ground upon rising, the "great silence" after night prayers until after breakfast the following morning, a "lesser silence" for an extended period after breakfast (some of the well-known and respected religious orders used to require silence as the common mode of behaving except during formal recreation times, at least from their novices), and even, in some of the sterner orders, sleeping on the ground or on bare planks were common practice at one time. They are no longer so frequently to be found and, although it is not something about which monks or nuns are prepared to talk, probably only the enclosed or contemplative orders now maintain such practices at all. Certainly they seem to have disappeared from the penitential routines of the active orders such as the Jesuits or Passionists. In other words, Opus has stayed where it was while other organizations have changed their practices to accommodate themselves to new understandings of the psychological damage that might be done.

Much less sensational than the penitential discipline of Opus, and attracting less attention though it may be far more damaging, is the requirement that: "Each week all members must talk familiarly and in confidence with the local director, so that a better apostolic activity may be organized and encouraged" (paragraph 255).

The "confidences" are a major part of the Opus structure, so much so that they are mentioned not only as one of the "pious customs," they are prescribed again as one of the "devout obligations" which members assume. They are, says paragraph 268, "an open and sincere conversation" with the director, so that superiors can have "a clearer, fuller, and more intimate" knowledge of members; that superiors will be assured thereby that members have a constant "will to sanctity and to the apostolate in accordance with the spirit of Opus Dei"; and so that there can be a complete openness and understanding* between subordinates and superiors. *Cronica* described them as follows:

> In the confidence in our relationship with our superior, a sincerity without ambiguities or circumlocutions—brute sincerity, rude when necessary . . . The Father reminds us "Foolish child, the day you hide some part of your soul from the director, you will have ceased to be a child, for you will have lost your simplicity."

These "confidences" figure large whenever one talks to ex-members. They are supposed to be an aid to an individual's

---

*The Spanish is "*intima efusión de ánimos y compenetración,*" which is considerably stronger than the English translation.

spiritual progress, a means by which the director comes to know intimately those under his or her charge. They therefore are supposed to be very detailed. María del Carmen Tapia recalled that members were expected to report to their directors upon their sex lives and problems—though the word "chastity" was preferred to sex. This was true even of married women who were supernumerary members.

None of this happens under what Roman Catholics call "the seal of the confessional," the pledge of absolute secrecy (even to the point of death if need be—the Church has martyrs to prove it) of what is revealed to a priest in the sacrament of confession. It has to be remembered that the directors are not clergy. They are unlikely to have had even the minimum training in techniques of counseling or hearing confessions which priests might expect to receive in the seminary. For example, Vladimir Felzmann was twenty-two years old when he came to take charge of Netherhall and so became director of Opus members attached to it. He may have been particularly gifted, but he could hardly have had the maturity and the wisdom to guide those under his charge.

The practice of "the confidence," more commonly known as a "manifestation of conscience," was at one time an important element of the life of religious orders, though generally practiced on an annual, or semi-annual, basis rather than the weekly one laid down for Opus members. It was, however, so obviously open to abuse that it was banned by the Catholic Church as long ago as 1890. The prohibition entered the Church's Canon Law, and was quite explicit. It was contained in canon 530 of the 1917 Code of Canon Law, the code in force in 1950 when Escrivá insisted upon the "confidence" or manifestation of conscience as one of the duties, not an optional extra, of members of Opus. This makes it even odder that the 1950 Constitution received Vatican approval.

Opus Dei superiors do not have to rely on the confidence alone, however, to gain information about their subordinates. There is also the circle. Like manifestation of conscience, the circle or chapter of faults has a long history in the tradition of religious orders in the Catholic Church. Members of a community gather in a circle (hence the name) and accuse themselves of faults against religious discipline and the common life. It can be a very painful experience for those chosen to undergo this type of humiliation under the guise of improving his or her spiritual life. In addition, there is fraternal correction, which can claim New Testament sanction. Someone who has noticed a fault in another first asks permission of the superior, then tells the erring member of the failing in the expectation that it will be corrected. The superior is then informed that the "fraternal correction" has taken place. To engage in such activities, says Felzmann, was regarded as evidence of zeal: there was pressure to find fault.

For Opus members the circles occur each week. They concentrate not only on personal defects, but also on how much each individual present has advanced the apostolate—which means to what extent members have "fished" (the Opus word) for new recruits, or have maintained and developed contact with those already hooked. Any who have failed in this apostolate are roundly rebuked, if not immediately then later on when the person in charge of the circle has reported upon it to the director.

Both circles and confidences take place in what the Catholic Church regards as the "external forum." To an extent they are public in that information so gathered about an individual can be used by superiors for what they consider to be his or her own good, or for the good of the institute. But there is also the weekly practice of confession laid down as an obligation upon members: "Let each member make a weekly sacramental confession to whichever priest may be designated" (paragraph 263). This rule then goes on to say, as is required by the law of the Church, that members may go to any priest they choose provided he has episcopal approval, and no account of the confession need be given to Opus superiors.

That is the rule. While making a nod in the direction of the requirement of Canon Law, Escrivá de Balaguer's advice to members of Opus puts it rather differently:

All my children have freedom to go to confession with any priest approved by the Ordinary [he is quoted by Cronica as saying], and they are not obliged to tell the directors of the Work what they have done. Does a person who does this sin? No! Does he have a good spirit? No! He is on the way to listening to the advice of bad shepherds . . .

You will go to your brothers the priests as I do. And to them you will open wide your heart—rotten if it were rotten!—with sincerity, with a deep desire to cure yourself. If not, that rottenness would never be cured . . . and doing this wrong, seeking a second-hand doctor who cannot give us more than a few seconds of his time, who cannot use the bistoury* and cauterize the wound, we would also harm the Work. If you were to do this you'd have the wrong spirit, you'd be unhappy. You wouldn't sin because of this, but woe to you! You would have begun to err.

This is a tantamount to telling members that, in practice, confession to a non-Opus priest is forbidden. And not only confession. A woman member of Opus who was thinking of leaving went to see Vladimir Felzmann. There was no question of sacramental penance, just advice was needed, and he gave it. On her return to her residence, however, she felt uneasy at having talked to a non-Opus priest without permission, and told her director what she had done. The director was furious, and immediately forbade her to receive Holy Communion for a period of two weeks. One may reasonably be puzzled about the basis of her authority to take such action. The director herself later came to believe she had acted too harshly: the punishment was reduced to one week's abstinence.

The reference to a "second-hand [rank?] doctor" in the passage quoted above is indicative of the founder's attitude to clergy who were not part of his own organization. It may be recalled that he started the Sacerdotal Society of the Holy Cross because he could not trust non-Opus priests with the formation of members along the lines he prescribed. María del Carmen Tapia recalls him making the quite extraordinary

*A bistoury is a scalpel. In the case of *Cronica* I did not have access to the Spanish version but only to an English translation. Though the standard of translation has improved considerably over the years, the early editions of the journal read rather oddly. In the passage quoted, for example, I suspect "second-rank" might be a more appropriate rendering of the original than "second-hand," but that is a guess.

claim that it would be better to die without the last rites rather than receive them from the hands of a Jesuit. Escrivá's suspicion of those who had not come under his influence was profound:

> As I have not ceased to warn you, the evil comes from within [the Church] and from very high up. There is an authentic rottenness, and at times it seems as if the Mystical Body of Christ were a corpse in decomposition, that it stinks. . . . Ask forgiveness, my children, for these contemptible actions which are made possible in the Church and from above, corrupting souls almost from infancy. (*Cronica*)

He added: "Our Lord has chosen us to be his instruments in these very difficult moments for the Church."

On the subject of priests, rather than prelates, and their qualifications as confessors, he told his "children": "You have the freedom of going to confession to whomever you want, but it would be crazy to place yourself in other hands which perhaps are ashamed of being anointed. You cannot be trustful," a piece of advice that comes very close to rejecting the fundamental Catholic teaching which goes back at least to St. Augustine at the beginning of the fifth century, that neither doctrinal orthodoxy nor personal holiness are required in the ministers of the sacraments.

Escrivá was obsessed with the sacrament of confession, both for members of Opus and for the Church in general. So, when he wrote, "The sanctifying function of the layman needs the sanctifying function of the priest who administers the sacrament of Penance, celebrates the Eucharist and proclaims the word of God in the name of the Church," it is noticeable that he puts the sacrament of penance first whereas most, if not all, Catholic theologians would have put first the celebration of the Eucharist.

However, it was not so much the theological import of Escrivá's teaching on the sacrament of penance that was and is disturbing, as the psychological impact it had upon those subjected to it. Confession in Opus becomes a major form of social control. Its use by members is restricted in practice to priests who are themselves members, and it is used to inspire feelings of guilt because of failure to live up to the highest ideals and thereby damaging the whole institution.

The section on confession in *Cronica* was read by a Jesuit priest, Father Brendan Callaghan, a clinical psychologist experienced in dealing with members of religious institutions who are suffering from psychological disorders. His notes on the document that he prepared for this book expressed his increasing alarm. Some of this alarm arose from strictly theological issues, some from the confusion that is contrived between "our Father" meaning God and "our Father" meaning Escrivá de Balaguer. There is, for instance, a constant use of the Gospel of John, chapter 10, verses 1–19, the story of the good shepherd and the sheepfold, as if the sheepfold were Opus itself and the bad shepherds who come to steal and slay were non-Opus priests who might be approached by members of the institution. "I read this passage [from *Cronica*] through several times," Brendan Callaghan remarked, "because I thought I was getting paranoid. But it's the only interpretation which makes sense. . . . I had hoped the bad shepherd might be a term for 'the evil spirit'—but no such luck." This is Escrivá's version of the New Testament passage, incidentally. The story does not itself identify the thieves and destroyers with shepherds.

On the section already quoted above about it not being a sin to go to a non-Opus priest but that anyone so doing is "on the way to listening to the voice of a bad shepherd," Callaghan comments: "This is telling people they are in bad faith, something I've encountered within Opus in its dealing with youngsters and prayer, and a highly manipulative approach."

He was pulled up short by the aphorism, "Filial fear is the gateway to love." "It kind of sums up the whole Opus approach, doesn't it," he commented. "It is a pity it's got nothing to do with the Gospel." With the constant intermingling of the fatherhood of Escrivá with the fatherhood of God, it is impossible to determine whether the filial fear is that of anyone toward God, or a member of Opus toward the founder. The confusion between the two appears intentional, a view which María del Carmen Tapia, with her many years as a member of Opus Dei, corroborates.

The effect upon the organization's members trained in a singularly devout, enclosed, and tightly controlled society can be devastating when it is suggested to them that there is some form of symbiosis between the will of God and the will of the founder whom they are taught to venerate. It puts them under enormous psychological pressure, shielded as they are from any questioning by people outside their group. "In our docility," *Cronica* told members, "there will be no limits." There has to be obedience of both heart and mind, for it frees members from a "sterile and false independence . . . that leaves a man in darkness when it abandons him to his own judgment."

That is the ideology of submission to which members commit themselves through their three vows—or the equivalent "fidelity," as Opus prefers to call it. And the confidences, the circles, and the sacrament of penance are all means to enforce it. Given the extremely strict rules the Church of Rome imposes upon the secrecy of the confessional, sacramental confession should, of course, lie outside the structure. But as can be seen by the insistence on going only to an Opus confessor, that is not so. Has confessional secrecy ever been abused? Not directly, perhaps, but Vladimir Felzmann relates a disturbing incident. After some time as a lay numerary he was ordained and returned to England where he heard the confessions of members. One day he was visited by senior Opus Dei officials. It had come to their attention, they told him, that someone had confessed to him the sin (as they saw it) of homosexuality, yet Felzmann had not informed Rome. That, pointed out Felzmann, would have been to breach the seal of the confessional. The officials grudgingly conceded the point, but told him he should have made the person involved, on the pain of not receiving absolution from his real or supposed sin, come back to him or to someone else outside the confessional in the form of a confidence, so that the information might be used. Felzmann protested to the point of tears that this could still technically be construed as breaking the seal. The senior members would not accept this, and rebuked him sharply for his want of loyalty to the organization.

Rather curiously, in the midst of Escrivá's reflections on confession, there occurs the following:

> A firm resolution: the first sacrifice is not to forget, in our whole life, what is expressed in Castile in a very graphic way: the dirty clothes are washed at home. The first manifestation of your dedication is not being so cowardly as to go outside of the Work to wash dirty clothes. That is if you want to be saints. If not, you are not needed here.

Again there is the moral blackmail, but that is not the reason for quoting this passage. Escrivá's use of the Castilian equivalent of "not washing one's dirty linen in public"—even, apparently, in the confessional (did he not trust non-Opus clergy to preserve the seal?)—makes it clear that one of his prevailing concerns was that of the secrecy of the organization, something not to be breached even in the sacrament of penance.

Though it will vigorously deny it is a secret society, secrecy, or "discretion" as members prefer to call it, is one of its hallmarks. In the interview with Peter Forbarth, Escrivá rejected the charge. "Any reasonably well-informed person knows that there is nothing secret about Opus Dei," he said. "It is easy to get to know Opus Dei. It works in broad daylight in all countries, with the full juridical recognition of the civil and ecclesiastical authorities. The names of its directors and of its apostolic undertakings are well known. Anyone who wants information can obtain it without difficulty."[1] This is all a little hard to take. The interview took place in 1966 when the policy of not making a full copy of the Constitutions available even to bishops who had Opus houses in their dioceses still prevailed. Much later, Henry Kamm's interview with Escrivá's successor, Mgr Alvaro del Portillo, was described by Professor Eric Hanson as "a fine example of how little information a disciplined organization can give to the media if it so chooses."[2]

The rationale for the secrecy/discretion is the apostolate. Lack of it, says paragraph 191 of the 1950 Constitution, "could prove a serious obstacle to apostolic work, could create problems within a member's natural family, or in carrying out his or her office or profession." Opus members were to keep silent about the names of other members; they could not reveal that they themselves belonged to the institute without express permission, even if they thought it would help the spread of the institute; in particular the names of those who had recently joined or, for whatever reason, recently left were not to be disclosed (paragraph 191). To maintain this secrecy there would be no special insignia (paragraph 192). Members were not to take part as a group in church services such as processions (paragraph 189). This can be observed even at a public mass to commemorate the death of Escrivá: though small groups of numeraries and other full members may sit together, men and women clearly separated of course, there is no public display of membership or solidarity. However, this solidarity becomes rather more evident after the mass when members meet together in the forecourt of the church.

Numbers were not to be revealed, and conversation with non-members on Opus Dei topics were banned (paragraph 190). The Constitutions themselves were to be kept secret, together with any documents published or to be published. The Constitutions were to be printed only in Latin: without the permission of Escrivá they could not be translated into a modern language. It should perhaps be said that the same restrictions on the publication of constitutions used to apply to the Constitutions of the Jesuits, and of other religious orders: they would be issued to members bearing the words "Ad usum tantum nostrum" ("For the use of 'ours' only"). Nowadays they are readily available in English to any inquirer.

Rather oddly, it is one of the duties of a local director to ensure that the Constitution is fully observed. At least until the publication of the 1982 edition, he or she has had to do this without having access to the Constitution itself. Of the ex-members interviewed, only María del Carmen Tapia said she had seen it at all, and then she had been allowed to study it only under the strictest conditions despite the fact she was at the time head of the women's section in Venezuela.

In *Camino* a whole group of maxims, numbers 639 ("Remain silent, and you will never regret it: speak, and you often will") to 656 inclusive, are devoted to the virtue of "discretion." Here, too, as in the 1950 Constitution, it is seen as an instrument of the apostolate. "If you keep a check on your tongue," Escrivá wrote in Maxim 648, "you will work more effectively in your apostolic undertakings." "Be slow to reveal the intimate details of your apostolate" (Maxim 643) can mean do not let parents know you are trying to recruit their son or daughter into Opus. "In some cases," wrote the Opus priest Father Andrew Byrne in the *Daily Mail* of 14 January 1981, "when a youngster says he wants to join we do advise them not to tell their parents. This is because the parents do not understand us."

It is, of course, one of Opus's requirements that its numerary members, male and female, should either have doctorates, or be capable of getting them. It is geared to education, and especially to university education: Escrivá de Balaguer boasted that he had spent most of his life in and around universities. One might have expected that the liberal education universities are expected to impart might have had some softening effect upon the harsh discipline and closed mentality of the organization, but one need encounter an Opus priest only quite briefly to discover that this does not happen.

In his report to his 1985 diocesan synod, the rector of the seminary of the diocese of La Rioja accused Opus clergy of "heresy-hunting" (see above, p. 78). He went on to say:

[The] sort of priest Opus Dei offers us is hardly suitable for our people, nor for the present post-Vatican II period. So we see in the priests who belong to the Sacerdotal Society of the Holy Cross and whom we meet the following failings, which it is hard to know how to cure: there is an individualism which shows itself in prayer, in the liturgy, in inter-parish and diocesan collaboration. . . . They believe themselves to belong to the "race of Melchisedek," the notion of the "dignity" of the priesthood prevailing over that of service. They display an ideological, retrograde traditionalism which is little in keeping with the notion of priesthood put forward in *Presbyterorum ordinis* [Vatican II's document on the priesthood] and is displayed in practice by the way they cling to "traditions" and systematically reject anything that smacks of *aggiornamento* by their fear of confronting the signs of the times, and by their failure to commit themselves to ordinary people and to the social apostolate.

There is nothing at all surprising about this. Though Escrivá was determined his members should be well-educated, it was education of a particular kind: "Culture, culture! Very good: let us be second to none in striving for and possessing it. But, culture is a means and not an end" (Maxim 345). To ensure that the learning of members was in accordance with the aims of Opus, centers of study were set up whose instructors were to be priests chosen "not only because of their learning but also because of their virtues and prudence" (1950 Constitution, paragraph 131). The scheme of studies included Latin and Greek, philosophy, theology, and church music—"together with knowledge of our institute," despite the fact that the Constitutions would not be available to the students (paragraph 134).

> The studies in philosophy and theology, as also the instruction of [non-Opus Dei] students in these disciplines, are to be carried out by professors who are entirely in line with the method, teaching, and principles of the Angelic doctor, and these [method, teaching, and principles presumably] are to be held as sacred,

says paragraph 136. The Angelic Doctor, as we have already seen, is, of course, St. Thomas Aquinas. "Thomism" underwent a strong revival in the nineteenth century which endured at least until the middle of the twentieth, if sometimes in a rather debased form. Escrivá de Balaguer would not have been alone in 1950 in encouraging the study of St. Thomas but, with that rigidity of thought which is typical of Opus, he insists upon an extremely "orthodox" (in the ecclesiastical sense) interpretation of Thomas. Other views are not tolerated.

When the journalist Henry Kamm went to the University of Navarra, Opus's show-case intellectual establishment, to research an article for the *New York Times,* the chairman of the Department of Philosophy conceded there were in his department no Marxists, or even people sympathetic to Marxism. He told Kamm that students might use any book in the library, though he admitted that there were some exceptions—Marxist works being prominent among them. But there were other restrictions: Kierkegaard, for example (a youth had apparently committed suicide after indulging in Kierkegaard), Schopenhauer was "very pessimistic," and Sartre "not very suitable for young students." "The philosophy shelves," Kamm noted, "are almost evenly divided between the permitted and the forbidden, the latter including Spinoza, Kant, Hegel, Kierkegaard, Nietzsche, Heidegger, John Stuart Mill, and William James."[3]

The list is an interesting one. It appears to be based on the *Index Librorum Prohibitorum* (the Index of Forbidden Books), which used to list all works of which the Vatican disapproved because they were, in the eyes of the censors, contrary to the belief of the Church or harmful to morals. Catholics were banned from reading them without explicit permission from the local bishop, a regulation widely ignored. The *Index,* in any case, has long since disappeared, abolished by papal decree of Paul VI. It seems that Opus is determined to preserve it even though Rome thinks the Catholic world can do without that degree of thought-control. Indeed, Opus even goes beyond its provisions: the philosopher and psychologist William James was never banned.

It is not simply that the University of Navarra has been slow in updating its practice, for the latest edition of the Opus Constitution reiterates the role of "the Angelic Doctor." When the reading matter allowed to members of Opus remains strictly controlled, as ex-members testify it does in accordance with Escrivá's Maxim 339 ("Books: don't buy them without advice from a Christian who is learned and prudent"), it is difficult to make sense of paragraph 109 of the new Constitution:

[Opus Dei] does not have its own opinion or common stance on any theological or philosophical question where the Church gives the faithful a freedom of view: members of the Prelature, within the limits laid down by the hierarchy of the Church which guards the Deposit of Faith, enjoy the same liberty as all other Catholics.

Opus, of course, is not alone in adopting a strongly traditionalist position on matters theological, though Opus is more traditionalist than most. At Easter 1986, Germain Grisez, an extremely conservative professor of Christian Ethics at a small college in Maryland, was invited to Rome. Opus Dei and the Institute on the Family attached to the Lateran University had asked him to address a conference, after which he was to go on to a public meeting arranged by Opus at its Rome study center. Grisez's views, ultra-orthodox to many, were deemed by Opus not to be sufficiently orthodox when he presented them at the conference. His invitation to address the public meeting was promptly withdrawn. Grisez decided to turn up at the meeting nevertheless, only to find the lecture theater closed to him. He was invited into the nearby English College by its Rector, and delivered his lecture there. Under the present Pope, the "restoration" of old orthodoxies has become a major program, directed by the Cardinal in charge of the Congregation for the Doctrine of the Faith, Josef Ratzinger. Into such a program Opus, which was engaged in a similar mission in Spain in the three decades following Franco's victory, fits very neatly. And nowhere is this more amply demonstrated than in the case of Liberation Theology.

This new perspective on theology may have its roots in European academic religious thought, but it was first developed in Peru in the 1960s. In 1968 there was a conference of CELAM—the Conference of Latin American Bishops—in Medellin, Colombia. Its purpose was to put into Latin American dress the conclusions of Vatican II which had come to an end just three years before. The documents drafted at Medellin were quite extraordinarily radical for the time, particularly when they addressed the issue of the Church's relationship to the conditions in Latin America under which it had to operate.

Their conclusions gave encouragement to a small group of Peruvian clergy who had studied together at university and worked together in the lay organization, Catholic Action. Their leader, who became a priest and eventually published the "grammar" of Liberation Theology, was Fr. Gustavo Gutierrez.

At the same time, however, there was something of an invasion of priests and nuns into Peru. For the most part they came from the United States, though some came from Europe, and for the most part they were people who had been in their studies at the time of Vatican II. Neither the sending churches nor the receiving church had any idea how to prepare these missionaries for their work in Peru. They went to the poorest areas, because that was where the need was greatest. They said mass, but they also tried to help to improve the conditions of those among whom they worked. It was a good time to be in Peru: the Velasco regime, though a military government, was basically progressive. Opportunities were there, but the priests and nuns, led by Gutierrez and his group, began to reflect upon what they were doing in the name of the Church. As they would now say, the practice (they call it "praxis") came first, the theory afterward. The theory emerged as Liberation Theology.

This development left Opus out on a limb. According to Peter Hughes, an Irish priest who once headed a group of missionaries working in the poorest *barrios* of Lima, before the Medellin conference Opus considered itself to be a powerful influence in the Peruvian Church. But it had absolutely no idea what was happening to the *campesinos,* the Peruvian peasants. In the euphoria engendered by Medellin, Opus felt marginalized, for as we have seen it was already at odds with the changes brought about by Vatican II. However, the CELAM elections of 1973 moved the organization sharply to the right, which gave Opus a breathing space. Opus members once again started making their presence felt, and the rather weak episcopal conference in Peru was incapable of coping with the flak Opus generated. The tactic was to talk about preparing the Church for the year 2000, no doubt an admirable idea in itself, but one which was intended to distract attention from the problems of the present, to abandon what was going on, and to ignore the grass-roots church which was slowly emerging.

Opus had influence increasingly through CELAM and the Peruvian bishops' conference (today at least five bishops are members of Opus and others are sympathizers, including the Jesuit Archbishop Vargas), and through the apostolic nuncio. By the spring of 1983 Opus thought it had enough support in the episcopal conference to launch an all-out attack upon Liberation Theology. Though they had, or appeared to have, the support of Rome, Opus failed to win the majority vote of the bishops when they gathered in Lima. In an extraordinary move, the conference was summoned to Rome to discuss the matter before Pope John Paul II. It seemed touch and go, but once again Opus lost, and lost decisively: the fracas may have had something to do with the clear shift of sympathy in the Vatican toward Liberation Theology. Cardinal Ratzinger, having been responsible for one very hostile "Instruction" to the whole Church on the topic, now wrote a much milder second document. The Pope likewise, in a letter to the Brazilian bishops' conference, expressed greater support than hitherto. According to Peter Hughes, Opus hostility to Liberation Theology in Peru has not abated, but for the time being has to take the form of sniping from the columns of the daily papers.

Despite such setbacks, nothing seems able to shake the confidence of Opus members in themselves. They are utterly convinced that they are right, just as their founder was:

> Not only will the Work never die, it will never grow old. . . . God brought His Work up to date once and for all by giving it the lay, secular characteristics which I have commented upon in this letter. We will never need to adapt to the world since *we are* part of the world. Nor will we have to follow in the wake of human progress for you are my sons—the ones who, together with the other people who live in the world, are bringing about this progress with your ordinary work.

The *prima facie* sense of this quotation from *Cronica* is that the Constitutions, in this case the 1950 Constitution, were definitive, fixed not just for a lifetime but for ever. In María del Carmen Tapia's words, Escrivá said his Constitution was eternal. *Cronica,* implicitly comparing Opus to the Virgin Mary, writes: "As we came to know the Work, we were enthralled to discover with greater clarity each day her profound attractiveness, her immaculate beauty." There is a strong sense of a divine vocation: "We have been chosen to convey God, to transmit the spirit of His Work; it is the only reason for our apostolic work. This confers on us the great responsibility to walk vigilantly in order not to change anything."

This high opinion of the institution places an obligation upon its members, when confronted by a book such as this:

> Tolerance or silence when faced with insinuated or public calumny—in good or bad faith—with inexact opinion, or with the mistaken judgment of persons or institutions, would be complicity, a clear sign of lack of love for our Mother and a serious attack upon our collective humility. This silence would be equivalent to denying the Work is divine.

A theologian might well be puzzled by the claim of divinity for Opus, which seems to put it on the same level as the Church itself. In any case the Church, though for Catholics a divine institution, is certainly not above criticism and is always open to reform: *"ecclesia semper reformanda."* Not true, it would seem, of Opus Dei.

Opus spokesmen (one does not hear of Opus spokeswomen) will be obliged by the above to spring to its defense. The tenor of their response will be easy to guess:

> Anyone who has done serious research on a scientific or historical subject will realize that a long list of quotations—which at first might give the appearance of a thorough study on the matter—can easily be based on unchecked or unreliable sources, or also doctored to suit a thesis.

So said the Revd Richard Stork, an Opus priest, writing an "Apologia pro Opere Dei" in the Catholic British monthly the *Clergy Review* for February 1986. I have indeed frequently quoted articles "published for internal use of members of Opus Dei," but they have not been "hacked around to produce a distorted picture"; they have been quoted at some length. Indeed the impact of the publication of *Cronica* in extenso might do more harm to the reputation of Opus than the few passages used. Fr. Stork does not even offer in mitigation that much of it was written and circulated a long time ago; he stands by it all.

Just what it is he stands by might be difficult to determine. When María del Carmen Tapia was in charge of the Opus Dei printing press in Rome she recalls that she had to produce new pages for Opus Dei journals, internal journals such as *Cronica,* which were sent to Opus Dei centers where the old pages, regarded as no longer ideologically sound, were removed and the up-dated doctrine was inserted. Vladimir Felzmann, on the receiving end of such missives from Rome, corroborated her story.

But that is not the central defense. What is fundamental to Fr. Stork's "Apologia" is the backing of the Church: "Can an institution, approved by the Catholic Church, be so wrong, so perverse, so stupid?" he asks, and goes on to hint, in a quotation from St. Thomas More, that Opus's opponents fall into the category of heretics. A Jesuit might smile ruefully at such a naive view of the Church, since the Church decided in its wisdom to suppress his order, only to revive it again nearly half a century later when wiser counsels prevailed.

More to the point, however, one might question the support which Opus has within the Catholic Church. Undoubtedly there are those in the Roman papal bureaucracy, and at a very high level, whose own vision of the Church coincides with that of Opus. Likewise it is true that well over a thousand prelates dutifully wrote to Rome soliciting the introduction of the cause of Mgr Escrivá de Balaguer for canonization as a saint.

Against that one might weigh the protests of the Spanish episcopate, and of other bishops, against the establishment of a personal prelature, the long delay in finding a suitable ecclesiastical formula to cope with Opus Dei's unusual Constitution, Escrivá's own evident distaste for much of what happened after Vatican II, and the opposition of some prelates around the world to the expansion of Opus activities in their dioceses. There have also been opponents of Opus among the more distinguished cardinals of the Roman curia. Cardinal Pironio, the Argentinian head of the Congregation for Religious and Secular Institutes under which it fell until it became a personal prelature, was certainly no friend. More importantly, nor was Cardinal Benelli, for many years Paul VI's closest adviser (he had become the future Pope's secretary in 1944), whom many wanted to see elected in succession to Paul. Benelli served for a time in the Madrid nunciature where he took a strong dislike to Opus both because he recognized the need to separate the Church from uncritical support of the Franco regime, and because he thought of Opus as an alternative church.[4] In the light of Benelli's opposition in particular, it is hard to accept the Opus assertion that it has had "continual and sustained papal support."

It is true that the spirit of Opus appeals to the present Pope. He can hardly have been indifferent if, as it is alleged, Opus money was sent for the support of Solidarity in Poland. The ban on public manifestations by Opus seems to be lifted for papal visits around the world. Banners proclaiming "*Totus Tuus*" ("wholly yours") mark the location of the organization's members in the cheering crowds. The Spanish journalist Pedro Lamet commented about John Paul II's visit to Spain that when the Pope spoke about the need to cling to traditional teachings, especially on contraception and birth control, the Opus groups applauded loudly. When he spoke about the need for social justice they were strangely silent.

For it is possible to point to important areas in which the spirit of Opus departs from the more recent tradition of the Catholic Church, and puts it at odds with the tenor of John Paul II's pontificate. These areas have to do with the Church's social concerns, and are the subject of the next chapter.

7

Politics and Business

In November 1985 a Munich court prevented the publication of a book which falsely alleged that certain Opus members had worked with right-wing death-squads in Chile.

On the other hand, the charge that Opus supports military regimes in Latin America is frequently made by the organization's critics, and is hotly denied by the organization.

The accusation will not go away. In various forms it is made by academics, journalists, and Catholic clergy. Professor Brian Smith, for example, teaches politics at the Massachusetts Institute of Technology. In his book *The Church and Politics in Chile* (1982), he considers Opus to be one of the forces disillusioned by the modest liberalism displayed by President Eduardo Frei between 1964 and 1970, and claims that its members were among the first chief administrators of the brutally oppressive military regime of General Pinochet which, in September 1973, overthrew the socialist government of Frei's successor, Salvador Allende.[1]

The Latin-American newsletter *Noticias Aliadas* has been more explicit. In December 1975, when it was edited by a Catholic priest, it published a story saying that Opus in Chile had begun to receive funds from conservative U.S. foundations as early as 1962; that it organized landowners against the modest agrarian reforms of Frei, and helped to create, with money from the CIA, the Sociedad Nacional de Agricultura which opposed the unions that had brought Allende to power.[2] The late Penny Lernoux, a Bogotá-based writer, claims: "Opus Dei and Fatherland and Liberty [a right-wing terrorist group] worked together in Chile during the Allende years, and General Juan Carlos Onganía, dictator of Argentina from 1966–70, seized power after making a religious retreat sponsored by Opus Dei."[3]

Camilo Torres was a Colombian priest turned revolutionary who took up armed struggle against his country's government after his failure to achieve greater social justice by democratic means. He was shot in February 1966. The officer in charge of the brigade which killed Torres, thereby turning him into a kind of ecclesiastical Che Guevara, and a hero for Catholic radicals in Latin America, is now a general. He helped edit an Opus-linked magazine in Bogotá. In Peru, during the June 1990 run-off for the presidential elections, it was reported that an Opus Dei member accompanied the right-wing candidate and well-known novelist Mario Vargas Llosa, in the final days of his—ultimately unsuccessful—campaign.[4]

On a wider scale, Penny Lernoux also claims that the German Catholic aid-agency Adveniat "gradually replaced the CIA in the 1970s as the helpmate of the military regimes,"[5] and that Adveniat was controlled by bishops sympathetic to Opus. (One of the members of that German hierarchy, Cardinal Höffner, Archbishop of Cologne, in August 1984 attempted to hand one of the parishes of his dioceses over to two priests of Opus. So great were the protests of the parishioners, however, that he had to abandon the attempt.) Further allegations of Opus-CIA links were made in the American journal *Mother Jones* for July 1983. After repeating Lernoux's charge that Opus and Fatherland and Liberty were linked, and adding that the latter, which eventually fused with Pinochet's secret police, was CIA-funded, the author of the article, Martin Lee, went on to claim that CIA money supported an Opus "think-tank," the Chilean Institute for General Studies.

As often as these assertions are made, however, Opus spokesmen and apologists deny that the organization has, as an organization, anything at all to do with politics. Clearly there is a contradiction between their assertion and other people's perception. Opus members would say it is all a fabrication of those who wish them harm, and this much certainly has to be granted:

no one interviewed for this book who has had knowledge of the internal workings of Opus has alleged that he or she was ever told which way to vote, or overtly subjected to right-wing propaganda. Nor in Latin America is there any indisputable evidence of direct Opus support as an organization for military dictatorships or any other form of regime, right-wing or otherwise.

Of the alleged examples of Opus's political involvement, the case of Spain (where there are thought to be about 35,000 members or some 40 percent of all members of the organization) was the most obvious, and—no doubt in consequence—is now the best documented and most comprehensively studied. There is no argument that, from the mid-1960s to the early 1970s, General Franco chose a number of his government ministers from the ranks of Opus members. Most commentators would regard the number of Opus ministers at any one time as surprisingly large. Opus might dispute the significance of this fact, but fact it is. Much more disputatious, however, is whether Opus in Spain intended to take control of the State, or whether it was coincidental that so many members were called to government office. Opus would, of course, have one believe the latter interpretation, but it is hard to credit. It has, moreover, been explicitly denied by Raimundo Pannikar, and he was in a position to know.[6]

In the late 1940s Pannikar was the editor of Spanish research institutes' (CSIC) flagship journal *Arbor*. It was the group of Opus intellectuals round *Arbor*, round the CSIC in general, and round Rialp, the publishing house founded in 1947 by Calvo Serer, which became prominent in Spanish politics. (Rialp had published various Escrivá writings.) A doctoral thesis written for New York's New School of Social Research argues that Calvo Serer's book *La Dictadura de los Franquistas* (The Dictatorship of the Franco-ists) published in Paris in 1973 provides evidence that Opus members acted in conjunction and conspiratorially in the effort to gain power in Spain, even while he denies it.[7] Pannikar is quite blunt: according to him they set out to see if they could take charge of the Spanish State—and nearly succeeded.

The movement into government positions began in 1951, just at a time when Opus influence in Spain seemed to be about to go into decline because of the replacement of Ibáñez Martín as education minister by Joaquin Ruiz Jimenez, a staunch Roman Catholic, but one with liberal views on politics and social issues. He was part of a brief liberalization of the Franco regime, which included the establishment of a Ministry of Information and Tourism. An Opus member became the ministry's first director general. Villar Palasi, who had close links with Opus, became its technical secretary. Information was a typical Opus concern: their senior positions in the new ministry gave these two considerable control over censorship, a burning issue in Spain until the end of the Franco era, and over propaganda for the regime through broadcasting and the press.

Villar Palasi's career was typical of the way in which members helped each other and their friends. In 1962 he became undersecretary for commerce, a post to which he was appointed by Alberto Ullastres, formerly Professor of Economics at the University of Madrid but from February 1957 Franco's Minister of Commerce. After three years serving in the Ministry of Commerce, Villar Palasi went as director to the Institute of Administrative Studies situated at the Center for Civil Servants at Alcalá, not far from Madrid. This institute was the brain-child of another Opus member, Laureano López Rodó. Rodó was a lawyer, formerly Professor of Administrative Law at the University of Santiago, and practiced law in partnership with another Opus member in Santiago who in 1956 became technical secretary general to the presidency, a form of secretary to the cabinet. This was a newly created post which he himself had advocated in an article, though Calvo Serer claimed it was his patronage which helped López Rodó into office. From his position he was able to streamline, or modernize, the Spanish government bureaucracy without changing its thoroughly conservative political stance. Indeed, it was López Rodó's belief that modern economies, and especially those in rapid development, were too complex for any other sort of government than a strongly authoritarian one.[8]

Also heavily involved in the modernization project was Gregorio Lopez Bravo. He had entered government in 1959 when Ullastres appointed him director general of foreign commerce. He became the key figure in the control of foreign trade at a time when Ullastres was still Minister for Commerce and another Opus member, Navarro Rubio, was Minister of Finance. In 1962 Lopez Bravo himself became Minister of Industry—a post he held until 1969 when he became Franco's Foreign Minister. He outlasted both Ullastres, his former patron, and Navarro Rubio, both of whom left the government in 1965, though at that point López Rodó was raised to ministerial status.

Opus was associated with the modernization of the Spanish economy through other means, most particularly perhaps by its highly competent business school in Barcelona, founded by two members in 1958 with the backing of the Banco Popular with its Opus Dei chairman. According to a disillusioned member, Alberto Moncada, the Banco Popular also backed ESFINA, a finance company set up in 1956 with Ullastres as its first president, to look after Opus's own business concerns and investment. Curiously, most of its own economic activities were not in the industrial sector which government ministers belonging to Opus were actively promoting, but in the services sector—banking, for example—and especially in information, with journals and a news agency. They may have seen the services sector as the one most likely to yield real growth, or the attraction may have been the opportunities it offered for propaganda and control.

One has to be clear about this. Opus spokesmen insist that the organization is a purely spiritual one. As such it does not, nor can it, have any banks under its control, publish any journals, involve itself in politics. To avoid confusion, then, it must be understood that the term "Opus Dei," when speaking of control of businesses or publications, is simply a shorthand for "individuals who happen also to be members of Opus Dei." So, for example, to say that *Mundo-Christiano,* a religious magazine, or *Telva,* a women's magazine (which shortly before the events of September 1971 to be described on the following pages, had published an article on the translation of *Camino* into Chinese), were Opus Dei enterprises would not be accurate. On the other hand, they were owned by Opus Dei members, and had a surprisingly large number of Opus Dei members working for them.

What is most significant in all this in the political life of Spain in the late 1950s and early 1960s is the way in which Opus members exercised patronage toward each other despite occasional personal antipathies (Navarro Rubio, for instance, was critical of López Rodó) and political disagreements (Calvo Serer backed Don Juan as successor to Franco; López Rodó and Valls Taberner—though both, claims Calvo Serer, were originally supporters of Don Juan—eventually went over to the side of Prince, now King, Juan Carlos, Don Juan's son). The degree of patronage, and the "conspiracy" factor, cannot but have been encouraged by the proximity in which some of the most powerful officials of the Spanish State lived. Laureano López Rodó, whose long career in government has been outlined above, Jorge Brosa, director of the Banco Español de Crédito, the country's largest bank, and Luis Valls Taberner, president of the Banco Popular, resided in the same Opus house. What, one critic has asked, did they talk about after night prayers?[9] (The answer, of course, should be nothing. If they were good members of Opus and kept the rules, they would have observed the great silence from night prayers to breakfast the following morning.)

From their several positions of influence, Opus members engaged in a very considerable modernization of Spanish government, financial, and industrial institutions, which was all to the good and long overdue. They did not, however, make any attempt to change the political structures. In accordance with the Opus rule no. 7 of the 1950 Constitution they "observe with the greatest respect the legitimate laws of the civil society" in which they find themselves. By their efforts to improve Spain's economic performance it could be argued that they helped significantly to preserve the political status quo, providing a rather better standard of living, especially for the middle-class. Though Calvo Serer later proclaimed himself a socialist (and his example is quoted by Opus members to demonstrate their political pluralism), what he wrote in the Madrid daily *ABC* could not have failed to please Franco: "Freedom of conscience leads to loss of faith. Freedom of speech to demagogy, mental confusion and pornography. Freedom of association to anarchy, and to the rejection of totalitarianism."[10] The particular value of Opus to Franco was that it was an undeniably Catholic movement which gave him the support which the Church in Spain had traditionally held out to the country's conservative rulers—and which the bishops of the Church were just on the point of withdrawing from the regime. This they did most dramatically at the Asamblea Conjunta.

The Asamblea was a gathering of Spanish bishops and representatives of the clergy of every diocese in Spain, which met in the week beginning 13 September 1971. Nearly one-third of all bishops in Spain had been appointed between 1969 and 1971. Influential in their selection had been the papal nuncios Mgr Luigi Dadaglio and his predecessor, Antonio Riberi, sent to Madrid in 1962. Riberi himself had succeeded Archbishop, later Cardinal, Ildebrando Antoniutti who had been an admirer of Opus and, it seems, had staffed the Madrid nunciature with its members. Riberi indicated to Paul Hofmann, when he was the *New York Times* correspondent in the Spanish capital, that it was impossible to talk openly in the presence of the domestic staff, and that he had already replaced Opus "nuns," in Hofmann's phrase, who had operated the nunciature's switchboard, and whom he suspected of listening to telephone conversations.[11]

The Concordat, or treaty, between the Vatican and Spain gave the Spanish government a veto over the appointment of bishops to dioceses. Despite this theoretical control over the nomination of bishops, the two nuncios, Riberi and Dadaglio, had managed to change the nature of the episcopate into a group of men much more critical of the Franco regime than their predecessors, who had endured the terrors of the civil war, had been. The result of the Asamblea was to distance the Church from the State. It wanted, among other things, a revision of the Concordat to free the Church from State control, and requested bishops who had places in the Spanish Parliament to resign them. So alarmed was the regime that a magazine which published a letter quoting great chunks of the Asamblea's conclusions was seized by the police.

Conservative churchmen and women had boycotted the Asamblea, which is perhaps one reason why the outcome was so radical. Opus, however, decided to play a role in its aftermath.[12] Naturally enough, the Asamblea was attacked by the Opus Dei press.

The story begins with a statement issued on 21 February 1972 by Mgr Guerra Campos, secretary of the Conference of Spanish Bishops, and one of the conference's most reactionary members. Later on, after he had been removed from all ecclesiastical office because of his opposition to the conference's policies, he was the only Spanish cleric the Franco regime could trust to appear on television. In the course of one extraordinary broadcast he reminded his audience that in the fourth century all the world seemed to turn Arian—become heretical—and only one bishop, Athanasius of Alexandria, held out for orthodoxy. Guerra Campos clearly saw himself as a latter-day Athanasius.

Inquiries had been made by some of the bishops, he asserted, about a document that had come from Rome. He did not at the moment have any such document, he went on, but would try to obtain it and send it out to members of the conference as soon as possible. That, it seems, was the first anyone knew of the document's existence.

That same evening Europa Press put out a story saying that it appeared that a Roman document existed which contained important observations on the Asamblea. The following morning only *Nuevo Diario* carried the story. Other papers denied the existence of any such document.

This denial goaded Europa Press to defend itself. It described the appearance of the document. *Nuevo Diario* followed suit, and on 26 February went on to claim not only that the document existed—by this time there was no doubt of this— but also that it was official, and had been sent to the Archbishops of Toledo (the Spanish primate) and of Madrid. It went on to quote Frederico Alessandrini, the Vatican's spokesman, saying that the Congregation for the Clergy had produced a document which it had not thought necessary to show either to any other department of the Roman curia, or to Pope Paul VI. This ought to have been warning enough to the papers that the document was not, after all, an official one, but Alessandrini's statement proved too subtle for the comprehension of the press opposed to the Asamblea. *Mundo-Christiano* printed a photograph of Cardinal John Wright, Prefect (director) of the Roman Congregation for the Clergy, with a note that the document had been sent with the consent of the Pope. It later transpired that it had not been sent with the Pope's approval, and that the photograph was not of Cardinal Wright but of fellow-American Cardinal Dearden, Archbishop of Detroit.

On 1 March the agency Cifra, a quasi-subsidiary of Efe, the official Spanish news agency, put out a summary of a hostile study of the conclusions of the Asamblea, prepared by *Mundo-Christiano*. But not until 4 March did both Cifra and Europa Press make available the full text of the document. Twice the Ministry of Information had stepped in to prevent its premature publication.

The much-heralded document proved to be a "study" of the conclusions of the Asamblea Conjunta, prepared by a group within the Sacred Congregation for the Clergy. To judge from the covering letter signed by Cardinal Wright and Archbishop Palazzini, secretary to the Congregation, it seems to have been intended for Cardinal Enrique y Tarancón, the liberal Archbishop of Madrid and architect of the Church's anti-Franco stance. But although he was the addressee, Tarancón was by no means the first to receive it. Indeed, on 21 February he had denied that the document even existed. In his opening speech at the episcopal conference in March, the Archbishop of Madrid spelled out the sequence of events. This was as follows: on 21 February at 9:30 P.M. a call came from a journalist asking Tarancón about the document—he denied there was any such thing; on 26 February at 1:30 P.M. he first saw a copy of the document, shown him by another bishop;

on 27 February at 10:30 A.M. Mgr Guerra Campos sent him photocopies of the document, together with the letter of Cardinal Wright—it was dated 9 February.

That last day, Sunday 27 February, was a crisis day for Tarancón. He considered resigning his post. By chance he was already booked to go to Rome the following day for a meeting on 29 February. In Rome he saw Cardinal Villot, the papal Secretary of State. Villot provided him with a letter. It read:

> The Sacred Congregation for the Clergy caused a study to be made of the documents of [the Asamblea Conjunta]. The considerations and conclusions of this study, of their very nature, do not possess a normative character, nor have they received higher approval, that is to say of the Holy Father, to whom in point of fact they were not submitted.

The Pope, too, saw Tarancón to assure him of his support. The next meeting of the Spanish bishops, at which Villot's letter was read, respectfully acknowledged the receipt of this "study" but gravely lamented "the faults in procedure with regard to [it] and especially culpable leakage to the press, tendentious presentation, and painful mistakes which have disturbed opinion." The meeting ignored the advice of the study to leave aside the first section of the Asamblea Conjunta's conclusions, and ratified them all. Mgr Guerra Campos was replaced as secretary of the conference of bishops. The affair of the Congregation for the Clergy's "study" was an unmitigated disaster both for those who commissioned it, and for those who tried to use it to reverse the Spanish bishops' about-turn on Church-State relations.

There was, naturally enough, a good deal of speculation concerning the identities of those who had prepared the letter. An Opus spokesman in Madrid claimed at the time to have heard five quite distinct versions. The Cardinal of Madrid, however, was told the identities. He had copies of letters from Mgr Benelli at the Secretariat of State to Cardinal Wright, from Cardinal Wright to Tarancón himself and to Cardinal Villot. As long as Tarancón remained Archbishop of Madrid the publication of the letters remained a threat to those responsible. It was not difficult, however, to make an informed guess concerning authorship.

The "study" was originally compiled in Spanish, then translated into Italian in an attempt to disguise its origins. Two authors were Spanish members of Opus: Alvaro del Portillo, then secretary general but now of course Escrivá de Balaguer's successor as head of the organization, and Salvador Canals. An aged Jesuit, Raimondo Bidagor, and a priest, Anastasio Gutierrez of the Claretian order, were also mentioned. The four Spaniards were all involved in the same department within the Congregation for the Clergy, the secretary of which, the pro-Opus Archbishop, later Cardinal Palazzini, was also thought to have had a hand in writing the "study." The text of this was passed on to Europa Press by another member of Opus Dei associated not with the Congregation for the Clergy but with the Commission for the Revision of the Code of Canon Law. Alvaro del Portillo was, at the time, also a member of this commission.

The affair of the Roman document reveals the degree to which Opus has been prepared to manipulate the media in pursuit of what it sees to be either its own good, or the good of the Church—though for Opus members the distinction is an unreal one: the good of Opus and the good of the Church are identical. In such a context it is easy to understand why Opus appears to put such a premium on the media, controlling magazines, television companies, schools of journalism. In many capital cities of Catholic countries—in Bogotá for example, or in Santiago in Chile—where they do not necessarily own a major daily newspaper, members are frequently to be found writing regular features. Archbishop John Foley, head of the Vatican's Commission on Social Communication (Vatican-speak for the mass media), though not himself a member, is believed to be very closely in sympathy with Opus. Russell Shaw, spokesman of the National Conference of Catholic Bishops in the United States (until he resigned in October 1987), and Joaquin Navarro-Valls, the spokesman of the Vatican itself, are both Opus members. Navarro-Valls is a numerary. Shaw, a long-time sympathizer with Opus, only joined as a supernumerary after becoming spokesman for the NCCB.

If they are loyal disciples of Escrivá these men are presumably motivated by Maxim 836 of *Camino:* "To serve as a loudspeaker for the enemy is the height of idiocy; and if the enemy is God's enemy, it is a great sin. That is why, in the professional field, I never praise the knowledge of those who use it as a rostrum from which to attack the Church." There is an extraordinary contrast between those words of Escrivá and the words of an acknowledged saint, Augustine of Hippo, no less opposed in his own day to the enemies of God than was the founder of Opus Dei in this century: "Who can possibly do full justice to the intellectual brilliance displayed by philosophers and heretics in defending their errors and incorrect opinions?" (*On the City of God,* 22.24.)

The affair of the Asamblea Conjunta, and the concern it demonstrated on the part of Opus that the Church should continue to support Franco's repressive regime, find a rationale in the writings of Escrivá de Balaguer. These show scant interest in the niceties of democracy and add up to reveal an attitude of mind which, politically, supports the establishment—always provided that the establishment allows room for Catholicism to flourish. Other considerations do not loom as large: "Do you not think that equality, as some people understand it, is synonymous with injustice?" (Maxim 46). "What crimes," Escrivá de Balaguer asked at the end of a series of maxims recommending "holy intransigence" and refusal to compromise, "are committed in the name of Justice!" (Maxim 400). If any Opus members were troubled by the oppression and injustice they saw about them, they would be consoled by Maxim 702: "You are worried. Listen: happen what may in your interior life or in the world that surrounds you, never forget that the importance of events or of people is very relative." And should any member be tempted by liberal values, he or she might seek consolation in Maxim 949: "Laugh at him! Tell him he is behind the times: it's incredible that some people still want to regard the stagecoach as a good means of transport. This is how I feel about those who persist in unearthing musty and periwigged 'Voltaireanisms' or discredited liberalisms of the nineteenth century." The Opus ideal eschews heroics: "You talk of dying 'heroically.' Do you not think that it is more 'heroic' to die a bourgeois death, in a good bed, unnoticed . . . than to die of love-sickness?" (Maxim 743). There are unlikely to be any Camilo Torres from the ranks of Opus Dei.

All of this spiritual training together with the solid bourgeois virtues (and deathbed) which Escrivá advocated and the Constitutions enshrined is likely to commend the members of the organization to military or otherwise repressive right-wing regimes, especially those that have forfeited the support of the official Church as in Chile, just as it commended Opus to Franco.

There is, in Bogotá, a Jesuit college directly across a narrow street from the presidential palace. On one of the several occasions when the Jesuits have run into trouble with the Colombian regimes it was seized by the State, and for a while not returned even when the Society was once more allowed to exist in the country. So another college was begun in the city with exactly the same name—leaving the Society now with two colleges both called San Bartolomé de la Merced. But the old college, the one close to the palace, goes back to the very beginnings of the country and it, or its equivalent in Medellin, Colombia's second city, have for generations provided education for the élite families, the ones which have produced president after president. But no more. The Colombian Jesuits are not among the most radical of their brothers in Latin America, but they are now regarded with suspicion. The élite families send their children to Opus Dei schools, where they will not be exposed to the new "theology of liberation" with its concern for the restructuring of society in the interests of greater justice for the poor.

Exactly the same is true of the Jesuit college in Santiago, the capital of Chile. There, just as in other countries of Latin America, the names of individuals in government who are either Opus members themselves or sympathetic to Opus are widely known within Church circles.

Apart from the case of Spain itself, the widespread influence of Opus elsewhere in Spanish-speaking countries does not constitute a conspiracy to take over the State in the interests of the Church as understood by members of Opus. Even were Opus interested in achieving political power as such, the experience of the Spanish débâcle—the assassination of Opus's protector Admiral Carrero Blanco in December 1973 led Franco to change the whole tenor of his government—would discourage it from trying, at least for a long time to come.

Much more important is the mind-set of a member of Opus, schooled along the lines indicated above. "Ignacio Valente" is the pseudonym of José Miguel Ibáñez Langlois, a priest of Opus and a regular contributor on literary topics to the Santiago daily *El Mercurio,* a paper sympathetic to Pinochet's government. On 5 October 1986 he wrote an apologia, "Twenty Years as a Critic":

> I have never written a prologue, never presented a book, I don't go to literary gatherings, go out to meals [*cenaculos*] or see other writers. Because of time: the priestly ministry fills my days and years, I want to write my own books of poetry and essays. But alongside this reason there is another, deeper one: I believe that a critic ought to keep a certain distance from the literary world, and a total absence from personal commitments. There is yet another motive: the conviction that, in general, the work is superior to whoever has written it. With some regularity I prefer books to their authors. I have friends among them, as is logical, but I treat them—in criticism—as if they weren't friends. I also have enemies, obviously, but I try to treat them the same way, as if they weren't enemies.

No doubt it was written for effect, but what is so chilling in this apologia is Ibáñez Langlois' boast that he lacks personal commitment to anything but his task of writing, and to his priestly ministry as a member of Opus. Other clergy in the same city, meanwhile, were out on the street demonstrating, being beaten by the police, arrested and harassed for their opposition to the brutal regime of General Pinochet. These are not themes to be found in Ibáñez's poetry.

"No. Opus Dei has nothing whatever to do with politics. It is absolutely foreign to any political, ideological, or cultural tendency or group." That is Escrivá de Balaguer, in his conversation with Peter Forbarth of *Time*.[13] The Opus apologist Julian Herranz, in an article entitled "Opus Dei and the Activity of Its Members," first published in Studi Cattolici, no.

31, July/August 1962, [14] is writing specifically of the political role, or lack of it as he sees it, of Opus Dei in Spain:

> Opus Dei is not to the right or to the left or to the center, as the aims of the Association are not political but spiritual. No doubt there are people who take it for a political party and laboriously strive to place it in one camp or other. Opus Dei however has no desire to come down to the realm of Caesar nor can it do so. But its members certainly can and are entirely free to do so in accordance with their own personal judgment and opinions. It was in order to clarify and affirm these points that the Secretariat of Opus Dei in Spain sent a note to the press in 1957 stating that "Opus Dei is a Secular Institute of the Catholic Church whose activities are directly and exclusively apostolic; in virtue of its very spirit, it lies outside the sphere of politics in any country. Opus Dei expressly disavows any group or individual using the name of the Institute for their political activities. In this field, as in their professional, financial or social activities, the members of Opus Dei, just as other Catholics, enjoy full freedom, within the limits of Christian teaching" (Madrid, July 12th, 1957).

This article by Julian Herranz has become something of a *locus classicus,* referred to whenever discussion of Opus turns, as it so often does, to the involvement of the organization in politics.

The argument, then, is that, as good citizens, Opus members may well find themselves playing a role in the government of their country. But that role is theirs by personal choice: it is not imposed upon them, nor is any political orientation imposed upon them by Opus itself. That is the claim. It sits oddly with paragraph 202 of the 1950 Constitution which insists that: "Public offices, and especially those which involve management, are the institute's particular means of its apostolate." Opus Dei as an institution keeps out of politics. "If that is true, then Opus ought to be playing a positive role in politics," said one distinguished Spanish theologian as the Church in Spain actively disengaged itself in 1971 from a regime supported by a number of Opus ministers.

But the truth is more complex. Opus spirituality and structures inculcate a view of life which is socially stratified, self-confessedly committed to the bourgeois ideal, highly disciplined and over-respectful of authority. In this world-view, the supreme value is human labor, more specifically human labor in the professions. In the article just quoted, Herranz cites an English member of the "Association" writing in the *Observer* for 26 August 1962. This individual had drawn attention to Opus members among the miners in the north of Spain then on strike against a government with Opus members among its cabinet ministers. And undoubtedly there are working-class members of Opus even outside the ranks of the women auxiliaries recruited to clean the residences of men. An Italian television film made to commemorate the fiftieth anniversary of Opus Dei, and with which Opus subsequently made much propaganda, featured a Manchester bus driver. He was Irish.

There would not, however, be many bus drivers, English or Irish, with the academic qualification of a doctorate necessary for the rank of numerary member, the only full membership. And as is quite clear, both from the 1950 Constitution and from that of 1982, Opus is primarily aimed at professional men and women—though it is true that the more recent Constitution does not make special mention, unlike the earlier, of people in government service (see 1950 Constitution, paragraph 4.2).

Opus Dei undoubtedly attracts Catholic businessmen to its ranks with its message of sanctification through work and its sympathetic understanding of the apostolate of the dinner table, the apostolate of not giving (see p. 108), and the blessing upon middle-class values (see pp. 108–9 and above). No doubt in theory such businessmen could embrace, and operate within, a wide range of political and social environments. But that is being unrealistic. When Opus members controlled the economy of Spain they developed private industry at the expense of public. It has been argued[15] that there were two main reasons for this. First, Opus's main political enemy in Spain was the *Falange* which, because of its support for Franco during the civil war, had been allowed to survive. Though fascist, it was technically a socialist party and supported nationalized industry. Secondly, it was good Catholic teaching that the State should not do for individuals what individuals could do for themselves. The State would provide optimum conditions for private enterprise to flourish, and step in only at that level where individual entrepreneurs could not operate for themselves.

So private enterprise was allowed to flourish. But in this climate business acumen of some Opus members took some sharp knocks. Spain suffered two major scandals involving Opus members and their businesses, the first that of Matesa in 1969, the second that of Rumasa in 1983.

Matesa (Magquinaria Textil de Norte de España Sociedad Anonima) was founded in 1956. It was based in Pamplona and employed some 2,000 people to make textile machinery. It was accounted one of the country's more dynamic businesses: at the time of its collapse in August 1969 it controlled seventy-five other firms both in Spain and abroad. Its growth was largely the result of acquiring, by somewhat doubtful means, a patent for a particular type of loom: payment was made for the patent in French francs which were smuggled out of Spain and shown on the balance sheet as royalties. Matesa improved the loom, but was short of money to launch it on the world market. The head of the company, Juan Vila Reyes, found the cash he needed from the Banco de Crédito Industrial, claiming that he wanted the money to finance wholly fictitious sales of his machines. This money, estimated to have been in the order of 5,000 million pesetas, was again smuggled out of the country, and sent back yet again as payment for goods; when the firm collapsed it had debts of around 10,000 million pesetas (about £75 million). For these crimes Vila Reyes was tried twice: the first time he was sentenced to three years in prison, and a hefty fine, the second time, when he was indicted on 424 separate charges, to 224 years in jail (the public prosecutor had demanded nearly 1,290 years) and he was ordered to pay back to the government about £70 million.

Vila Reyes learned his business skills at the Opus-run business school in Barcelona. His legal adviser, Villar Palasi, who was Minister of Education at the time the scandal broke, moved in Opus Dei circles; Lopez Bravo was the Minister for Industry who had approved the loans. Another member of Opus, Mariano Navarro Rubio, had been governor of the Bank of Spain at the time of the frauds, and had to resign. Vila Reyes admitted giving a modest £12,000 to his old Opus school. Rumors at the time put the sum much higher: a commission set up by the Spanish Parliament failed to determine how much was contributed by Vila Reyes to the University of Navarra in Pamplona, but there were allegations (although denied by Opus) that the sum was 120 million pesetas and that, in total, donations to Opus were in the region of 2,400 million pesetas, including substantial gifts to Opus headquarters in Rome, to a university in Peru, and to American student residences.[16] These rumors were all denied by the Opus spokesman in Madrid. The fact that an Opus Dei-trained businessman went to jail for substantial fraud could not, however, be denied.

The second major scandal involved Rumasa, at one time one of Spain's largest enterprises in private hands. It owned eighteen banks and well-known chain stores such as Galerias Preciados and the Spanish branch of Sears Roebuck. The firm would have been better known in the United Kingdom for its wine companies (its head came from Jerez) with brands such as Dry Sack sherry. It also owned the Augustus Barnett chain of liquor stores in Britain. In all, there were 245 companies under the Rumasa umbrella. It collapsed in February 1983 with liabilities exceeding its assets by some £1,000 million.

The founder of Rumasa, and its head until the take-over by the Spanish government, was José María Ruiz-Mateos (Rumasa stands for Ruiz-Mateos Sociedad Anonima). After the collapse of his empire he fled to London and was eventually arrested in Germany. He was extradited to Spain on condition that the charges against him be relatively minor. Imprisoned for a time in Madrid, he was later released and never put on trial and ran in an election for the European Parliament as the candidate of the José María Ruiz-Mateos Voters' Association. The distinguished London-based weekly *The*

Economist described his subsequent behavior, and that of his family, as "increasingly dotty."[17]

While in London Ruiz-Mateos told journalists that he had given large sums of money to political parties, to individual political leaders, and to trade unions. Though he said he sympathized with its aims, he denied he was himself a member of Opus Dei.[18] This is not true; he was indeed a member. In his diary of his imprisonment he records that, alongside a holy picture of the Virgin Mary embracing her son, he put a picture of Escrivá de Balaguer upon the table of his cell.[19] While in prison in Madrid, he was visited by members of Opus and threatened with expulsion. He had donated considerable sums of money—some £7 million was mentioned—to an educational institute based in the Channel Isles and associated through its directors with Opus in the UK. When, early in 1983, the BBC was preparing a television program about Opus, researchers were puzzled by the way in which the Opus-controlled Netherhall Educational Association (NEA) in Hampstead had managed to raise the money, to some extent by cheap loans in foreign currencies, to finance its very considerable property purchases.

The Netherhall Educational Association came into being in 1964, but it was not quite the first Opus organization to be registered in the United Kingdom. In 1954 Michael Richards and a Spanish priest, Juan Antonio Galarraga, both giving their address as 18 Netherhall Gardens, established a charitable trust for "the Roman Catholic society established according to the Canon Law of the Roman Catholic Church as a Secular Institute known as 'The Sacerdotal Society of the Holy Cross and Opus Dei.'" After more than a quarter of a century of existence it had never filed accounts with the Charity Commissioners, something which, hardly surprisingly, the commissioners found disturbing.

The 1954 trust deed indicated that the purpose of the trust was "the advancement of the Roman Catholic religion." It gave the trustees "absolute discretion" over the buying and selling of property, stocks and shares, securities, and so on. They were to be appointed—and dismissed—by the "National

President," in other words the Opus regional counselor, who had complete control over the nomination of trustees of the Sacerdotal Society. When the Sacerdotal Society became a registered charity in 1965 it listed the ownership of three properties, Oxford's Grandpont House (see above, p. 65), a house in Manchester, and the headquarters of Opus in the UK, 6 Orme Court in Bayswater in London. By that time, however, the Trust had already disposed of a number of other properties, including 16 and 18 Netherhall Gardens, which had been handed over to the Netherhall Educational Association, formed in 1964, with seven directors, all but one of whom lived in known Opus Dei properties. Technically the NEA had purchased the houses for £60,000, but the £60,000 had been donated for that purpose by the Sacerdotal Society.

Although the NEA has regularly filed its accounts, it was, however, summoned to the High Court, Chancery Division, in February 1979 to explain why it had failed to register three mortgages in contravention of the Companies Act. Their records reveal a very considerable number of expensive property purchases in pursuit of the stated object of "education within the Christian ideal." The charity expanded its property at the Netherhall site with a mortgage for more than £250,000 from the (now defunct) Greater London Council and a £75,000 grant from the British Council on the understanding that 80 percent of its hostel accommodation be made available to students from abroad.[20] Among its many purchases were Dawliffe Hall, on the Chelsea Embankment, which in 1980 became the property of the Dawliffe Educational Foundation, along with neighboring Shelley House, bought in 1976 for nearly £500,000, and sundry other properties both in London and scattered around the country. The Dawliffe Educational Foundation appears to be the operating charitable trust of Opus's women's section.

Many of the properties owned by the NEA or the Dawliffe Educational Foundation are in London, and in prime locations. Orme Court seems especially favored, since Opus has now purchased, in addition to no. 6, its original acquisition and still Opus Dei's British headquarters, nos. 1, 4, 5, 7, and 10 Orme Court at a cost of well over £1 million. There seems to be somewhat less interest in the North of England, though the Greygarth Association Ltd. was set up by the NEA in 1974 with particular responsibility, it would seem, for the Opus apostolate in the North.

It is clear from the NEA's accounts that quite substantial loans came from abroad in dollars, Swiss francs, or marks, at remarkably favorable rates of interest. By September 1983 unsecured loans in foreign currencies at rates of interest of between zero and three percent amounted to £1.5 million. Dawliffe and Greygarth enjoyed similar loans, if of lesser value. NEA's "associated charities" also made money available, as in 1980 did the big hotel and catering group Trust House Forte. In this last case the sum was not particularly large in terms of Opus's budget for house purchasing, a mere £50,000 as an interest-free loan. Four years later, in August 1984, Lord Forte made £50,000 over to Netherhall House.[21] As charities, the Sacerdotal Society and its off-shoots can solicit covenants, donations upon which a charity can recoup from the Inland Revenue any income tax which has been paid. It is normal practice for members of religious orders to covenant any income they may earn to their order. Presumably the same holds true of Opus, and convenanted income does figure on the NEA's balance sheet—though not perhaps to the extent that might be expected. It could, however, be the case that some of the sums made available by "associated charities" such as the Dawliffe Educational Foundation are raised by means of covenants taken out by numerary members.

There has also been a concerted attempt to raise money from other sources. In 1970 the Netherhall House Trust was set up precisely to further the work of Netherhall House. Among its first eight trustees were Sir George Bolton, then just ending a thirteen-year stint as chairman of the Bank of London and South America, and Sir Philip de Zulueta, also a distinguished banker, though for many years before he resigned from the civil service, private secretary to successive prime ministers. Each year, directors of the NEA have made a point of thanking the members of the trust for the work they have done in raising money to pay off the mortgage on Netherhall. The sums contributed by the trust have been variable, and while at times not inconsiderable, have been in no way comparable with the loans made available from abroad at rates way below those charged commercially. Yet the sources of this generosity have not been disclosed.

Links between Opus in Ireland and in Britain have been close. Even before the Sacerdotal Society was set up as a trust in London, Michael Richards went to Dublin to help create University Hostels Limited. The founding directors of this company, besides Richards, were Cormac Burke and Richard Mulcahy. All three subsequently became priests of Opus. In Dublin as in London the rules were the same: directorships of companies associated with Opus were controlled by the chief Opus representative of the country. University Hostels attracted a wide range of distinguished investors—including two conservative bishops and John Costello, a former Irish Prime Minister—but they can only have given their money as an act of generosity to Opus, since the prospectus made it clear that little or no return was to be expected on the shares, and the shares on offer carried no voting rights. The Irish monthly magazine *Magill* reported that the shares in 1983 were held largely by the Lismullin Scientific Trust and the Tara Trust, both of which operate out of the same address, an Opus Dei residence.

To some extent the pattern in Ireland mirrors that in England: the Opus company owns considerable properties in prime locations, but perhaps because of the nature of Irish society, the organization has apparently been able to diversify its interests rather more than in the United Kingdom. It has, for instance, through an educational development trust, moved into secondary education in Ireland as in Spain and some countries of Latin America. The schools it has established in Dublin are aimed, claims Roche, "at the élite of Dublin society." They are popular: pupils may travel ten or twenty miles to attend them. They are, of course, segregated by sex. Roche clearly regarded the fees as high at £460 a year in 1983; English parents sending their children to independent schools would have regarded that as very reasonable. What they might find odd, however, is the educational development trust's way of finding what surely must be a considerable shortfall in the costs of the schools. In 1975 it established a company called the Park Industrial and Provident Society. For every child they send to schools run by Opus, parents are required to advance an interest-free loan (£ 1,200 in 1983) to the Park Industrial and Provident Society.

Opus also has considerable publishing interests in Ireland. Scepter Publishers Limited began in 1959 in Dublin, one of a chain of similarly-named companies round the world, as a vehicle for marketing Opus Dei titles, including *The Way*. Again according to Roche, it ceased trading in 1978. These titles were then passed on: several of the books used while writing this study, for example, were published by the Four Courts Press, founded in 1969 by Michael Adams, a numerary member of Opus. It also produces books and pamphlets written by Dr. Jeremiah Newman, perhaps the most conservative of all the Irish bishops. Mr. Adams also is the managing director of the Irish Academic Press which bought out the assets of the Irish University Press which collapsed in 1974 with assets of £1.4 million. Mr. Adams had been a director of Irish University Press.

Scepter apparently still lives on in the United Kingdom. It operates out of 1 and 2 Leopold Road, a property near Ealing Common underground station purchased for nearly £100,000 in 1974, which also houses Westpark, a study center for boys. It was the English Scepter which in 1977 published Bernal's *Msgr Escrivá de Balaguer,* quoted earlier in this book. Apart from Escrivá's latest collection of maxims or aphorisms, *The Forge,* published in January 1988, Scepter UK does not seem to have been notably active of late, though the *Scepter Bulletin* continues to appear ten times a year. A slight publication priced at 70p, it contains a mix of pious articles, conservative in tone, and lengthy sections of papal utterances, taken from the weekly (the Italian version is daily) English-language edition of *Osservatore Romano,* the Vatican newspaper. It is not unusual, of course, for religious groups to produce monthly or quarterly journals: in the United Kingdom, to take but two instances, the Dominicans run *New Blackfriars* while the Jesuits have *The*

Month. But in both these cases the affiliation of the magazine is clear, and is acknowledged. Unless one were aware that its editor, John Horrigan, was the Opus spokesman in London, it would be impossible to gather from *Scepter Bulletin* to which group it belonged.

Opus will say, of course, that this company, like most of the others, is not an Opus Dei company at all, but belongs to members of Opus. Strictly speaking that may be true. Apart from the trust set up in 1954 as the Sacerdotal Society of the Holy Cross and Opus Dei, the other legal entities through which its members operate frequently include non-members. They are known as "common works." There are also "co-operative works" in which numeraries and supernumeraries collaborate and which they wholly own, though there may be non-members in their employment. Publishing companies are typical examples of the former kind, schools of the latter. But it is a sophistry to distinguish either of these kinds of enterprise from purely Opus Dei ones. First, all profits made by numerary members in whatever capacity accrue to Opus itself. That is the consequence of the obligation of poverty which they have taken upon themselves. Even supernumerary (or married) members are under pressure to give as much as possible to the organization. Secondly, no numerary member certainly, and probably no supernumerary member either, will enter upon a business enterprise without having discussed it at length with his or her director; the obligation to be entirely open with the director applies in this sphere as in any other. And there is a third point:

> Members of Opus Dei, whether they are acting individually or through associations which might be cultural, artistic, financial, and so on, do so through what are known as "auxiliary societies." In their dealings, these societies are equally subject to obedience to the hierarchical authority of the Institute. (1950 Constitution, paragraph 9)

Every five years, according to paragraph 375 of the same document, the administrator general is to undertake a visitation of the administration in each of the regions of Opus. "He will take the opportunity of this visitation to inspect the auxiliary societies as well."

What makes it all the more strange, is that Opus does not really have any need to be quite so coy. It is perfectly reasonable for it, as a body, to be involved to some extent in the business of earning money. All, or nearly all, the religious organizations of the Catholic Church have to do likewise, and they have their legal personas in order to operate: the British Jesuits, for example, are known legally as "Trustees for RC Purposes Rgd," a marvelous catch-all title. Few if any organizations, however, can dispose of the sort of sums of money which were required to make the purchases Opus made in Britain since it first became a recognizable entity in 1954.

That Opus is rich can hardly be denied. Ruiz-Mateos himself admitted to giving around 4,000 million pesetas (about £20 million at today's exchange rate) to the organization in Rumasa's twenty-three years of life. Larrain Crusat, a Chilean company whose rise under the free-enterprise regime of U.S.-trained economists, known as the "Chicago boys," in the late 1970s and subsequent fall mirrored that of Rumasa, is reported to have been giving Opus 10 million pesos a month at a time when the Chilean currency was stable at around 40 pesos to the dollar.[22] Quite apart from such gifts, regional administrations send 10 percent of their income to Rome while local residences forward 10 percent of their income to the regional administration. Any extra donations or money left over also goes to Rome. María del Carmen Tapia calculates that the women's section in Venezuela in the mid-1960s was sending between $10,000 and $12,000 a year to the Institute for the Works of Religion (*Istituto per le Opere di Religione,* or IOR in its Italian abbreviation). She believed it was going to the training of priests and the support of a women's college.

This bank began in 1887 as a fundraising vehicle for Church work around the world; it was then called the Administration of the Work of Religion. Pope Pius XII provided its new name in 1942, and widened its role so that it might hold, and invest, money on behalf of religious orders and other Church-related enterprises which needed to move money around the world. It is located inside the Vatican City State, and therefore is not on Italian territory, which puts it outside Italian banking law. It is a merchant bank rather than a clearing bank, though for people associated with the Vatican it can act in the latter capacity. Between the Vatican City State and the Republic of Italy there are, of course, no customs barriers or other checkpoints. The IOR, therefore, has been a source of temptation to any Italian trying to find a way round his country's exchange controls. From 1971 until recently its chairman was Archbishop Paul Marcinkus, a Chicago-born prelate of Lithuanian background who seems to have acted both as bodyguard to the Pope and as tour manager. Marcinkus's considerable bulk was much in evidence on papal tours around the world until warrants for his arrest limited his movements to the confines of the Vatican City State—by far the smallest country in the world, being only one-third of the size of the next smallest, the Principality of Monaco.

Marcinkus went to the IOR in 1968, at a time when the Vatican was trying to diversify its investments. One of those consulted with this end in view was Michele Sindona, a Sicilian banker who had strong links to the Mafia, and was sometime partner of David Kennedy of the Continental Illinois. In March 1980 he was jailed for twenty-five years in the United States on sixty-eight counts of fraud and similar charges arising from the collapse of his Franklin National Bank in 1974, but was later brought back to an Italian prison to answer charges about the collapse of his Banca Privata Finanziaria, also in 1974. He died on 22 March 1986 in an Italian prison after drinking poisoned coffee. In the same year as Sindona's banks collapsed, the IOR reported heavy losses— its total losses are estimated to have amounted to around $200 million[23]—sustained through the Banco di Roma per la Svizzera, a subsidiary half-owned by the IOR, half by the Banco di Roma. The executive said to be responsible for these losses was subsequently found dead upon a railway line.

At about this time, Archbishop Marcinkus was developing links with the Milan-based Banco Ambrosiano, and in particular with a one-time colleague of Sindona who was busy expanding the Ambrosiano, Roberto Calvi. On 18 June 1982 Calvi was found hanging under London's Blackfriars Bridge.

One of the reasons for the development of these contacts, and the establishment of other overseas banks by the Ambrosiano in which Marcinkus came to play a considerable role, was the Vatican's urgent need for cash. During the 1970s, its financial situation became increasingly fragile, a situation generally disguised under Pope Paul VI but publicly acknowledged by Pope John Paul II. This was the time when Pope Paul had refused Opus Dei the status of personal prelature Escrivá de Balaguer had been seeking; the Pope might be persuaded to reopen the matter, reasoned Escrivá, if Opus contributed some of its considerable funds in the direction of the IOR. The sum agreed was for Opus to provide 30 percent of the Vatican's annual costs.[24] The Vatican allegedly wanted Opus money to come to the IOR indirectly, through the Banco Ambrosiano. Opus, on the other hand, wanted payments to be made through the banks controlled by Rumasa in Germany, Switzerland, England, Latin America, and elsewhere. Rumasa's Swiss bank was the Nordfinanzbank in Zurich whose managing director, together with four Opus members, constituted the board of the Limmat-Stiftung, an Opus Dei foundation also in Zurich which has links with Opus Dei banks around the world. The Nordfinanzbank and its managing director Arthur Wiederkehr had shares in Calvi's enterprises.[25]

Though Ruiz-Mateos produced evidence of large-scale donations to Opus funds, it is far from clear that the agreement to support the Vatican's crumbling finances was ever put into operation. For one thing, Pope John Paul II proved more sympathetic to Opus's aims than Pope Paul had been. And for another, the Banco Ambrosiano was in trouble. The Bank of Italy began its inquiries into its operations, and into its connections with the IOR, as long ago as 1978. Certainly the collapse of the Banco Ambrosiano put an end to any Opus involvement there may have been in an attempt to sort out the Pope's money worries. But now there was no longer any need to protect the over-stretched Rumasa. Less than a year after the death of Calvi that too had collapsed and, like Calvi before him, Ruiz-Mateos had fled to London.

Unlike so many of those who have been major actors in these financial dramas, Ruiz-Mateos is still alive. He has accused several members of Opus as having collaborated in the expropriation of Rumasa, among them Luis Valls Taberner of the Banco Popular. For his public utterances he has been threatened with expulsion from Opus, of which he originally denied he was a member. The Opus press office in Madrid was forced to make a statement. It confirmed that

> on 24 May [1986 Opus] made known to Don José María Ruiz-Mateos that his way of acting and his frequent declarations over some considerable time are not in accordance with the spiritual and formative obligations which he freely entered into with Opus Dei, and he ought to correct them. The Prelature has never failed to offer him that help, solely and exclusively spiritual, to which he has a right, and which in fact he has refused. . . .
>
> On the other hand we again deplore that he continues to repeat assertions and arguments which have been denied on many occasions since 10 January 1986 because they lack any foundation whatever. On that date this office said that no director of Opus Dei had been involved in any agreement in relation with Rumasa. Nor has José María Ruiz-Mateos been given suggestions, advice, or promises of any kind with reference to remaining in Spain or leaving the country, nor with the technical defense of his person and his legitimate interests. It lacks any sense to attribute to Opus Dei the consequences of personal and free acts, or to expect from the Prelature any kind of protection or support in professional, social, economic, or political matters.

Which all seems a mite ungenerous from an organization to which not only Ruiz-Mateos himself, but many members of his close family, had devoted much of their lives, and a great deal of their money.

The Vatican, meanwhile, though it has refused to accept responsibility for what the Italians graphically call the "crack" Ambrosiano, has made some reparation: $250 million, less discount for paying all at once, was made over to the Ambrosiano creditors in May 1985. How the Vatican, poverty-stricken as it came to be, could find such a sum has not been explained. The Vatican is now concerned that Opus be allowed the same exemption from taxes in Spain which other ecclesiastical organizations such as religious orders, dioceses, parishes, and so on, enjoy under the Spanish Church-State agreements. If it is to come under the agreements, then it has to reveal a good deal about itself, its aims, structure, and so on. It does not want to do so. If the matter goes before the Spanish Parliament it is quite likely that the whole Church-State relationship on the matter of taxation would be aired, and the result may well not be beneficial to the Church.[26] On the other hand, if Opus Dei does not qualify for tax-exempt status, then a major source of revenue to the Church would be put in jeopardy. No wonder the Vatican has raised the question with the Madrid government.

If indeed Opus can dispense large sums, then the fatal visit of Calvi to London may reflect the banker's belief that Opus could bail him out. Both Signora Calvi and his son have claimed that he was expecting Opus to mount a rescue operation. They have said that he was thinking of going to Spain: instead he came to England. Was it because he believed the center of Opus's financial operations was in the City of London?

8

Sectarian Catholicism

In the index to the English version of *Camino* there is no entry
between PROFESSIONAL FORMATION ("see *Formation, professional*") and PRUDENCE. But an entry is to be found in the
Spanish edition: PROSELITISMO. Closer examination reveals
that the English text prefers APOSTLES, WINNING NEW.
Throughout the text has been bowdlerized. "Proselytism—it is
a certain sign of true zeal" has become "The search for fellow-
apostles. It is the unmistakable sign of true zeal" (Maxim 793),
while "Prayer is the most effective means of proselytism" has
been translated as "Prayer is the most effective means of winning new apostles" (Maxim 800).

Cronica, on the other hand, displays no such delicacy over
the use of the word "proselytism."

> Proselytism in the work is precisely the road, the way to
> reach sanctity. . . . No one can be dispensed from doing it,
> under any circumstances. Not even the sick can be dispensed
> because it would be as much as dispensing them from being
> saints. . . . Only if we are proselytistic will we live our voca-
> tion completely. When a person does not have the zeal to
> win others it is because his heart is not beating. He is dead.
> And we can apply to him those words of Scripture: "Iam
> foetet, quadriduanus est enim" (John 11:39)—"He is already
> decayed [literally, he stinks] for he is dead four days." Those
> souls, even though they were in the Work, would be dead,
> rotten, iam foetent. And I, says the Father, do not get any-
> where with cadavers. I bury cadavers.

The problem about translating *proselitismo* as "winning
apostles" is that it gives quite the wrong impression. Apostles

are preachers of the Gospel. The primary end of Opus Dei's proselytism, on the other hand, is to win recruits for itself: "to promote in the world the greatest possible number of souls dedicated to God in Opus Dei for the service of the Catholic Church and for the good of souls." Opus Dei comes first.

To seek recruits is a central obligation, it is something that has to be manifested each week in the circles: how far has an individual fulfilled his task of "fishing"—the Opus word—for new members: "It is time to count. How many vocations have you brought?" "Our personal apostolate," *Cronica* goes on, "is directed in the first place to fit our friends into the work of St. Raphael." The apostolate of St. Raphael is the Opus Dei term for the pursuit of young members ("I don't say," the Father concludes, "that we cannot find vocations among older people, but that . . . is a difficult thing") who might then, if suitable, be further recruited into the full, celibate membership (the apostolate of St. Michael) or formed as fathers of families (the apostolate of St. Gabriel). "'How frankly you laughed when I advised you to put your youthful years under the protection of St. Raphael so that he'll lead you, as he did the young Tobias, to a holy marriage, with a girl who is good and pretty and rich,' I [Escrivá] added jokingly."

Those with friends among members of Opus may be disturbed to learn that this friendship is regarded as a means to attract new recruits. Once they have been won, the professionals take over to provide formation in the ways of the organization.

> The Father himself has taught us the precise way to build the spiritual edifice of the youngsters. And he has given us well-defined norms for the courses of formation, which "are the essence of the work of St. Raphael," and which therefore are unchangeable, identical for all the circumstances of place and time.

The erstwhile friends then move on to further "fishing" expeditions.

The favored spot for "fishing" is the good Catholic school, with or without the encouragement of the school authorities. One distinguished foreign correspondent for a British newspaper complained that his Benedictine headmaster had urged him to fraternize with Opus: its members continued to pester him long after he had, he thought, made it clear he was not interested in the organization. In a girls' public school not far from London, on the other hand, the headmistress banned Opus from its premises after she discovered pupils newly arrived from Spain being invited to unauthorized meetings on the lawn at 5:00 P.M. with Opus priests.

Once a youngster has been hooked, the next step is the youth club. No fair-sized Opus house is complete without one, or two. The Tamezin club for girls, for example, operates out of Dawliffe Hall on London's Chelsea Embankment. There are similar centers for both recreational and study purposes in several of the London properties mentioned earlier. There are lectures, discussion groups, guidance with school work (have "some of the more advanced fellows clear up the more obscure points for some of the young ones"), excursions, and so on. Those who attend are unaware they are being carefully vetted:

> Before a fellow takes part in the weekly class, better still before he can attend the class of formation, the Director has to talk to him alone. . . . In that private conversation with the youngster who intends to attend the courses make him see—the Father indicates—that our house is not a place for recreation (we don't have, nor will we have, even a billiards table). It is rather an unpleasant place, where they often ask you if you pray etc., if you are good to your parents . . . if you study.

The Opus Dei "club" is to become a second home: "The fellows are not going to a club or to a friendly society. They are coming to their house." Alienation of children from their families goes hand-in-hand with the creation of dependency upon Opus:

> To direct this growth there is the talk with the priest and conversation which each youngster has with whomever is working with him, in order to tell, in the confidence of younger brothers, their little secrets and worries of all kinds. In the beginning it is difficult for them. Afterward, they need it.

The reward for the most loyal members of the clubs and study groups, for those who have bared their souls to the priests and to the director, for those who are most malleable, is the selection for the annual Easter pilgrimage to Rome. This is a highly-charged affair of camaraderie, religious zeal, and the carefully cultivated sense of belonging to an élite group. "By the time you've gone on the Easter pilgrimage, you're just begging to join," one disillusioned ex-member told the Liverpool weekly *The Catholic Pictorial*.[1] And that is when the problems start.

In a letter to the *Daily Mail,* Andrew Byrne, a priest of Opus, admitted: "In some cases when a youngster says he wants to join we do advise them not to tell their parents. This is because the parents do not understand us." A young man who had studied economics at Manchester University, and lived in a university hostel near a residence belonging to Opus Dei was befriended by a member of Opus. The friendship followed the usual path, and he was approached as a possible candidate. When he said he would first talk it over with his parents, his friend told him not to do so, because, as Fr. Byrne said, they might not understand. "I did not tell my parents until after I had joined," the "friend" added, "they were upset at first but they've gradually come round."[2]

Reports of sons being alienated from their families, possibly because of the greater freedom Opus Dei allows to its males, are much less frequent than stories of daughters being alienated. These accounts follow patterns familiar enough to any who have come across the charges regularly leveled at new religious movements, or "cults" as they are more popularly known. "I saw her behavior change," one mother said of her daughter who had gone to Lakefield, the Opus Dei catering college in Hempstead, London, after a careers talk at school. "She used to be a marvel of a daughter, and now she has become secretive and introverted."[3]

Restrictions on girls appear to be based upon the fear that, should they be exposed to family events, ties of affection would quickly be restored. Attendance at baptisms or weddings is regarded as particularly dangerous. At least two former members of Opus in England have reported that their decision to leave was confirmed by Opus's refusal to allow them to be bridesmaids at their sisters' weddings. Visits home are very few, and strictly regulated: a couple of nights a year are all that is permitted. When a father, a lorry-driver, met his daughter in London she decided on the spur of the moment to return home with him for a visit. An Opus superior rang the house and accused the father of kidnapping his own daughter.

While such stories could be multiplied, they have to be treated with a certain caution. Opus Dei is new and relatively unknown. Some of the parents have said they would not have objected—or not objected so much—had their daughters chosen to join one of the well-established sisterhoods. In many cases puzzlement is the greater because children have not only joined Opus without telling their parents, they have first of all converted to Roman Catholicism from some other denomination or none, after working or studying in the hot-house atmosphere of one of the Opus residences.

Stories of parental opposition to children joining religious communities, even of kidnapping and attempts at "deprogramming," are nothing new in the history of the Church. St. Thomas Aquinas in the thirteenth century met opposition from his family when he wanted to join the comparatively new Dominican Order, was taken prisoner by his brother and, according to legend, subjected to temptations to persuade him to adopt another kind of life. In the sixteenth century Stanislaus Kostka was forced to flee from his brother, and risk his father's considerable anger against the Society of Jesus in Poland, in order to enter the Jesuits. Opus could well claim in this instance at least to stand in a venerable tradition.

But traditional practices have changed. It would now be unthinkable for any of the major religious orders, male or female, to accept a candidate, at least one under the age of twenty-one, who did not have parental approval to join. Nor would any order recruit into membership someone under the age of at least eighteen or thereabouts, as they consider younger people rarely attain sufficient maturity to make the sort of life-long commitment which adherence to a religious order normally requires.

These considerations clearly disturbed Cardinal Hume, Archbishop of Westminster, after the London *Times* in January

1981 published a highly critical, page-length feature about Opus, based chiefly upon the experiences of Dr. John Roche. "Insofar as it is established within the diocese of Westminster," he declared, "I have a responsibility, as bishop, to ensure the welfare of the whole local Church as well as the best interests of Opus Dei itself." He went on:

I have made known to those responsible for Opus Dei in this country what I consider to be the right recommendations for the future activity of its members within the diocese of Westminster. I now wish to make public these four recommendations. Each of them arises from one fundamental principle: that the procedures and activities of an international movement, present in a particular diocese, may well have to be modified prudently in the light of the cultural differences and legitimate local customs and standards of the society within which that international body seeks to work.

These recommendations must not be seen as a criticism of the integrity of the members of Opus Dei or of their zeal in promoting their apostolate) I am making them public in order to meet understandable anxieties and to encourage sound practice within the diocese.

The four recommendations are as follows:

1. No person under eighteen years of age should be allowed to take any vow or long-term commitment in association with Opus Dei.

2. It is essential that young people who wish to join Opus Dei should first discuss the matter with their parents or legal guardians. If there are, by exception, good reasons for not approaching their families, these reasons should, in every case, be discussed with the local bishop or his delegate.

3. While it is accepted that those who join Opus Dei take on the proper duties and responsibilities of membership, care must be taken to respect the freedom of the individual; first, the freedom of the individual to join or to leave the organization without undue pressure being exerted; secondly, the freedom of the individual at any stage to choose his or her own spiritual director, whether or not the director is a member of Opus Dei.

4. Initiatives and activities of Opus Dei, within the diocese of Westminster, should carry a clear indication of their sponsorship and management.

These "Guidelines for Opus Dei within the Diocese of Westminster," as they were entitled, were dated 2 December 1981. Though, in a closing paragraph, the Cardinal claimed to be "confident that these four guidelines will in no way hinder Opus Dei in the apostolic work to which it has committed itself, but will help it to adapt to the traditional spirituality and instincts of our people," readers will by this point in the book be aware of how contrary they are to Opus Dei attitudes and practices. It is therefore questionable how far they are observed. One young man who joined Opus at seventeen and has since left[4] claims that when he raised the matter of the Cardinal's statement, he was told they were merely guidelines, not rules, and that Opus was therefore not obliged to follow them. On the other hand, two women assistant numeraries[5] were adamant that, although it might not be a good idea to tell one's parents, nobody was admitted until they were more than eighteen years of age. That might technically be true, though recruitment certainly begins before that age. The fourth guideline requires "clear indication" of Opus's activities within the diocese of Westminster. In its lengthy report for the year ending 30 September 1986, the Netherhall Educational Association makes no mention anywhere that this limited company controls not only Netherhall but also Ashwell House[6] in west London and Grandpont in Oxford as international halls of residence for students; Lakefield Housecraft and Educational Center, Elmore (Orme Court), Westpark in south-west, and Kelston (a club and study center for school boys) in south London; the Wickenden Manor Conference Center in Sussex and Dunreath in Glasgow. The latter has a board of directors made up exclusively of Opus Dei members who all give as their addresses Opus Dei houses in London or Manchester, and none of whom receives remuneration for their services. The report states that: "The principal objects of the Association are the advancement of education and the training of character in accordance with Christian principles and ideals." In none of this is there mention that Opus is in any way involved, a remarkable oversight, one would have thought, in the light of the Cardinal's wishes in the matter. But even greater problems arise with another aspect of the third guideline, the freedom to leave the organization.

Maria Angustias Moreno was a long-time member of Opus in Spain who, after her resignation, wrote about her experiences. Her account occasioned many letters from other former members: twenty signed a public letter of support. These twenty were visited by two priests from Opus, the first contact some of them had had since they left many years before. They were told that Maria Angustias had been a lesbian, and a practicing lesbian, during her days in Opus Dei, and that is why she had been dismissed. No evidence was produced, she alleges in her book *La otra cara del Opus Dei*,[7] beyond one of the priests touching the cloth of his soutane to indicate that, as a clergyman, he must be worthy of trust. Maria, who had previously been warned by Opus that they would use things known against her without specifying what it was that was known, felt she had no alternative but to seek legal redress. She was eventually offered a full apology before her lawyer for the things said against her, but she wanted the apology repeated in open court. In this she failed time and again for technical reasons, clearly to her mind because of the machinations of Opus.[8]

Angustias Moreno's account seems to verge at times on the paranoid. It is difficult to believe that any religious organization whose members are dedicated to the pursuit of holiness would behave in the way she describes. But María del Carmen Tapia too experienced problems. Some time after she had left Opus she decided to go to a university in the United States. She had of course studied while a member of the organization, but had never been given any form of certificate or diploma. When certificate of attendance at these courses was requested by the American university, Opus replied that she had never taken them. Tapia went to the Vatican to ask for help. She was told there were several other people waiting like herself for certification of the studies they had undertaken while in Opus Dei. Eventually Opus sent to the Vatican a statement that "unless the members pass a revalidation of their studies, Opus Dei never keeps a record of the studies taken."[9]

No attempt was made to prevent Tapia herself from leaving Opus. On the contrary. She was, as she puts it, "fired personally by the Founder," but in quite remarkable circumstances.

In 1965 she was summoned to the Rome headquarters where she was put virtually under house arrest for eight months. She was allowed no communication with the outside world either by telephone or by letter. A sympathetic numerary from Venezuela opened a numbered postbox for her, but this was discovered and the numerary severely punished. Tapia's refusal to reveal the number of her postbox was described by a woman official of Opus's central directorate as a mortal sin. She was informed that anyone who asked for her would be told she was either sick or absent. Over a period of three months her hair went white. She asked if she might return to her family in Spain: she was refused permission.

While head of the female section in Venezuela, Tapia had been one of the most liberal of Opus Dei superiors, battling for equality of opportunity with the men for the women under her charge, giving permission to them to go to confession to the priest (of Opus) of their choice, something of which Opus disapproves, and complaining at the amount of direction they used to receive from Rome. Because of these alleged "crimes" she was accused of damaging the unity of the organization. When she failed to admit her guilt or evince remorse, she was required by the founder to resign, but warned never to mention what had happened in Rome. Apart from her passport, Opus kept hold of all her personal documents. As she left she was forced into a confessional. An Opus Dei priest warned her that no matter how much penance she did for various "crimes," she was unlikely to be saved.

In her account in the *National Catholic Reporter* she describes the "ill-mannered" and insulting treatment she received at the hands of the Founder. She concludes "My astonishment is infinite when I hear now that Monsignor Escrivá is in the process of beatification."[10]

Similarly strange events surrounded the departure of Raimundo Pannikar from Opus Dei. When he became unhappy with life within its confines, instead of dispensing him from his commitments his Opus superiors sent him to India. (His father was Indian.) He was told he could be freed from the obligation of poverty, could find a bishop in whose diocese he might work and, as long as he wrote occasionally to Opus, no problems would arise. There was only one condition: he could not return to Europe without permission.

Pannikar kept to this condition, even when an important interchurch institute was established at Tantur in Israel and he was appointed by Pope Paul VI as one of the Catholic founder members. Pannikar himself, mindful of his promise not to return to Europe without permission, said he could not come to the first meeting of this governing board. He was, however, given permission to attend the second. On his way he arranged to meet a French woman, at her request, in Zurich: Opus alleged that he was having an affair with her.

While in Europe he agreed to go to Bonn to give a lecture for the archbishop of Utrecht. While he was there he was persuaded to fly to Rome because Mgr Escrivá de Balaguer wished to see him. As soon as he arrived in Italy he was met by two Opus priests who said they were taking him to see the founder, but once in the car they changed their story. Escrivá was very tired just at that moment, they would take him somewhere else, and he would see the founder the following day. The next day he was indeed taken to Escrivá, but only for the beginning of a quasi-trial before a form of jury, in which he was accused of all kinds of misdemeanors. He refused to answer or to sign any paper. A report was presented to the Congregation for Religious and Secular Institutes under which Opus still came—this was 1966—but it was laughed out of court. An audience with the Pope had been arranged; he was not allowed to go. His mother telephoned from Barcelona; she was told he was not in Rome. Finally he was dismissed from Opus, put on a non-stop flight back to Delhi, and told to find a sympathetic bishop. He became a priest of the diocese of Benares, and later Professor of Religious Studies at the University of California, Santa Barbara.[11]

These were people who were thrown out of Opus in curious circumstances. A more common experience, it would seem, is of people who find it difficult to leave. A Colombian Jesuit reported suicides. So has John Roche, who says he knows directly of one Opus Dei suicide in Kenya.[12] The case of Michael Richards, mentioned above as the first English recruit and later a priest of Opus Dei, is particularly strange. As a priest he became chaplain to university students at Bangor in North Wales. But after a while he appeared to lose all interest in himself, and in living. According to another chaplain he was required to take regular medicine, but he failed to do so. He would sit up long hours, sometimes all night. He wasted away. Eventually he was found dead in his sister's seaside home of natural causes, though he seems to have destroyed himself through neglect.

Whatever the difficulties that might be put in the way of someone trying to leave Opus, these are perhaps not the real problem. "When you leave you become a non-person, and no one who is a member is allowed to help you," says María del Carmen Tapia. "When a person leaves Opus he or she is on the street, financially, spiritually, psychologically." This was the experience of John Roche whose own sister, still a member, would have nothing to do with him, though this has recently changed. He tried to sue the organization for the return of the money which he put into it, but failed on a technicality. Opus's Constitutions in any case make specific mention of people trying to get their money back. They rule it out.

But the real problems are spiritual and psychological. Tapia recalls the founder saying that "any person who has belonged to Opus would not want to belong to any other Institution." It is not hard to understand why. It is all in *Cronica*. There is this, for example:

> [Opus Dei's] spirit is above all geographical, historical, social, or cultural boundaries. It transcends as well the evolutionary development over the ages. . . . As a result, as long as there are men on earth, there will be Opus Dei . . . [our internal law] by the will of God contains everything necessary for our sanctification and our effectiveness. That is why it is holy, unchangeable and everlasting. . . . God has entrusted this treasure to us. Our first obligation, then, is to guard and defend it exactly as we have received it. . . . There will never

come a time, now or in the centuries to come, in which circumstances would advocate habitually abandoning some part of our internal law.

Nor, added the founder addressing his "sons," "will we ever have to follow in the wake of human progress."

In this vision, central to the ideology of Opus Dei, the organization is perfect, like God immutable (though there have, of course, been several changes in its legal status, each accompanied by a new Constitution), and offering to all, regardless of time and place, the certain hope of salvation through work. Pannikar recalls that in the early 1940s, when he first joined, Opus Dei was a form of "counter-culture," a serious acceptance of the demands of Christianity in contrast to the conformist practice of Catholicism which Escrivá de Balaguer and the first members believed they saw all about them. It has become, however, not simply a serious commitment to the following of Christ, but the only true way in which the teachings of Christ can be understood. Just like Christianity which, until relatively recent times, did not accept that non-believers could be "saved" and achieve eternal happiness in heaven, members of Opus are taught to think the same of their own organization. It is the one sure hope of salvation. Hence the enormous emphasis on winning converts, on proselytizing, on encouraging people to "whistle" as the Opus jargon has it. According to John Roche, every member is supposed to have at least fifteen friends suitable for recruitment, of whom a third are being worked upon to "whistle" at any one time. "None of my children can rest satisfied if he doesn't win four or five faithful vocations each year," says the founder in *Cronica*.

Raimundo Pannikar described the organization as the "last remnant of that militant messianism which is endemic in the Abrahamic religions."[13] The Abrahamic religions (Judaism, Christianity, and Islam) are all marked by claims to be the only true faiths. Each periodically has to endure outbursts from fundamentalist groups within them which attempt to recall backsliders to what they see as the primitive, true faith. In Christianity's case, at least, such groups preach their message in the context of a (to them) decadent society which they believe to be the prelude to the last days.

Opus, says Pannikar, wants to save the world from itself in the name of God—but on Opus's own terms. Opus's terms, of course, are identical with those of the founder. All grace leading to salvation comes to Opus Dei members through the founder. It is through the grace of the founder that you are what you are. Hence the traumas suffered by those who leave. Too often they themselves believe, and faithful Opus Dei members believe of them, that because they have cut themselves off from this source of grace, put themselves outside this divinely inspired and unchangeably perfect institution, they are destined to be damned for all eternity. "The devil acts quickly," said Janet Gould to her mother when explaining why she could not briefly abandon the Opus residence to return home on a visit, "and he will do if I leave here."[14]

The impact upon Opus members is predictable. They are cut off, early in life, from their natural family. They are taught to believe that salvation is impossible, certainly now that they are members of Opus, save through the organization they have joined. It supplies their family life, their total environment, at least as far as everything that is not professional activity is concerned, and in many cases, especially for women, that as well. When they are disillusioned, therefore, the emotional impact is overwhelming. People who wish to leave have no one to turn to, no one, outside Opus, with whom they have been allowed to build up a sufficiently close relationship that they might confide in them. And they have also been brought up to believe that in breaking ranks they are committing the most heinous sin possible for them. Salvation is mediated through Opus. Without Opus the former numerary is damned.

Similarities between Opus Dei and some of the new religious movements are striking. It is not hard to make revealing comparisons between organizations such as the Unification Church—the Moonies—and Opus. However, such comparisons do not always work: Opus has throughout its life sought, and eventually received, the approbation of the Holy See. Despite its many detractors, it remains an accepted part of

Roman Catholicism, with entries in the Vatican's yearbook, and the directories of Catholic Churches around the world. On the face of it, the notion that Opus might be classed as a new religious movement or sect which is operating within Roman Catholicism would seem paradoxical and highly unlikely. Paradoxical or not, the question has to be addressed: is Opus Dei a reputable part of Roman Catholicism or is it a sect at odds with the Church which gave it birth? Carol Coulter, an Irish journalist, included a chapter on Opus in her book *Are Religious Cults Dangerous?* She concludes: "The suspicion must remain that the Catholic Church has its own cult, protected up to now by the highest levels in the Church itself."[15] So is the Roman Catholic Church divided against itself? Is the monolith—though in truth the Church has seemed a monolith only to those outside its embrace—about to crumble? For the problem is more widespread than Opus alone.

Not so long ago the Holy See was expressing its concern at the growth in Latin America of Protestant sects, particularly those of an evangelical variety. It has good reason for its alarm, as even a brief visit to the poorer *barrios* of the big cities rapidly reveals. The expansion of such sects, almost invariably of a distinctly conservative theological type, has been the subject of considerable study. Much less attention has been paid, however, to an equally alarming development within Roman Catholicism itself: the emergence of right-wing groupings.

Some of these, Communión y Liberación, for example, are known in Europe under an equivalent title. Others, such as Fiducia in Chile or the Peruvian Sodalitium Vitae, are homegrown products. They have distinctive identities. No doubt there are similarities between the Protestant and Catholic sects which sociologists could swiftly point out. Much more striking, however, are the contrasts. The Protestant sects appeal to the poor and the dispossessed, the Catholic ones to the rich and the privileged. The former vigorously reject Rome in the name of the Reformation; the latter display unquestioning loyalty—albeit of their own kind. The former eschew politics and thus, as a distinguished liberation theologian, Jon Sobrino, once put it, cut their converts off from their historical responsibilities. The latter do just the opposite, regarding the Church as the buttress of the State and expecting the State to be, in return, the patron of the Church. The former are frequently Pentecostal, seeking consolation from the almost unbearable burden of the daily struggle for existence in the discontinuities created by the unpredictable coming of the spirit. The latter take refuge in the security of a well-tried value system: in tradition, the family, and property. This is, in fact, the name of one such group—Tradición, Familia y Propriedad—active in various parts of Latin America.

Yet in spite of these differences the success of both Protestant and Catholic sects in attracting recruits seems to have the same origin: the changing role of the official Church within political structures.

For political structures to operate at all there has to be a degree of consensus among those who work within them, and those who are governed by them. When that national consensus breaks down, a country becomes ungovernable. The most obvious, though least attractive, way of restoring a semblance of order in such circumstances is through military dictatorship. But while it may be possible to impose order, it is not possible to impose consensus, to create a new system of values, or to win acceptance by force of a social structure which does not reflect the needs and aspirations of the majority of the people.

In the past, the Catholic Church in many countries, particularly Latin American countries, has been part of that national consensus. It has been closely involved with the State, appearing to give the State divine authority over those it governed. The presence within a country of a papal nuncio; his attendance, and that of other prelates, at State occasions; State recognition of religious festivals—these and many other signs have demonstrated that the State has the blessing of the Church and that the Church legitimizes the State.

But it is precisely such a role which the Catholic Church has either ceased to play, or at least is no longer so sure about. Its retreat from this role has left a vacuum into which the Catholic sects have rushed.

It is, of course, necessary for there to be a degree of consensus within the State. It is also proper that Christians should play a part in forming that consensus, but with the arrival of Liberation Theology in the 1960s the method of doing so has radically altered. The Church was accustomed to operate as if the State and its citizens, the State and society, were identical, and they are not. It has addressed governors rather than the governed. Liberation theologians, on the other hand, have turned their attention away from the State and toward the people, toward society.

This difference in perspective between the official Church and liberation theologians may be yet another reason why it has taken Rome so long to come to terms with this new theological phenomenon. It may also explain why Catholic social teaching, of which there is a great deal and to which much lip-service is paid, has made so little impact upon people's lives. In all of its social teaching the Church has hitherto addressed the State. To take a recent example, Pope John Paul II's September 1981 letter to the whole Church, known as *Laborem Exercens,* admirable though it may be in what it says about the dignity of human work, has little of comfort for the unemployed. It deals with the State and its employment policies, not with people and their problems.

No one could say that of the theology of liberation. Certainly no one could say that after attending a catechetical instruction in a *barrio* of Santiago in Chile, or after having listened to freedom songs sung in the churches of the shanty town around Lima or up in the hills above Bogotá.[16] And of liberation theology Opus, as has been seen (pp. 124–27), is the sworn enemy.

Opus is the doyen of the neo-conservative movements within the Catholic Church. It is the most powerful, with members in high office in governments of Catholic countries round the world, and in influential posts in the media and in business. As a personal prelature, it is the only one able to provide a cradle-to-grave service for its devotees, not only sacramentally in the Church, but in many places educationally as well, albeit in distinctly conservative, inevitably single-sex, schools. It serves all echelons of society in some form, but its preferred clientele is the professional élite, as its Constitutions make clear. Catholics of this class who had, in many countries, a privileged access to the organs of State through their Church, have been "disenfranchised" by the "option for the poor" embraced by the hierarchies of many Third World countries. As an alternative means of access they have turned to these new movements, and especially to Opus Dei.

The reasons for Opus Dei's popularity are clear enough and have been vividly described by the Brazilian theologian Leonardo Boff. Early on in his controversial book *Church, Charism and Power,* Boff talks of various "models" of the Church, different kinds of styles of operation.[17] In one of these models he describes the Church as "mother and teacher" or, in Latin, *Mater et Magistra,* using the famous opening words of one of the letters of Pope John XXIII on social problems.

It is typical of this model of the Church, says Boff, and it must be emphasized he does not have Opus in mind at this point, that "the Church allies itself with the dominant classes that control the state, organizing its projects around these classes, giving rise to colleges, universities, Christian political parties and the like." It does not, however, neglect the poor. On the contrary, they rank high in its list of priorities, as they do with Opus which can claim, in all justice, to run agricultural and industrial schools, training schools in domestic service for women, and so on. "A vast network of assistance programs are established, leading the Church to become a Church *for* the poor rather than a Church *with* or *of* the poor." Boff then goes on to a description of the theological stance of this kind of Church, which applies perfectly to Opus within the Church:

> On a doctrinal level, this Church is conservative and ortho-
> dox. It is suspicious of any innovation. Dogma is rigid; and
> vision, legalistic, confined to those in positions of power
> within the Church, the hierarchy. There is the ever present
> appeal to authority, especially to that of the Pope [one might
> add, in the Opus context, of the founder]; preaching is
> priestly and devoid of prophetic witness. The deposit of faith
> [a Roman Catholic term for the definitive revelation of God
> in Jesus Christ] is presented as complete and perfect; nothing
> can be added to it and nothing can be taken away from it.

All social practices must be derived from it. The Church emerges, fundamentally, as *mater et magistra*, mother and teacher: it has an answer to every question taken from the deposit of faith, formed by Scripture, tradition, the magisterial [i.e. of the hierarchy] teachings, and a specific understanding of natural law.

According to his model, Boff continues, there is a straightforward relationship between Church and State as if between two forces, the Church understanding itself, just as does the State, in terms of law and power. It is a model of the Church which appeals to the State, because although it still allows the Church a voice in political matters insofar as they have moral implications, it both restricts the Church's room for more direct intervention in the political arena, and in any case compromises the Church by its close links with the political powers that be. Although Boff himself does not use this kind of language, it is another formulation of the nineteenth-century description of Church and State as two "perfect societies," each autonomous in its own sphere, though linked because both had in common the people subjected to their power. It is this theory upon which many generations of priests were brought up—and that includes the present Pope. One explanation of John Paul II's apparently ambiguous attitude to political action on the part of churchmen and women, supporting it in Poland and seeming to condemn it in Latin America, may well be that in the former instance, the Church is attempting to return to the old "two perfect societies" model, whereas the liberation theologians of Latin America reject any such formulation, siding with the people—with society—rather than with the State.

That Opus Dei should share with the Pope the same attitude to overt political action, while leaving its members free to act politically as they wish, namely in a generally conservative mold, fits precisely into this framework of the Church as "mother and teacher," described by Boff. In his book *Jesus and Politics: A Scriptural Study of Messianism,* the Opus Dei priest (though of course it nowhere describes him as such) José María Casclaro brings his essay to an end with a passage which might have been written to confirm Boff's description:

The Church, insofar as it is Christ's body is, like its Lord, above ideologies, political regimes, social movements, pressure groups, parties, professional and national bodies etc., while still being deeply interested in and concerned about these human affairs although from a lofty perspective. But all these things, all these very often noble human affairs, are still ephemeral and changeable. What was at one time regarded as being *the* final stage of a long process, becomes absolutely a thing of the past. All this is, then, unstable and changing. Christ, the Church, are on the other hand eternal, just as their mission is eternal.[18]

The conjunction of ideologies between the Pope and Opus, together with their similar views on the place of work at the center of life, may help to account for John Paul II's apparent sympathy toward Opus Dei. One experienced Vatican observer, however, has remarked that Opus's influence in the present pontificate has "peaked."[19] Events at the Synod of Bishops in Rome in October 1987 may suggest a reason.

During the Synod there was much talk about "movements," by which those present meant organizations such as Communión y Liberación—in practice better known in its Italian dress as Communione e Liberazione. Bishops with dioceses were unhappy about these movements because they were outside their control, and often displayed, as Opus does, strongly conservative traits. Opus, however, proudly stood aside from these debates. As a personal prelature it was no longer a movement: it had achieved a juridical independence to which other movements still aspired.

The Vatican, on the other hand, has favored movements. There may be intra-Roman Catholic reasons for this: the movements are centralist, and so is the Vatican, alarmed at the increasing independence displayed by conferences of bishops around the world. But there is another, perhaps more significant, reason. Movements can be mobilized, can be used by the Roman powers that be; Opus insists that it takes no collective action—its members may be active, but only as individuals. As has been seen, this is Opus's constant retort to critics who accuse it of political interference in the conservative interest. But during an increasingly interventionist papacy, that stance of

Opus may decrease its value to the Vatican, and therefore also decrease the Vatican's interest in Opus's future development.

Nonetheless, as this study has shown, the central authorities of the Roman Catholic Church have displayed considerable interest in the organization over its sixty-year existence and this interest makes it difficult to conceive of Opus as a cult or new religious movement or sect. It appears on the face of it to be an integral part of a worldwide Church, recognized as such by the Church authorities.

Religious sects have been a subject of considerable study in recent years, both as individual movements and as a rather more general concept.[20] As a general concept, the analysis of the characteristics of sects is particularly associated with Dr. Bryan Wilson of All Souls' College, Oxford. In his article "The Sociology of Sects," he remarks that "sect" used to be a pejorative word in a religious context, applied to "a movement committed to heretical belief and often to ritual acts and practices that departed from orthodox religious procedures."[21] He then goes on to describe the various characteristics displayed by sects. They tend (1) to be exclusive; (2) to claim a monopoly on the complete religious truth; (3) to be lay, though they may develop a body of professional organizers; (4) to deny "special religious virtuosity" to anyone except, perhaps, their own founders and leaders; they (5) are voluntary—an individual chooses to be a member; (6) are concerned to sustain standards, with sanctions against the inadequate or wayward; and (7) demand total allegiance. He also adds (8) that sects are protest groups, either against the Church, though he thinks this less likely given what he sees as the weakened state of the Church, or against secular society.[22] Elsewhere Dr. Wilson comments that:

> Sects have a totalitarian rather than a segmental hold over their members: they dictate the member's ideological orientation to secular society; or they rigorously specify the necessary standards of moral rectitude or they compel the member's involvement in group activity.[23]

Into most of the above categories Opus Dei fits with great ease. It is exclusive (1) at various levels as has been seen: in its selective recruitment and in the secrecy with which it surrounds itself. It would be untrue to say that it claims to have a *monopoly* of religious truth (2), but its members are utterly convinced that the interpretation of the Roman Catholic faith to which they adhere is the only orthodox version: witness Mgr Escrivá de Balaguer's exhortation to his faithful after Vatican II. That it is a "lay" organization is one of its proudest boasts (3), even though technically it is a clerical institute within the Church and is undoubtedly clerically dominated. It is also one of its characteristics that it depends almost entirely upon the writings of its founder, and is molded wholly by his spirituality. It therefore neatly complies with characteristic (4) as listed by Dr. Wilson. Recruitment procedures, Opus's internal discipline, and the total commitment required of members, coincide with points (5) to (7).

Whether Opus could ever be described as a "protest group" is, perhaps, rather more problematic, although, as Pannikar pointed out, it started off in a "counter-cultural" mold. In more recent years it has displayed distinct unwillingness to conform to the changes which followed in the wake of Vatican II, and is a committed opponent of Liberation Theology, espoused by many churchmen throughout the world. If the comparison made above between Boff's "Mater et Magistra" model of the Church and Opus is valid, then it would certainly be the case that Opus is espousing a theological outlook which, no matter how attractive it may be to churchmen in high office, has declined deeply in popularity in the Church at large since Vatican II.

The danger of the arguments advanced above to show that Opus displays many of the characteristics of a sect is that they might prove too much. Within the Roman Catholic Church and, in different ways, in other Christian denominations, there exist religious orders. These are groups of varying size, ranging from less than a hundred to many thousands of men or women (the groups are almost all single-sex) who dedicate themselves to God under a particular rule of life, and generally, though not always, share a common life in monasteries or convents. They include such well-known bodies within Catholicism as the Society of Jesus (the Jesuits), the Order of Preachers (the Dominicans), or the Franciscans in their different forms. Should the arguments advanced to show Opus to be a sect apply equally to religious orders then those arguments would be meaningless: it would be foolish to argue that such well-established bodies as the Jesuits, Franciscans, or Dominicans were sectarian when they have done so much to promote the well-being of the Roman Catholic church as a whole.

The sociology of religious orders has not attracted as much interest as that of sects: one of the few substantial books on the subject is Michael Hill's *The Religious Order,* which is for the most part a study of the revival of this kind of institution in the Church of England, rather than a full-scale investigation of the phenomenon. He does, however, provide a definition of orders which distinguishes them from sects. "The religious order," he writes, "is a collection of religious virtuosi with an uncompromising interpretation of the Gospel ethic which is sanctioned by the Church but is not put forward as necessary for all," a definition which fits neatly into Roman Catholic theological categories.[24]

Within this theological thinking there is a distinction (though one, it has to be said, which is no longer much in favor) between precepts and counsels. The precepts are those interpretations of the Gospel ethic obligatory on all; the counsels are those embraced only by religious enthusiasts (or in Hill's language "virtuosi") and recognized as not binding on all. In practice these interpretations are given concrete shape in the three vows of poverty, chastity, and obedience.

On this criterion, however, Opus falls into the sectarian class, rather than the religious order. It does not believe that its own interpretation of the Gospel is only one among many competing versions.

> We are the remnant of the people of Israel. We are the only ones who, having remained faithful to God, can still save the Church today. Given the state of the Church today, it seems as if it were abandoned by the Holy Spirit. We are the ones who can save the Church by our faithfulness to the Father.[25]

This is a perfect expression of one type of sectarian thinking, called by Wilson an "Ark of the Covenant" sect—the only ones who hold firm to the true faith. Russell Shaw, once spokesman for the American Catholic Bishops, contrasts the American Church with the Catholic Church. Members of the latter "take their lead on matters of spiritual and moral substance for the most part from orthodox Roman Catholicism as articulated by John Paul II," he says. He identifies Opus with this group. The American Church, on the other hand, led by the bishops who were for a good number of years his employers, have parted from such orthodoxy.[26]

For Opus members, their rule and spiritual life, applicable as it is to married couples, single people, even young people, is the way that all Christians would live and worship, were they but to be aware of it. The essence of "proselytism" in Opus Dei is precisely the conviction that the whole world is to be converted to Escrivá's understanding of the Gospel message.

Opus, then, displays very many of the characteristics which sociologists discover when they analyze religious sects and sectarian behavior. Yet "what has characterized the Opus Dei even after the Second Vatican Council has been its extreme orthodoxy."[27] That is José Casanova's view, but he then goes on to throw doubt upon Opus's fundamental Catholicity. "Escrivá basically reiterates the main themes of Luther and Calvin, ideas which were analyzed by Max Weber as determinant of the Protestant ethic,"[28] he says, and then goes on to isolate three elements. Escrivá's teaching, he claims, (1) puts an end to the "hierarchical structuring of both this world and the other world"; (2) insists that salvation is to be found in worldly activities; and (3) proclaims a universal call to perfection.

If these are the marks of "Protestantification" as Casanova claims, then the whole Roman Catholic Church is turning Protestant, at least since Vatican II. And no Church whose founder preached "You, therefore, must be perfect, as your heavenly Father is perfect" (Matthew 5:48) is going to deny a universal call to perfection. Casanova's criteria require a little more nuance.

Take this last point about the call to perfection, for example. Certain Protestant groups develop it further. They believe there is a small, predestined "elect" who will go to heaven and the rest of humankind is damned. This is a view which has been decisively rejected by the Catholic Church. According to its teaching no one can be certain of salvation. Not so Opus members, however. Their salvation is guaranteed by the Father/Founder:

> When the years pass you will not believe what you have lived. It will seem that you have been dreaming. How many good and great and wonderful things you are going to see!. . .
> *I can assure you that you will be faithful, even though at times you will have to suffer. Besides, I promise you heaven.*[29]

While avoiding the obvious dangers of predestinationism, Escrivá de Balaguer manages to assure his followers they are not simply a spiritual élite but a religious elect. This would seem scarcely compatible with orthodox Catholic doctrine.

Again, no Catholic could deny that the vast majority of human beings have to work out their salvation in the midst of the "world"—though very many of them nowadays would be uneasy about the rather derogatory understanding of "the world" to be found in much traditional piety. On the other hand it is a Calvinistic, rather than a Roman Catholic, outlook which so stresses professional success that such success comes to be looked upon as a sign of God's favor. Other charges of heterodoxy are sometimes aimed at them. They are occasionally accused, for instance, of falling into the error of Pelagianism, believing that, with the guidance of the founder's wisdom, they can attain sanctity by their own efforts.

All great heresies have their origin in a determination to cling on to out-moded formulations, and Opus's major error lies in its staunch conservatism. "We are among the most committed defenders of the notion that undebatable truth exists. Doctrine is not debatable," said Fr. Rolf Thomas, a member of the organization's general council.[30]

Opus has stayed where it was at the beginning of the 1940s, and that means for Catholic theology, intellectually in the early years of the century, when Pius X launched his bitter attack upon historical scholarship as applied to the religious sciences. Antonio Fuentes teaches scripture at the University of Navarra. In 1987 Dublin's Four Courts Press published his *Guide to the Bible,* a quite remarkable work. In it he upheld the view that Moses wrote the first five books of the Bible, and that the author of the Book of Isaiah was a single individual. In doing so he cited the authority of Vatican statements of the first decade of this century. These opinions, and many others in this *Guide,* flatly contradict scholarly opinion both inside the Catholic Church and outside it. Often enough, on the authorship of the Pauline letters, for example, Fuentes does not even allow his readers to know that views different from his own are widely held. This is the mind-set of the Catholicism of the first half of the twentieth century, utterly convinced that it alone possesses the truth, no matter how bizarre its official line.

The Roman Catholic Church has moved on, and moved on fast, since then, and especially after Vatican II which Escrivá de Balaguer so much disliked. Yet Opus, in the dress of its clerics, in the style of worship in its chapels, in its rule-bound spiritual counseling, or in the teaching of its theological faculties and, apparently, its departments of Scripture, is an anachronism. There is no reason to doubt the sincerity of its members' belief that they preserve the true faith. The vast majority of the remaining 850 million members of the Church hold to a rather different orthodoxy.

It was remarked by the Founder of Christianity that "Every kingdom divided against itself is laid waste, and no city or house divided against itself will stand" (Matthew 12:25). A sect, holding to heterodox beliefs, does precisely that: it divides the Church against itself. Naturally, Opus members deny they divide the Church. Their response—predictable as always—is to claim the approbation of successive popes and many bishops. As this book has pointed out, such hierarchical support is difficult to substantiate. Popes before the present one can hardly be said to have been enthusiastic in their endorsement of Opus, and for every bishop who welcomes Opus into his diocese it is clear there are many who either will not accept them, or are unhappy at finding them installed within their jurisdiction when they take up their appointments.

To silence their critics, it is a common Opus tactic to appeal to history, in particular to the formation of the Society of Jesus in the middle years of the sixteenth century. It is true that the foundation of the Jesuits was accompanied by controversy, some of it because there had been a decision that no further religious orders were to be permitted, but more because the Society constituted a new manner of life within the Church, as does Opus Dei today. Because of the similarity of the works they undertake and the speed of their growth, comparison between Opus and the Society is inevitable. But within its first sixty years the Jesuits had produced four acknowledged saints, provided theologians for the popes, and sent missionaries to India, Japan, and China to enter as far as possible into the culture of the peoples they were to evangelize. They were, for the most part, liberal-minded men of open outlook, and it was for that reason they clashed with the more traditional members of the Church establishment.

In the case of Opus Dei it is just the opposite. It is with the liberal-minded that they clash. As missionaries they do not enter the culture of the people among whom they work, but see it as their task to mold the culture of their neophytes to the traditional model of Christianity they have themselves learned. Of their saints it would be improper to speak; after all, it took time enough to canonize even so widely popular a figure as Francis Xavier. In Escrivá's lifetime Opus introduced the cause of "God's engineer" (see p. 34). That has now been put on the back-burner while the all-important canonization of Escrivá de Balaguer himself is promoted.

Should this happen—despite the best efforts of some ex-Opus members who worked closely with the founder—it will be hailed as a triumph by the organization. It will be regarded by them as the final accolade of approval by the Church upon Escrivá's foundation. In itself, however, canonization is simply a declaration by the Church that the person thus honored is in heaven, and worthy to be shown public veneration. And that his or her promoters have the wealth to pay for what is a distinctly costly process.

Opus, on the other hand, will argue that the authorities in the Vatican would not go ahead with such an undertaking unless they were wholly behind it, because they have only the good of the whole Church at heart. That is not very convincing, particularly if it is true that the Vatican bank, through its involvement in the Banco Ambrosiano, was giving financial support to despotic regimes in Latin America which engaged in the persecution of priests and nuns who worked with the poor and the oppressed. The Banco Ambrosiano scandal, the rise of Opus and other similarly sectarian organizations within Roman Catholicism, are all evidence of a Church which is today divided against itself.

As María del Carmen Tapia said to me in August 1984, speaking across a table littered with coffee cups in New York's Barbizon Plaza Hotel: "In a hundred or in fifty years the Church is going to say that we were wrong to approve Opus Dei."

9

The Apotheosis of the Founder

In his book *Cults, New Religions and Religious Creativity* Geoffrey Nelson comments:

> Many religious leaders who attract a following build an organization through which their experiences can be transmitted to future generations, but the transmitted experience ceases to have any transformatory power for the individuals who receive it. The organization grows and comes to dominate the lives of whole populations, because of the power which the "message" gives the leaders (priests) over the lives of their followers. The control that these "priests" have enables them to prevent the mass of the people from questioning the authenticity of the "message," and allows them to persecute those who point out that the benefits of contact with God can only be had through personal experience.[1]

There can be little doubt about Escrivá de Balaguer's personal magnetism, about his "charism" to use that much-abused term. Nor is there any doubt that people followed him and that he provided a form of spiritual guidance which they needed at the time. Some who have left Opus Dei would like to believe that the path it has now taken is a betrayal of his fundamental insight, that he never meant it to be the secretive, somewhat sinister, highly regulated, manipulative organization it has become.

A new collection of his aphorisms, drawn from notes Escrivá jotted down over the years in copybooks and published under the title *The Forge,* would seem to prove the contrary.[2] Opus has become exactly what its founder intended. Aphorism 466 reads:

The enemies of God and of his Church, manipulated by the devil's unremitting hatred, are relentless in their activities and organization.

With "exemplary" constancy they prepare their cadres, run schools, appoint leaders and deploy agitators. In an under-cover way—but very effectively—they spread their ideas and sow, in homes and places of work, a seed which is destructive of any religious ideology.

What is there that we Christians should not be ready to do in order to serve our God, of course, always with the truth?

The clear answer is to use the same methods as "the enemies of God and of his Church"—though, "of course, always with the truth." It fits Opus perfectly.

The image of Escrivá which was projected suited both his vanity and the need of his followers to believe that the man they followed, and the organization they had joined, were something quite out of the ordinary. This was most obvious in the stage-management of the visits Escrivá de Balaguer paid to various countries, particularly in the last few years of his life. Great crowds were assembled, in stadia, in conference centers, always of the faithful. He was greeted everywhere with rapturous applause. He spoke. The crowds responded with enthusiasm, and he moved on to the next triumph. His most banal phrases were taken up and, as has been seen with the advice he gave to Vázquez (see p. 12), treated as if they were the greatest wisdom. Bernal faithfully reports these, and indeed so many other *obiter dicta* that one begins to wonder whether the founder was followed everywhere by a disciple carrying a tape-recorder. Many of the gatherings were video-recorded for posterity, and questions were carefully planted in the audience to allow the founder to give apparently spontaneous spiritual advice.

In the extraordinary campaign to present Escrivá de Balaguer as a heroic figure, Vázquez draws attention to the academic honors he attained. Because of his knowledge of both law and theology, he claims, Escrivá de Balaguer in 1957 became a member of the Vatican's Pontifical Academy of Theology and a consultor (i.e., adviser) to the Sacred Congregation of Seminaries and Universities. Two years later he was appointed to the Pontifical Commission for the Authentic Interpretation of Canon Law. Later still he became Grand Chancellor of the Universities of Navarra and of Piura in Peru.

However, these are all by way of being honors rather than marks of respect for Escrivá's deep learning. The two universities cited are, of course, institutions of Opus itself. In contrast, the vast celebratory volume for the fiftieth anniversary of the foundation of Opus, *Mons. Josemaría Escrivá de Balaguer y el Opus Dei,* produced by the Faculty of Theology of the University of Navarra[3] does not have an article on "Mgr Escrivá: Theologian" or anything similar, though there are mentions of his "teachings." The article by L. F. Mateo-Seco, "Obras de Mons. Escrivá de Balaguer y estudios sobre el Opus Dei" (The works of Mgr Escrivá de Balaguer and studies on Opus Dei), contains thirty pages dedicated to the works, and twice as many to the studies on Opus Dei. The thirty pages are, however, very illuminating. His published writings are few, and are mainly spiritual. Among the "writings," Mateo-Seco includes interviews he gave which were collected and published by his devotees. "Learned and academic writings" consist of *La Abadesa de las Huelgas* (first published in 1944 but then reproduced by an Opus Dei publishing house in Madrid a decade later and much reviewed by Opus Dei reviewers) and lectures—frequently lectures on the occasion of receiving or, in his capacity of Grand Chancellor, bestowing, honorary doctorates. "Quite obviously," remarks Mateo-Seco, "Mgr Escrivá de Balaguer spent his best efforts on tasks very different from those of writing monographs on history, law, or theology."[4] Quite obviously.

To make up for the lack of publications, Opus Dei hagiographers dwell lovingly on the number of editions of Escrivá's works in different languages. *Camino,* for example, has, according to the same article, appeared in thirty-six editions in Spanish, and in translation into no less than thirty-five languages, making 189 editions in all. One is constrained to wonder why. Why has it appeared in Esperanto, for example? Who has benefited from translations in Albanian or Amharic? The

Santo Rosario (The Holy Rosary) has not done quite so well, but Mateo-Seco still delights to tell us that there have so far been sixty-three editions in fourteen different languages, and *Via Crucis* (The Way of the Cross) in nineteen editions in eight languages, and so on. Never mind the quality, as they say, feel the width.

One of the more bizarre efforts to present Escrivá de Balaguer as a man of great wisdom and insight is the Navarra Bible, two volumes of which have so far appeared in English translation from, naturally, a publishing house associated with Opus, the Four Courts Press in Blackrock, Dublin. The idea of a translation and commentary on the Bible "accessible to a wide readership," says the preface, was a "project entrusted to [the University of Navarra] by the apostolic zeal of the university's founder and first chancellor, Monsignor Josemaría Escrivá de Balaguer."

The commentary quotes many authorities, but none of them contemporary biblical scholars of a standing acknowledged by their peers in the field of scriptural exegesis. Instead there are ample quotations from the "magisterium," the official teaching of popes and councils, and from ancient Christian writers of great standing such as Augustine, John Chrysostom, or Thomas Aquinas. And from Escrivá. He is cited alongside these luminaries as if their equal. Not surprisingly, perhaps, if Escrivá's successor as head of Opus is to be believed. In the introduction to *Es Cristo que pasa* (forty-five editions in eight languages) he comments that in his exposition of the scriptures the founder "has discovered new lights, aspects which had remained hidden down the centuries."[5]

Learned though members—at least numerary members—of Opus are expected to be, it is not for their scholarship or lack of it that they are chiefly known. It is, of course, around the question of Opus Dei's "socio-political affiliation" that there has been most debate. Escrivá's own brand of political belief is not easy to define. Obviously he opposed the Spanish republicans in the 1930s, and espoused what came to be called National Catholicism in Spain. When he fled Madrid he went, as has been seen, via France to the headquarters of Franco's nationalist forces. His organization was identified with the spiritual "reconquest" which followed the defeat of the republicans in 1939. Personally, however, he does not seem to have been a follower of Franco. He was much more attracted to the monarchical, Carlist tradition in Spain which Franco, if he did not abolish it, put into cold storage for the greater part of his period as ruler of Spain.

Carlism, which Franco managed to integrate into the *Falange,* the only party permitted during his domination of Spain, drew its strongest support from the region in which Escrivá de Balaguer grew up. Its twin pillars were an authoritative Church in an authoritative monarchy. It was opposed to constitutional monarchy and parliamentary democracy. Nothing written either by Escrivá's admirers or by his critics, dwells at length upon his political leanings—apart from his obvious detestation of the Left, something which was hardly surprising in the light of his experience in Spain in the 1930s. But the Carlist tradition corresponds well enough with the clues he has left us in *Camino* and elsewhere. The monarchical tradition also fits in with the pursuit of a title, for titles of nobility have little significance in a republican constitution. And it also coincides with the love of *"grandeza,"* grandeur, which Escrivá de Balaguer displayed in his lifetime, despite his protestations of humility.

Maybe it was a reaction against the sudden poverty into which his family had been plunged, but everything which surrounded Escrivá de Balaguer had to be of high quality. This was true not just for Escrivá personally, but for all numerary members. Their poverty was not to be like that of members of religious orders. Escrivá took a close personal interest in the choice of furniture and fittings. For himself, only the best would do. His private chapel in the Opus Rome HQ in Viale Bruno Buozzi was richly, even opulently, decorated; he displayed it with pride to important visitors.

He was constantly and fastidiously concerned with detail of decor. Giuseppe Corigliano, an Opus spokesman in Rome, told John Thavis of the National Catholic News Service that he recalled a time when a small decorative cannon had been "badly placed" in an Opus Dei center. "Many members passed by, and either didn't notice or didn't fix it," Corigliano said. "The Founder called the members in and said that to ignore a detail like that meant they did not live the love of God. Some people cried, they were so moved."[6]

María del Carmen Tapia commented that everything with, or off, which Escrivá de Balaguer ate had to be of high standard. The plates were of the best porcelain, the cutlery of silver. According to an archbishop taken to lunch there in 1965 during the last session of the Vatican Council, the crockery was gold-plated. The archbishop (although at the time he was only a bishop, and newly consecrated) is a man of considerable social conscience. He found the gold plates impossible to reconcile with his expectation of Christian living in a man of such distinction in the Church. He also found the exquisitely prepared and perfectly served food impossible to eat.

It is often not so much Escrivá's good taste as his vulgarity that strikes one. During a visit to the Brazilian city of São Paulo* in May 1974, Escrivá de Balaguer was addressing the customary large crowd, gathered on this occasion in the Palace of Conventions, Anhembi Park. He told the assembled women:

> When your husband comes back from work, from his job, from his professional tasks, don't let him find you in a temper. *Do yourself up, look pretty and, as the years go by, decorate the façade even more, as they do with old buildings. He'll be so grateful to you.*[7]

Neither is his famed good taste always apparent in his best-known book, *Camino*. Maxim 367, for example, reads:

> The choicest morsel, if eaten by a pig, is turned (to put it bluntly) . . . into pigflesh! Let us be angels, so as to dignify the ideas we assimilate. Let us at least be men, so as to convert our food into strong and noble muscles, or perhaps into a powerful brain capable of understanding and adoring God. But let us not be beasts, like so many, so very many.

*It is noticeable that neither in Bernal nor in Vázquez, when there is any description of Escrivá's travels to the Third World, is there any mention of the depressed situation of so many millions of Catholics attempting to eke out a living there.

This, I would suggest, is hardly the language or the sensitivity of a master of the spiritual life. That, however, is how members of Opus wish to portray him.

The process of turning Escrivá de Balaguer into a saint had begun long before his death: it was something he connived at. The failings from which he suffered were nothing out of the ordinary, but they were hardly compatible with the degree of sanctity needed for canonization. He was, for instance, distinctly vain. He was vain about his appearance, always dressing with great care. He was vain about his family background, such as it was. His mother was a simple, middle-class woman of Barbastro. The portraits which he had painted presented her as splendidly dressed and, according to those who met her, quite out of keeping with her character. He himself for a time wore a skullcap, according to Bernal, to compensate for his youthful appearance[8] and to give him a guise more suited, in his own eyes, to his dignity as a founder of a major organization within the Church.

There was more than a touch of vanity, too, in the way in which he kept himself remote. Though in his early days in Madrid he had chosen Jesuits as his spiritual directors, he was later to turn against them. When Pedro Arrupe was elected Superior General of the Society of Jesus he wrote to the heads of all religious orders and congregations in Rome saying that he would like to pay them a fraternal visit. The courteous reply from all but one was the same: it was they who should be visiting him. The only head of a religious organization who made no response was Escrivá, as head of Opus Dei. Arrupe telephoned him five times, it is claimed. He was told Escrivá de Balaguer was not at home. According to one version of the story, when the two did eventually meet for lunch, conversation was almost entirely non-existent, though not for Fr. Arrupe's want of trying.

In Bogotá, a Spanish-born Jesuit told a similar story. Although he had himself joined the Society, the rest of his brothers and sisters were more closely allied with Opus Dei than with the Jesuits. One sister and brother-in-law paid a visit to Rome. Because of their close association with Opus in Colombia they had solicited, and had promptly been granted, an interview with Escrivá de Balaguer. He received them with considerable warmth. The following day their Jesuit brother had arranged for a meeting between his sister and her husband and Fr. Arrupe. While they were waiting to talk to Arrupe the Bogotá-based Jesuit fell into conversation with Arrupe's secretary who was himself a Jesuit priest. It was explained that the day before the three of them had met Escrivá. The secretary expressed his surprise. Fr. Arrupe, he told them, had been waiting for three years to be granted just such an interview.

The inaccessibility of the founder was all part of the game, part of the myth which was carefully and conscientiously being built up around him. He was an important, busy man.

It is not expected of a master of the spiritual life that he should prepare for his own canonization. In Barbastro Opus has acquired the house in which Escrivá was born, together with an adjoining property, as a kind of shrine. The shrine of the Virgin Mary at Torreciudad, where Escrivá de Balaguer had been "cured" in 1904, was taken over. Money was raised by a series of appeals instigated by Escrivá for the shrine to be enlarged. Now it has an esplanade capable of holding 40,000 pilgrims, a tower with thirteen bells all named after titles of the Virgin Mary (one of the largest is called Dolores, one of the smallest Carmen). There is a crypt with forty confessionals and various other embellishments quite out of keeping with the simple sanctuary it had once been when Escrivá was taken there by his mother. The spiritual direction of the place was, and is, in the hands of Opus. It is being promoted by them as one of the shrines of a "*ruta Mariana*," which includes the great shrine of Lourdes and the ancient national shrine of Spain, El Pilar. Tours to it are promoted from an office in Lourdes.

In Torreciudad in typical Opus mode, priests tout for confessions. This "touting" for custom was reported by a distinguished English Catholic priest, dressed at the time informally and not recognizable as a clergyman. While visiting Torreciudad from Lourdes he was approached by an Opus priest in the crypt of the shrine and asked if he wanted to go to confession.

But it is not just Escrivá's birthplace or the shrine where he was "healed" that receive this sort of treatment. There are plaques on houses in which he lived. Objects which belonged to him have been collected and are displayed. Even the baptismal font in which Escrivá de Balaguer was christened has been taken from Barbastro cathedral and re-erected in Rome. It had been destroyed in the course of the Spanish Civil War: what Escrivá received from the town-council of Barbastro were the fragments of the font, which he had moved to Rome and there reconstituted.

The remains of his parents were transferred on his instructions from a Madrid cemetery to the crypt under the Opus residence in Diego de Leon in Madrid. He gave orders that he, too, was to be buried in a crypt, that of the oratory dedicated to the Virgin Mary in the main residence in Rome. He chose the inscription for his tombstone:

PECCATOR

ORATE PRO EO

GENUIT FILIOS ET FILIAS

(A sinner, pray for him. He gave birth to sons and daughters.) On this, however, he did not get his way. The marble slab which covers his mortal remains simply says "El Padre," The Father. Fresh flowers always lie on the grave. His devotees flock there. They are to be found praying day and night: it is the only place where men and women of Opus Dei are allowed to associate.

"Keep me there for a while, then send me to a public church because I don't want you bothered," someone close to him heard him say: moving a grave to a public church is clear evidence of a *cultus* or devotion.

Despite all this, Escrivá repeatedly claimed to be a humble man. He loved to call himself a "mangy little donkey" (he signed himself "b.s." = *burrito sarnoso* in letters to his confessor in his early years in Madrid). So much so, in fact, that he collected models of donkeys—Opus headquarters in Rome was full of them. When an admirer asked for a portrait, Escrivá gave him a figure of a donkey, roughly cast in metal. "Here you are," he said, "a portrait of me. That is me, a little donkey.

I wish I were always God's little donkey, his instrument for work and for peace."[9] He spoiled this display of humility, however, by letting it be known that, while in prayer, he had once said, "Here you have your mangy donkey" and had received the reply from on high, "A donkey was my throne in Jerusalem."

Visions are a common occurrence among saints. Yet apart from the story of the foundation of Opus related earlier, these words are the only instance mentioned by the hagiographers, for all their devotion, of a directly supernatural intervention in Escrivá's life. On the other hand, rumors that he did have visions, especially of the Virgin Mary, were and are current within Opus.

He was, finally, someone who had a proper sense of his own dignity. "In my life," he is quoted in *Cronica* as saying, "I have already known several Popes, many cardinals, a multitude of bishops. But on the other hand, Founders of Opus Dei, there is only one!"

Such, then, is the man whose holiness of life and orthodoxy of doctrines are now formally on trial in the Vatican. The Roman Congregation for the Causes of Saints, which controls such things, gave permission for the process to begin leading to the beatification and eventual canonization of Mgr Escrivá de Balaguer on 30 January 1981. Opus Dei spokesmen report it is proceeding apace: the first stage was formally concluded in November 1986. Opus believes it has sufficient evidence for the two miracles usually required before a canonization process can be completed. A Spanish Carmelite nun and a Peruvian girl both claim to have been cured of cancer at Escrivá's heavenly intercession. "It's in the bag!" says Opus.[10]

Canonization of Mgr Escrivá de Balaguer is very important to the organization he founded. Though the granting of the personal prelature was a clear mark of papal favor, recognition of his sanctity will be the Church's final seal of approval both on Opus and upon its founder's teaching as a sure guide for souls. Though Opus annually marks the day of Escrivá's death with public, and well-publicized, masses, veneration for him has scarcely reached beyond the ranks of the Opus faithful. "If the

Pope ever declares Escrivá de Balaguer a saint," said the Archbishop mentioned above (p. 194), "I will accept it as a decision of the Church. But I will never be able to understand it."

Given the power, and the wealth, of Opus Dei the canonization of its founder seems inevitable. John Roche and other ex-members have been leading a campaign to subvert the process, but they have had little luck: Escrivá has friends at court.

These negotiations take time, however, no matter how much Opus through its influence may succeed in speeding the process up. Perhaps the Archbishop will not have to come to terms with St. Josemaría Escrivá de Balaguer in his lifetime.

In the Catholic Church at large, however, I suggest that the zenith of Opus's fortunes has been reached—and may have been passed. Though in numbers the most numerous of the conservative groups within the Church, it is no longer the most influential. That position is held by the Italian-founded "Communione e Liberazione," whose constitution is much more avowedly activist.

And it may be that the sympathies of a supposedly conservative Pope are turning against the organization to which he gave this still unique status of personal prelature. In his letter on "The social concerns of the Church" published in February 1988, Pope John Paul II showed himself much more favorably disposed than hitherto toward the proponents of Liberation Theology, the doctrine which Opus has so steadfastly opposed in the name of orthodoxy.

It is, I firmly believe, a basic tenet of Christianity that faith in Jesus Christ should be a liberating force in people's lives, that it should free them to become more themselves, more in charge of their own destinies. Opus with its rules and regulations, its censorship, its control of the minutiae of members' day-to-day living, its class-related structures, its association with élites of wealth and of power, as I have attempted to describe in this book, could not claim to be a force for liberation. And to the extent that it fails this test, it is not merely, as a sect, less than Catholic.

It is less than Christian.

Notes

Chapter 1. In Search of Opus

1. Guy Hermet, *Los Católicos en la España Franquista,* vol. 1. Madrid: Siglo XXI, 1985, p. 266. He is quoting Daniel Artigues, *El Opus Dei en España: su evolución ideológica y política.* Paris: Ruedo Ibérico, 1971, p. 127.

2. There was a brief report of the sacking in the London Catholic weekly, *The Tablet,* 5 December 1987, and a rather fuller account in the same paper, 9 January 1988, p. 41.

3. Russell Shaw, "Judged by Opus Dei," *The Tablet,* 27 February 1988.

4. María del Carmen Tapia was one of my chief informants. Material reproduced in this book is taken from the tapes of a day-long interview in New York's Barbizon Plaza Hotel, 23 August 1984.

5. See Janet Jacobs, "Deconversion from Religious Movements: An Analysis of Charismatic Bonding and Spiritual Commitment," *Journal for the Scientific Study of Religion,* vol. 26, no. 3, 1987, pp. 294–308.

6. Vladimir Felzmann, "Why I Left Opus Dei," *The Tablet,* 26 March 1983, p. 288.

7. Ibid., p. 287.

8. Luis Carandell, *Vida y Milagros de Monseñor Escrivá de Balaguer, Fundador del Opus Dei* (The Life and Miracles of Mgr Escrivá, Founder of Opus Dei). Barcelona: Editorial Laia, 1975, and frequently reprinted.

9. For the names of other decorations, see Carandell, op. cit., pp. 78–83.

10. For the letter see Andrés Vázquez de Prada, *El Fundador del Opus Dei.* Madrid: Ediciones Rialp, 1983, p. 349.

11. Salvador Bernal, *Msgr Josemaría Escrivá de Balaguer, Profile of the Founder of Opus Dei.* London: Scepter, 1977, p. 33.

1. Pedro Rodriguez et al. (eds.) *Mons. Josemaría Escrivá de Balaguer y el Opus Dei en el 50 Aniversario de su Fundación*. Pamplona: Ediciones Universidad de Navarra, 1982. The second edition, 1985, is the one used here.

2. Lucas F. Mateo-Seco, "Obras de Mons. Escrivá de Balaguer y estudios sobre e Opus Dei" in Rodriguez et al. (eds.), op. cit., pp. 469–572.

3. Vázquez, op. cit., p. 15.

4. Bernal, op. cit., pp. 106–7. Bernal is quoting Alvaro del Portillo— hence he puts "saw" in inverted commas.

5. Ibid., p. 34. The emphasis is Bernal's.

6. Felzmann, op. cit., p. 288.

7. Though I have talked to Raimundo Pannikar about Opus on at least three different occasions, most of the information used in this book comes from a long interview of 2 September 1984, which took place between Heathrow Airport and Oxford, and then continued long into the afternoon in his lodgings in Oxford.

8. Cf. Vázquez, op. cit., p. 117.

9. The section which follows is taken from my article "Being Fair to Opus Dei," *The Month*, August 1971, and is here reprinted by permission of the editor.

10. It was not revived until the recognition of the Opus Dei-sponsored University of Navarra at Pamplona in 1962.

11. Carandell, op. cit., p. 180.

12. Vázquez, op. cit., pp. 139, 163, 170.

13. For these, and further references, see Giancarlo Rocca, *L' "Opus Dei": Appuniti e Documenti per una Storia*. Rome: Edizioni Paoline, 1985, pp. 44–45.

14. See Vázquez, op. cit., p. 101.

15. Vázquez, op. cit., pp. 138–39.

16. Lucas F. Mateo-Seco, "Studios de Mons. Escrivá y Estudios sobre el Opus Dei," in Rodriguez et al. (eds.), op. cit., p. 470.

17. See the opening chapter of Maria Angustias Moreno's *La otra cara del Opus Dei* (Barcelona: Editorial Planeta, 1978) for an account of the early years by a former member in which she claims that the role of Escrivá's family has been much exaggerated.

18. Quoted in Rocca, op. cit., p. 20.

19. These figures are given in Bernal, op. cit., p. 232. See also Frances Lannon, *Privilege, Persecution and Prophecy*, pp. 201–2. Franco's forces, in contrast, executed 14 Basque priests.

20. For National Catholicism, see Frances Lannon's "Modern Spain: The Project of a National Catholicism," in Stewart Mews (ed.), *Religion and National Identity*, Studies in Church History, vol. 18. Published

for the Ecclesiastical History Society by Basil Blackwell, Oxford, 1982, pp. 567–90, and the same author's *Privilege, Persecution and Prophecy: The Catholicism Church in Spain, 1875–1975*. Clarendon Press, 1987, especially pp. 220–21.

21. Vázquez, op. cit., p. 227.
22. Ibid., pp. 22–23.

Chapter 3. The Years of Expansion

1. Vázquez, op. cit., p. 232.
2. Bernal, op. cit., p. 114.
3. Ibid., p. 146.
4. Vázquez, op. cit., p. 239.
5. Ibid., p. 234.
6. The document is quoted in full in Rocca, op. cit., pp. 138–44.
7. Cf. Vázquez, op. cit., pp. 237–38 and Rocca, op. cit., p. 33.
8. Rocca, op. cit., p. 36, and see the documents at the back of his book.
9. Ibid., pp. 55ff.
10. Bernal, op. cit., p. 324.
11. Vázquez, op. cit., pp. 252–53.
12. Rocca, op. cit., p. 64.
13. Ibid., pp. 74–79.
14. Rocca, op. cit. The two sections to which reference is made in this chapter are pp. 66–79 and 106–15.
15. Salvador Canals, *Secular Institutes and the State of Perfection*. Dublin: Scepter, 1959, p. 127. The original Spanish edition was published by Ediciones Rialp.
16. Ibid., p. 128.
17. They are currently most readily to be found in Rocca, op. cit., pp. 168–71.
18. J.-M. Escrivá de Balaguer, *Conversations with Monsignor Escrivá de Balaguer*. Manila: Sinag-Tala, 1977, p. 50. The interview quoted was with Peter Forbarth of *Time*, 7 January 1966.
19. Vázquez, op. cit., p. 297, and Bernal, op. cit., pp. 300–301.
20. John Lyons, *The Australian*, 28–29 and 30 November 1987.
21. Vázquez, op. cit., p. 359.
22. Daniel Artigues, *El Opus Dei en España*. Paris: Ruedo Ibérico, 1971, pp. 9–10.
23. Escrivá de Balaguer, *Conversations*, op. cit., pp. 54–55.
24. Vázquez, op. cit., p. 298.
25. Ibid., pp. 302–3. This was just three years before my own arrival in Oxford as an undergraduate. The story of Grandpont was my first introduction to Opus Dei: I even had a friend who lived there—briefly.
26. Vázquez, op. cit., p. 297.

Chapter 4. A Change of Status

1. See Vázquez, op. cit., p. 364.
2. Pedro Rodriguez, *Particular Churches and Personal Prelatures*. Dublin: Four Courts Press, 1986.
3. *Vida Nueva,* no. 1463, 26 January 1985, pp. 16–18.

Chapter 5. The Constitutions of 1982

1. Rocca, op. cit., p. 111 and Michael Walsh, *The Tablet,* 16 October 1982.
2. These details are taken from the 1985 edition of the *Annuario Pontificio,* p. 1029.
3. See *The Constitutions of the Society of Jesus,* translated by George F. Ganss. St Louis, MI: Institute of Jesuit Sources, 1970, p. 119.

Chapter 6. The Spirit of Opus

1. Escrivá de Balaguer, *Conversations,* op. cit., pp. 49–50.
2. Eric O. Hanson, *The Catholic Church in World Politics*. Princeton, NJ: Princeton University Press, 1987, p. 376.
3. Henry Kamm, "The Secret World of Opus Dei," *New York Times Magazine,* 8 January 1984.
4. See Sandro Magister, *La politica Vaticana e l'Italia 1943–1978*. Rome: Riuniti, 1979, pp. 379–80. I am grateful to Peter Hebblethwaite for this reference.

Chapter 7. Politics and Business

1. Brian Smith, *The Church and Politics in Chile*. Princeton, NJ: Princeton University Press, 1982, pp. 139 and 338.
2. *Noticias Aliadas* is published in Lima. The issue from which the remarks were taken is dated 4 December 1975.
3. Penny Lernoux, *Cry of the People*. New York: Doubleday, 1980, p. 305.
4. "Peru's Catholics believe in agnostic" *The Independent,* June 1, 1990. The article made the point that Vargas Llosa had the support of the Archbishop of Lima, and of Opus Dei, even though he was not a believing Catholic.
5. Ibid.
6. Private conversation, see chapter 2, note 7.
7. José Vicente Casanova, *The Opus Dei Ethic and the Modernization of Spain*. Unpublished doctoral thesis, New York New School of Social Research, 1982.
8. Argued in Casanova, op. cit.
9. Artigues, op. cit.
10. Quoted in Hermet, op. cit., vol. 1, p. 113. Hermet's book originally appeared in French in 1981, but by chance I came across the Spanish version.
11. Paul Hofmann, *Anatomy of the Vatican*. London: Hale, 1985, pp. 229–30. Pages 229–35, entitled "God's Octopus," and the following section, to p. 242, "Apostolate of Penetration"—both discuss Opus.

12. The story which follows is adapted, with the present editor's permission, from my piece "Spain on the Move," *The Month*, June 1972.

13. Escrivá de Balaguer, *Conversations,* op. cit., p. 44.

14. I read a separately published English version, nineteen pages in length, the last six pages being a bibliography on Opus in double columns. The article in its English dress carries no indication that I can discover of printer, publisher, or copyright holder.

15. By Casanova, op. cit.

16. *Le Monde* (English edition), 29 July 1970.

17. "Rumasa Rides Again," *The Economist,* 3 June 1989, p. 115.

18. See Stephen Arias, "How Mateos Rose and Fell: The End of a Reign in Spain," *Sunday Times,* 24 April 1983.

19. See Santiago Aroca in *Tiempo*, Madrid, 11 August 1986.

20. Escrivá de Balaguer referred to Netherhall House as a hostel for students from Africa and Asia. Escrivá de Balaguer, *Conversations,* op. cit.

21. Nicholas Perry, "Unliberation Theology," *New Statesman,* 1 March 1985, p. 21.

22. This figure was quoted by a journalist on *Hoy,* a Chilean magazine started by a group of writers who left *Ercilla* when it was taken over by Crusat and became a vehicle for interests close to Opus Dei.

23. Martin Lee, "Their will be done," *Mother Jones,* July 1983, p. 37.

24. So it is alleged by José María Bernáldez, *Tiempo,* 1 August 1983.

25. See Peter Hertel, "International Christian Democracy," *Concilium,* vol. 193, no. 5, 1987, pp. 95–105, especially p. 102.

26. *Vida Nueva,* 31 October 1987, pp. 8–9.

Chapter 8. Sectarian Catholicism

1. *Catholic Pictorial,* 29 November 1981. The other quotations are all taken from various issues of *Cronica.*

2. Private conversation, 14 November 1987. The young man in question joined the Society of Jesus instead.

3. Mrs. Sylvia Loffler of Poole, Dorset, reported in *The Universe,* 18 May 1984.

4. I have read a lengthy, unpublished interview with this former numerary, but I did not meet him myself; the text was passed to me by the interviewer in whom I have every confidence.

5. See note 4—the same applies.

6. The 1986 report indicates that this property is to be handed over "to an associated charity, Dawliffe Hall Education Foundation Limited in October 1986."

7. Maria Angustias Moreno, *La otra cara del Opus Dei*. Barcelona: Editorial Planeta, 1978. The detailed account of this campaign of detraction and the author's attempted defense occupy chapters 5–8, pp. 113ff.

8. See ibid., pp. 163–200 for a detailed account of this.

9. See chapter 1, note 4.

10. For her account, see the *National Catholic Reporter,* 27 May 1983.

11. See chapter 2, note 7.

12. John Roche is quoted here, and elsewhere in this chapter unless otherwise noted, from an unpublished document he drew up entitled "The Inner World of Opus Dei."

13. During the conversation referred to in chapter 2, note 7.

14. Quoted in the *Catholic Pictorial,* 13 September 1981. Ms. Gould has since left Opus.

15. Carol Coulter, *Are Religious Cults Dangerous?* Dublin: Mercier Press, 1984, p. 43.

16. My remarks about the new Catholicism sects and their function originally appeared in *The Tablet,* 15 November 1986. I thank the editor for permission to quote them here. On the Church's social teaching, see Michael Walsh and Brian Davies (eds.), *Proclaiming Justice and Peace.* London: Collins, 1985.

17. Leonardo Boff, *Church, Charism and Power.* London: SCM Press, 1985. The section under discussion occurs on pp. 4–5 of this edition.

18. José Maria Casciaro, *Jesus and Politics: A Scriptural Study of Messianism.* Dublin: Four Courts Press, 1983, p. 62.

19. Peter Hebblethwaite, the Vatican correspondent for the American weekly *National Catholic Reporter,* in a private conversation.

20. Dr. Eileen Barker has been a particular help in this area of research, and her *The Making of a Moonie* (Oxford: Basil Blackwell, 1984) is one of the best studies of individual sects available.

21. Bryan Wilson, "The Sociology of Sects," in B. Wilson (ed.), *Religion in Sociological Perspective.* Oxford: Oxford University Press, 1982, p. 88.

22. Ibid., p. 91.

23. Bryan Wilson, "Sect Development," in B. Wilson (ed.), *Patterns of Sectarianism.* London: Heinemann, 1967, p. 24.

24. Michael Hill, *The Religious Order.* London: Heinemann, 1973, p. 49.

25. Maria Angustias Moreno quoting an Opus priest in her book *El Opus Dei: Anexo a una Historia.* Barcelona: Editorial Planeta, 1976, p. 61. Though I have read this book, I have taken the quotation from José Casanova's article "The First Secular Institute: The Opus Dei as a Religious Movement-Organization," *Annual Review of the Social Sciences of Religion,* vol. 6, 1982, p. 273. I have slightly adapted the translation given by Casanova to emphasize the "faithful remnant" notion, an Old Testament concept much in vogue in theological circles in the 1970s and early 1980s.

26. Russell Shaw, "Judged by Opus Dei," *The Tablet,* 27 February 1988.

27. Casanova, op. cit., p. 256.

28. Ibid., p. 257.

29. *Cronica,* 1971/1, italics added.

30. Fr. Rolf Thomas quoted in *Time,* 11 June 1984, pp. 74–75.

Chapter 9. The Apotheosis of the Founder

1. Geoffrey Nelson, *Cults, New Religions and Religious Creativity*. London: Routledge and Kegan Paul, 1987, p. 10.
2. Escrivá de Balaguer, *The Forge,* London: Scepter, 1988. The Spanish edition was published in 1987 by Rialp.
3. Rodriguez et al. (eds.)., op. cit.
4. Op. cit., p. 498.
5. Quoted in Mateo-Seco, op. cit., p. 483.
6. Quoted by *NC News Service* (a publication of the U.S. National Conference of Catholic Bishops), 6 November 1984.
7. Bernal, op. cit., p. 52. Italics added.
8. Ibid., p. 324.
9. Vargas, op. cit., p. 318.
10. Nicholas Perry, "Unliberation Theology," *New Statesman,* 1 March 1985.

Bibliography

The bibliography contains books and articles, including the main newspaper articles, which I consulted in the course of preparing this book. I have added a small number, marked with an asterisk, which I could not see but which I believe worth commending to the attention of anyone who wishes to pursue the subject further. I have also omitted a number of Opus-inspired pieces on personal prelatures which do not add significantly to those included below. There were, of course, a number of briefer notices which were invaluable, particularly in the Madrid weekly *Vida Nueva* and in the news service *Katholische Nachrichten Agentur* (KNA). I have also not made special mention of reference books: of these the *Dizionario di Istituti di Perfezione* was most frequently consulted.

Aris, Stephen. "How Mateos Rose and Fell: the End of a Reign in Spain," *Sunday Times*, 24 April 1983.

Aroca, Santiago. Three articles, *Tiempo*, 4, 11, and 18 August 1986.

Artigues, Daniel. *El Opus Dei en España: su evolución ideológica y politica*. Paris: Ruedo Ibérico, 1971.

Balthasar, Hans Urs von. "Integralismus," *Wort und Wahrheit*, December 1963.

Balthasar, Hans Urs von. "Friedliche Frage an das Opus Dei," *Der Christliche Sonntag*, 12 April 1964.★

Balthasar, Hans Urs von. Interview on Swiss television, reprinted in *Trenti Giorni*, June 1984.★

Barker, Eileen. "Free to Choose? Some Thoughts on the Unification Church and Other Religious Movements: I and II," *The Clergy Review*, October and November 1980.

Barker, Eileen. "Doing Love: Tensions in the Ideal Family," in Gene G. James (ed.), *The Family and the Unification Church*. New York: Rose of Sharon Press, 1983.

Barker, Eileen. "The Limits of Displacement: Two Disciplines Face Each Other," in David Martin, John Orme Mills, and W. S. F. Pickering (eds.), *Sociology and Theology: Alliance and Conflict*. Brighton: Harvester, 1980.

Belingardi, Giovanni. "L'Opus Dei é potente ma lo deve al Cielo" (an interview with Alvaro del Portillo), *Corriere della Sera,* 7 December 1985.

Bernal, Salvador. *Msgr Josemaría Escrivá de Balaguer, Profile of the Founder of Opus Dei*. London: Scepter, 1977.

Bernáldez, Jose Maria. "El caso Rumasa salpica al Vaticano y al Opus," *Tiempo,* 1 August 1983.

Boff, Leonardo. *Church, Charism and Power*. London: SCM Press, 1985.

Burns, Jimmy. "Spanish Socialists Keep Their Promise on Rumasa," *Financial Times,* 6 March 1985.

Byrne, Frank and Willie Kealy. "Inside Opus Dei," *Sunday Independent,* Dublin, 16 August 1987.

Calderoni, Pietro. "La cassaforte dell'Opus Dei," *L'Espresso,* 4 May 1986.

Calderoni, Pietro and Maurizio de Luca. "Bancus Dei," *L'Espresso,* 6 April 1986.

Canals, Salvador. *Secular Institutes and the State of Perfection*. Dublin: Scepter, 1959.

Carandell, Luis. *Vida y Milagros de Monseñor Escrivá de Balaguer, Fundador del Opus Dei*. Barcelona: Editorial Laia, 1975.

Carey-Elwes, Columba. "Understanding Opus Dei," *The Tablet,* 26 March 1983.

Casanova, José V. "The First Secular Institute: The Opus Dei as a Religious Movement-organization," *Annual Review of the Social Sciences of Religion,* vol. 6, 1982.

Casanova, José V. *The Opus Dei Ethic and the Modernization of Spain*. Unpublished Ph.D. thesis, New School of Social Research, New York, 1982.

Casanova, José V. "The Opus Dei Ethic, the Technocrats and the Modernization of Spain," *Social Science Information,* no. 1, 1983.★

Casciaro, José M. *Jesus and Politics: A Scriptural Study of Messianism*. Dublin: Four Courts Press, 1983.

"Castles outside Spain," *The Economist,* 30 August 1969.

Codex Iuris Particularis Operis Dei. Rome, 1982.

Comblin, José. "Las ideas sociales de mons. Escrivá de Balaguer," *Servir,* 16/85, 1980.★

Constituciones del Opus Dei (printed as Appendix 4 of Jesús Ynfante's *La prodigiosa aventura del Opus Dei,* q.v.).

Cooper, N. B. *Catholicism and the Franco Regime*. Beverly Hills and London: Sage Publications, 1975.

Correa, Raquel. "A fondo hoy: Rodolfo Rodriguez, sacerdote," *La tercera de la hora,* Santiago, 18 November 1979.

Coulter, Carol. *Are Religious Cults Dangerous?* Dublin: Mercier Press, 1984.

Cumming, John. "Opus Dei—Not so Black or White as It Is Painted," *Catholic Herald,* 3 September 1982.

Dalmau y Olivé, M. J. *Contrapuntos al Camino del Opus Dei*. Barcelona: Editorial Portic, 1970.

Davies, Rachel, "Foreign Law Defence Disallowed in Rumasa Case," *Financial Times,* 15 January 1985.

de Zulueta, Tana. "Can the Pope's Bank Manager Survive?" *Sunday Times,* 11 July 1982.

de Zulueta, Tana and Francesco d'Andrea. "Is the Vatican Going Broke?," *Observer,* 1 June 1980.

de Zulueta, Tana, et al. "Death of God's Banker," *Sunday Times,* 13 February 1983.

del Portillo, Alvaro. *Interview, Doctrine and Life,* April 1985.

di Sales, Michael. "Opus Dei against the Family?," *New Oxford Review,* March 1984.

"A Dynamic Enterprise," *Le Monde* (English edition), 29 July 1970.

Earle, John. "Sindona, Calvi and Their Vatican Link," *The Times,* 12 July 1982.

Echeverria, Lamberto de. "Analisis juridico de la nueva Prelatura," *Vida Nueva,* 9 July 1983.

Echeverria, Lamberto de. "El 'Opus Dei' y sus 'secretos,'" *Vida Nueva,* 15 March 1986.

Escrivá de Balaguer, J.-M. *Camino* (14th ed.). Madrid: Rialp, 1957.

Escrivá de Balaguer, J.-M. Interview in *ABC,* Madrid, 24 March 1971.

Escrivá de Balaguer, J.-M. *Christ Is Passing By*. Manila: Sinag-Tala, 1974.

Escrivá de Balaguer, J.-M. *Conversations with Monsignor Escrivá de Balaguer*. Manila: Sinag-Tala, 1977.

Escrivá de Balaguer, J.-M. *Holy Rosary*. Dublin: Four Courts Press, 1979.

Escrivá de Balaguer, J.-M. *Friends of God*. London: Scepter, 1981.

Escrivá de Balaguer, J.-M. *The Way*. Blackrock, Dublin: Four Courts Press, 1985.

Escrivá de Balaguer, J.-M. *The Forge*. London: Scepter, 1988.

Felzmann, Vladimir. "Why I Left Opus Dei," *The Tablet,* 26 March 1983.

Fernández, M. Isabel. "El Opus Dei en Chile," *Ercilla,* 7 May 1980.

Fornés, Juan. "El perfil juridico de las Prelaturas Personales," *Monitor Ecclesiasticus,* vol. cvii, no. 4, 1983.

G., L. D. "Los testaferros de Ruiz Mateos," *Tiempo,* 1 August 1983.

Gillard, Michael. "A Hammer Blow for the Archbishop," *Observer,* 5 September 1982.

Gillard, Michael and Lorana Sullivan. "Calvi. The Deal that Never Was," *Observer*, 27 June 1982.

Gonzalez Ruiz, J.-M. "Opus Dei y politica en España," *Sábado Gráfico*, 10 April 1971.

Gould, Margaret. *The Unacceptable Face of Opus Dei*. Unpublished manuscript.

Hebblethwaite, Peter. "Opus Dei: Lifting the Veil of Mystery," *National Catholic Reporter*, 27 May 1983.

Hermet, Guy. *Los Católicos en la España franquista* (2 vols). Madrid: Siglo XXI, 1985.

Herranz, Julian. "Opus Dei and the Activity of Its Members," *Studi Cattolici*, no. 31, July–August 1962.

Hertel, Peter. *"Ich verspreche euch den Himmel."* Dusseldorf: Patmos, 1985.

Hertel, Peter. "International Christian Democracy (*Opus Dei*)" in Gregory Baum and John Coleman (eds.). *The Church and Christian Democracy: Concilium 193*, no. 5 for 1987.

Hill, Michael. *The Religious Order*. London: Heinemann, 1973.

Hofmann, Paul. *Anatomy of the Vatican*. London: Hale, 1985.

Holmes, J. Derek. *The Papacy in the Modern World*. London: Burns and Oates, 1981.

Horrigan, John. "Winning Recruits in Opus Dei," letter to *The Clergy Review*, December 1985.

Illanes, José Luis. *On the Theology of Work*. Dublin: Four Courts Press, 1982.

"Informe presentado en la Asamblea Sacerdotal de la Rioja," *Vida Nueva*, 26 January 1985.

Jacobs, Janet. "Deconversion from Religious Movements: An Analysis of Charismatic Bonding and Spiritual Commitment," *Journal for the Scientific Study of Religion*, vol. 26, no. 3, 1987.

Jacquet, Lou. "Opus Dei: 30 Years in Chicago," *Chicago Catholic*, 16 February 1979.

Jenkins, Loren. "Scandal Goes to Spain's Highest Court," *Guardian*, 20 May 1970.

Kamm, Henry. "The Secret World of Opus Dei," *New York Times Magazine*, 8 January 1984.

King, Ronald. "Opus Dei," *Sunday Times* magazine, 30 May 1971.

Komisar, Lucy. "Church in Peru Curbs Radical Priests," *Miami Herald* (International edition), 20 August 1986.

Lannon, Frances. "Modern Spain: the Project of a National Catholicism," in Stewart Mews (ed.) *Religion and National Identity*, Studies in Church History, vol. 18. Oxford: Basil Blackwell, 1982.

Lannon, Frances. *Privilege, Persecution and Prophecy: the Catholic Church in Spain, 1875–1975*. Oxford: Clarendon Press, 1987.

Lee, Martin A. "Their Will Be Done," *Mother Jones*, July 1983.

Longley, Clifford and Dan van der Vat. "Profile of Opus Dei," *The Times,* 12 January 1981.

Lustig, Robin. "Scandal in the Vatican," *Observer,* 15 August 1982.

Lycett, Andrew. "How the Moonies are Clouding a Freedom Issue," *The Times,* 30 July 1984.

Lyons, John. "The One Who Got Away," *The Australian,* 28–29 November 1987.

Lyons, John. "Opus Dei: Doing God's Work," *The Australian,* 28–29 November 1987.

Lyons, John. "Where the Zealots Start Recruiting," *The Australian,* 30 November 1987.

M., J.-P. "L'Opus Dei: une 'Association secrète'?," *L'Actualité Religieuse,* April 1986.

Magister, Sandro. "Cristo fra i massoni," *L'Espresso,* 11 May 1975.

Magister, Sandro. "I manager di Dio," *L'Espresso,* 17 November 1985.

Magister, Sandro. "Santa facciatosta," *L'Espresso,* 2 March 1986.

Magister, Sandro. "Il polipo di Dio," *L'Espresso,* 9 March 1986.

Magister, Sandro. "Amore e cilicio," *L'Espresso,* 16 March 1986.

Magister, Sandro. "Primo, obbedire," *L'Espresso,* 6 April 1986.

Magister, Sandro. "I nomi dell'Opus," *L'Espresso,* 25 May 1986.

Mazzuca, Alberto. "Ció che il Vatican non vuole dire sul crac Ambrosiano," *Adista,* 9–11 March 1987.

Moncada, Alberto. *Los hijos del Padre.* Barcelona: Argos, 1977.*

Moreno, Maria Angustias. *El Opus Dei, Anexo a una historia.* Barcelona: Editorial Planeta, 1976.

Moreno, Maria Angustias. *La otra cara del Opus Dei.* Barcelona: Editorial Planeta, 1978.

Navarro-Valls, Raphael. "Das 'Opus Dei' als Beispiel einer Personal-prilätur im neuen Recht,'" *Theologie und Glaube,* 2, 1985.

Nelson, Geoffrey K. *Cults, New Religions and Religious Creativity.* London: Routledge and Kegan Paul, 1987.

Nichols, Peter. "The Scandal Touching the Heart of the Vatican," *The Times,* 26 July 1982.

Norddeutscher Rundfunk. "Aufwärts! Mit heiliger Unverschämtheit," transcript of a program transmitted 4 March 1984.

Odone, Christine. "Held in the Grip of Religion," *Independent,* 22 May 1988.

O'Grady, Desmond. "How Long Can the Vatican Dodge the Ambrosiano Flak?," *Catholic Herald,* 10 September 1982.

Olmi, Massimo. "L'Opus Dei: Son évolution canonique," *Etudes,* December 1986.

Ombres, Robert. "Opus Dei and Personal Prelatures," *The Clergy Review,* August 1985.

"Opus Dei en Chile," *Mundo del Domingo,* Santiago, 11 May 1980.

Ostling, Richard N. "Building God's Global Castle," *Time,* 11 June 1984.

Perry, Nicholas. "Unliberation Theology," *New Statesman,* 1 March 1985.

"Politicians Face Exposure Threat as Trial Opens," *Guardian,* 9 April 1975.

Prezzi, Lorenzo. "Le migrazioni giuridiche dell'Opus Dei," *Il Regno-Attualitá,* 18, 1985.

Quaranta, Guido. "Divisi dall'Opus," *L'Espresso,* 23 March 1986.

Raw, Charles. "Ambrosiano: a Rumasa Link," *Sunday Times,* 20 May 1983.

Raw, Charles and Tana de Zulueta. "Archbishop Tried to Hide Vatican Links with Ambrosiano," *Sunday Times,* 27 March 1983.

Rocca, Giancarlo. L' "Opus Dei": *Appunti e documenti per una storia.* Rome: Edizione Paoline, 1985.

Roche, John. *The Inner World of Opus Dei.* Unpublished manuscript.

Roche, John. Letter to *The Clergy Review,* January 1986.

Roche, Maurice. "The Secrets of Opus Dei," *Magill,* May 1983.

Rodriguez, Pedro. *Particular Churches and Personal Prelatures.* Dublin: Four Courts Press, 1986.

Rodriguez, Pedro, Pio G. Alves de Sousa, and José Manuel Zumaquero (eds.). *Mons. Josemaría Escrivá de Balaguer y el Opus Dei en el 50 Aniversario de su Fundación* (2nd ed.). Pamplona: Ediciones Universidad de Navarra, 1985.

Ruiz Gallardon, J. M. Review of Jesús Ynfante's *La prodigiosa aventura del Opus Dei, ABC,* Madrid, 24 October 1970.

Ruiz-Mateos, J.-M. "La carcel es un cementerio para seres vivos," *Tiempo,* 11 August 1986.

Scobie, William. "The Amazing Tale of Licio Gelli," *Observer,* 11 October 1987.

"Shadow over Spanish Politics," *Financial Times,* 2 October 1969.

Shaw, Russell. "The Secret of Opus Dei," *Columbia Magazine,* March 1982.

Shaw, Russell. "Judged by Opus Dei," *The Tablet,* 27 February 1988.

Sieve, Harold. "Uneasy Calm in Sunny Spain," *Daily Telegraph,* 21 August 1970.

Sisti, Leo. "Caso Sindona: L'ultima memoria," *L'Espresso,* 6 April 1986.

"Skeleton in the Technocrat's Closet," *Le Monde* (English edition), 29 July 1970.

Steigieder, Klaus. *Das Opus Dei—eine Innenansicht.* Cologne: Benziger, 1983.

Stork, Richard A. P. "Apologia pro Opere Dei," *Clergy Review,* February 1986.

Sullivan, Lorana. "Why Calvi Came to London," *Observer,* 22 August 1982.

Sullivan, Lorana. "Argentina: The P2 Connection," *Observer,* 19 September 1982.

Tapia, María del Carmen. "Good Housekeepers for Opus Dei . . . ," *National Catholic Reporter,* 27 May 1983.

Thavis, John. Series of articles in *NC News Service,* 6 November 1984.

Thierry, J.-J. *Opus Dei, A Close-Up.* New York: Cortland Press, 1975.

"La transformiación (juridica) del Opus Dei," *Vida Nueva,* 3 November 1979 (a study which never appeared—see p. 00).

Tuininga, M. et al. "L'Opus Dei: révélations sur un corps d'élite," *L'Actualité Religieuse dans le Monde,* 15 November 1983.

Tully, Shawn. "The Vatican's Finances," *Fortune,* 21 December 1987.

Vázquez de Prada, A. *El Fundador del Opus Dei.* Madrid: Ediciones Rialp, 1983.

Walsh, Michael J. "Being Fair to Opus Dei," *The Month,* August 1971.

Walsh, Michael J. "Spain on the Move," *The Month,* June 1972.

Walsh, Michael J. "Opus Dei's New Status," *The Tablet,* 16 October 1982.

West, William. "Opus Dei: 'Exploding the Myth' about Its Activities," *The Australian,* 1 December 1987.

Wilson, Bryan. "Sect Development," in Bryan Wilson (ed.), *Patterns of Sectarianism.* London: Heinemann, 1967.

Wilson, Bryan. *Religious Sects.* London: Weidenfeld and Nicolson, 1970.

Wilson, Bryan. "The Sociology of Sects," in Bryan Wilson (ed.). *Religion in Sociological Perspective.* Oxford: Oxford University Press, 1982.

Wilson-Smith, Peter. "Calvi: Questions Still to Be Answered," *The Times,* 3 August 1982.

Ynfante, Jesús. *La prodigiosa aventura del Opus Dei: Genesis y desarrollo de la santa mafia.* Paris: Ruedo Ibérico, 1970.

Zizola, Giancarlo. *La restaurazione di papa Wojtyla.* Rome and Bari: Laterza, 1985.

Index

Abancay, Peru, 1, 2
ABC, Madrid, 137
Adams, Michael, 153
Adveniat aid-agency, 132
Albareda Herrera, José María, 37, 38
Alessandrini, Frederico, 139
Allende, Salvador, 131, 132
Alphonso XIII, King of Spain:
  abdication, 1931, 28
Angustias Moreno, Maria: on prob-
  lems of leaving Opus Dei, 168
Annuario Pontificio, 84
Antoniutti, Mgr Ildebrando (later
  Cardinal), 62, 137
Apostolic Ladies (Damas
  Apostólicas) of the Sacred Heart
  of Jesus, 19, 24–25, 29, 32
Arrupe, Fr. Pedro, 195, 196
Asociación Católica Nacional de
  Propagandistas, 26–27
Augustine of Hippo, St., 116, 192
  On the City of God, 142
Australian, The, 6

Baggio, Cardinal Sebastiano, 73,
  74–75
Banco Ambrosiano, 156, 157, 158,
  187
Banco di Roma per la Svizzera,
  156, 157
Benelli, Cardinal, 129, 140

Bernal, Salvador, 34, 50, 190, 194n
  hagiographical approach to
    Escrivá, 12, 13, 23
  *Msgr Josemaría Escrivá de Balaguer,
    Profile of the Founder of Opus
    Dei,* 12, 153
  on Opus Dei, 23
Bidagor, Raimondo, 141
Boff, Leonardo
  on Church as "mother and
    teacher", 177–78, 181
Bolton, Sir George, 151
Botella, Francisco, 37
Britain
  Banco Urquijo Hispano-
    Americano, London, 158
  Opus Dei activities, 149-51, 153
  Opus Dei HQ, 149
  Trustees for RC Purposes Rgd
    (British Jesuits), 154
British Council, 150
Brosa, Jorge, 136
Burke, Cormac ,152
Byrne, Fr. Andrew, 121, 164

Callaghan, Fr. Brendan: alarm at
  Escrivá's identification with God
  the Father, 117
Calvi, Roberto, 156, 157
  death under Blackfriars Bridge,
    156, 157, 159

Calvi, Signora, 159

Calvo Serer, Sr., 134, 136–37
    La Dictadura de las Franquistas, 133

Camino, (The Way), 3, 4, 31, 33, 39, 41, 43, 135–36, 152, 191–92, 193
    Maxim 28 on marriage, 51
    Maxim 61 on lay disciples, 43–44
    Maxim 178 on cross without figure, 56n
    Maxim 339 on advice about books, 26, 123
    Maxim 345 on culture, 122
    Maxim 367 on beasts and men, 194
    Maxim 457 on the Father, 106
    Maxim 463 on charity, 108
    Maxim 525 on Catholic patriotism, 25
    Maxim 563 on guardian angels, 107
    Maxim 677 condemning honors, 14
    Maxim 800 on winning apostles, 161
    Maxim 836 on not praising enemy, 141–42
    Maxim 905 on patriotic fervor, 37
    Maxim 946 on women's role, 109–10
    Maxim 974 on dinner-table apostolate, 109
    Maxim 979 on not giving, 108
    maxims on childhood, 106
    maxims on discretion, 120–21
    maxims on manhood, 106
    maxims opposed to liberalism, 142
    maxims supporting establishment, 142
    pelagian attitude, 107, 184
    style of spirituality, 107–8

Canals, Salvador, 141
    Secular Institutes and the State of Perfection, 58

Carandell, Luis, 27

Carrero Blanco, Adm., 144

Casanova, José, 183

Casciaro, José María: Jesus and Politics: A Scriptural Study of Messianism, 178-79

Casciaro, Pedro, 35, 37

Catholic Action, 124–25

Catholic Pictorial, The, Liverpool, 164
    on Opus Dei induction for girls, 111

Central Intelligence Agency (CIA), 131, 132

Cesarini, Virginia Sforza, 51

Chile
    alleged Opus Dei political role, 131–32
    Chilean Institute for General Studies, 132
    Fatherland and Liberty terrorists, 132
    Fiducia sect, 174
    Opus Dei influence, 143
    Sociedad Nacional de Agricultura, 131

Cicognani, Cardinal Amleto, 70–71

Cicognani, Cardinal Gaetano, 41

Cistercian abbey of Pontigny: legal base for Mission de France, 71

Clergy Review, 127

Colombia
    Jesuit decline and rise of Opus Dei, 143
    Medellin Bishops Conference (CELAM), 1968, 125, 126

Comblin, José, 6

Commentarium pro Religiosis, 59–60

Comunión y Liberación, 174, 179

Conference of Latin American Bishops (CELAM), Medellin, Colombia, 1968, 124–25, 126

Congregation of the Oratory (Oratorians), 63–64

Consejo Superior de Investigaciones Cientificas (CSIC), 38

Arbor journal, 38, 133
Constitutions of Opus Dei, 1982,
    8–9, 52, 69–70, 87–89, 146
    Apostolic letter *Ut sit* at begin-
        ning, 84
    concern with letter of law, 102
    Declaratio of Sacred Congregation
        of Bishops, 85
    Non Ignoratis letter from founder,
        85–86
    Nuper Nuntiatum letter from
        Alvaro del Portillo, 86–87
    on admission of members, 90–91
    on care of new members, 92
    on clergy, 92–93
    on cultivation of natural virtues,
        96
    on dismissal from prelature, 92
    on duties of faithful, 89–90
    on duties of new members, 92
    on means of sanctification of
        members, 89
    on nature and purpose of
        prelature, 88–89
    on obedience, 95
    on oblate and supernumerary
        priests, 93, 97
    on Opus Dei's apostolate, 97–98
    on Opus Dei's government,
        98–100
    on political attitudes, 95
    on question of secrecy, 95–96
    on relation with local bishops,
        94, 101–2
    on religious education, 96–97
    on spiritual practices, 94–95
    on those not to be admitted,
        91–92
Corigliano, Giuseppe, 193–94
Costalunga, Mgr Marcelo, 75
Costello, John, 152
Coulter, Carol: *Are Religious Cults
    Dangerous?*, 174
Craven, Bishop, 65
Cronica, Opus Dei journal, 106,

    112, 115n, 116, 117, 126–27,
        128, 198
    on proselytism, 161
    on spirit of Opus Dei, 171–72

Dadaglio, Mgr Luigi, 137
Daily Mail, 121, 164
Dawliffe Educational Foundation,
    150
Dawliffe Hall, 150
Tamezin club, 163
Debate, El, 26–27
Dell'Acqua, Cardinal, 14
Divine Light Mission, 10
Dominic, St., 11
Dominicans, 32, 165, 182
    Angelicum University, 63
Duncan, Ken, 1, 2

Economist, The, 4
Eijoy Garay, Mgr, Bishop of
    Madrid, 41, 42
    criticism of Opus Dei, 40–41
Escrivá de Balaguer, Carmen, 15,
    30, 32
Escrivá de Balaguer, Don José, 15,
    16
    death of, 1929, 16–17
Escrivá de Balaguer, Josemaría, 3,
    10–11, 48, 75, 78, 81, 84, 169,
    170
    Abadesa de las Huelgas, La, 191
    attitude to women in Opus Dei,
        109–10
    biographies, 12–13
    Carlism attractive to, 193
    Consideraciones espirituales, 30–31,
        32
    decorations, 14
    encourages "family" life in Opus
        Dei, 55
    Es Cristo que pasa, 192
    family, 14, 15
    fondness for England, 65–66
    Forge, The, 153, 189–90

foundation of Opus Dei, 13, 19,
  23-24, 27, 28
honors, 190–91
identification with God the
  Father, 117–18, 172
inscription on tomb, 197
keeps old-fashioned religious distinctions, 57–58
life and career: childhood, 15;
  religious education, 16–17;
  ordained priest, 1925, 17; law
  studies, 16; priestly advancement, 17-18; teaches law, 18,
  19; chaplain to Apostolic
  Ladies, 19; design for Opus
  Dei, 22–24, 27–28, 30;
  becomes chaplain to
  Augustinian nuns, 1934, 29;
  appointed to living, 29; founds
  DYA Academy, 30; sets up
  first residence, 30; founds
  women's section of Opus Dei,
  32–33; in hiding during
  Spanish Civil War, 35–36;
  escapes from Spain to France,
  36; returns to Franco Spain,
  1939, 36–37, 192–93; adopts
  Franco's conservative ideology,
  37; gets priests for Opus Dei,
  37, 43-45; prepares for international expansion of Opus Dei,
  45; visits Rome, 1945, 47;
  appointed "domestic prelate"
  to pope, 50; visits Latin
  America, 1970s, 69; unhappy
  with Opus Dei as secular institute, 69–70; desire for Opus
  Dei to be "prelatura nullius",
  71; death, 1975, 72; successor's
  tribute to, 72–73
luxurious style of living, 193–94
magnetism, 189
Maxims, see Camino
Non Ignoratis letter, 69–70, 85, 86
on confession, 114-15, 118–19

opposed to reform of standard
  mass, 68–69
opposed to Second Vatican
  Council, 67–68, 128
opposed to Liberation Theology,
  69
pilgrimage to Avila, 1935, 31
post-Civil War work for school
  of journalism, 27
practice of flagellation, 30, 111–12
projected image, 190
promises salvation to members,
  184
receives title of Marques of
  Peralta, 1968, 14
remoteness, 195–96
route to apotheosis, 189–99
suspicion of non-OD
  churchmen, 115-16
vanity, 195
veneration of houses and objects
  connected with, 196–97
Via Crucis, 192
vulgarity, 194
Escrivá de Balaguer, Santiago, 14, 29
Europa Press, 138, 139, 141

Felzmann, Vladimir, 10, 21, 68,
  109, 113, 115, 118, 128
  on founder of Opus Dei, 10
  on ossification of Opus Dei, 23
Foley, Archbishop John, 141
Forbarth, Peter: quotes Escrivá,
  62–63, 70, 119, 144
Forte, Lord, 151
Four Courts Press, 153, 184, 192
Francis, St., 11
Francis Xavier, St., 186
Franciscans, 23, 32, 82, 182
Franco, Gen. Francisco, 36, 37, 38,
  106, 124, 133, 136, 137, 143,
  144, 193
Frei, Pres. Eduardo, of Chile, 131
Fuentes, Antonio: Guide to the Bible,
  184-85

Galarraga, Juan Antonio, 65, 149
Gilroy, Cardinal, 61
Greater London Council, 150
Grimshaw, Joseph, Archbishop of
    Birmingham, 65
Grisez, Germain, 124
Guerra Campos, Mgr, 138, 140
Gutierrez, Anastasio, 141
Gutierrez, Fr. Gustavo, 125

Hanson, Prof. Eric, 119
Hebblethwaite, Peter, 3
Henry VIII, 11
Hernández y Garnica, José María, 44
Herranz Julián, 70
    "Opus Dei and the Activity of Its
    Members", 14–45, 146
Höffner, Cardinal, 132
Hofmann, Paul, 137
Horrigan, John, 153
Hughes, Peter, 125, 126
Hume, Cardinal: "Guidelines for
    Opus Dei within the Diocese of
    Westminster", 165–66

Ibáñez Langlois, José Miguel:
    "Thirty Years as a Critic", 144
Ibáñez Martin, José, 37, 38, 39, 134
Iglesia-Mundo magazine, 135, 139
Ignatius, Loyola, St., 4, 11, 88
Institución Libre de Enseñanza, 25
Institute for the Works of Religion
    (Vatican Bank), 155–56
    connections with Banco
        Ambrosiano, 156, 157
    losses through Sindona banks'
        collapse, 1974, 156
Ireland
    Opus Dei activities, 151–53
    Opus Dei schools, 152
Irish Academic Press, 153
Irish University Press, 153

Jesuits, see Society of Jesus
Jiménez Vargas, Juan, 24

John Chrysostom, 192
John XXIII, Pope, 67, 71
    Mater et Magistra letter, 177
John Paul II, Pope, 6–7, 72, 75,
    126, 129, 157, 176
    Laborem Exercens letter, 176
    "Social concerns of the Church"
        letter, 199
    sympathy with Opus Dei, 129,
        179
    Ut sit letter, 84–85
Joseph Calasanctius, St., 16
Juan, Don, 136
Junta para Ampliación de Estudios e
    Investigaciones, 25–26

Kamm, Henry, 119, 122
Kennedy, David, 156
Kennedy, Fr. 7
Kianda School, Nairobi 61
Kostka, Stanislaus 165
Krishna Consciousness, 10
Küng, Hans, 6

Lakefield catering college,
    Hempstead, 164
Lamet, Pedro Miguel, 6, 129
Larrain Crusat company: contribu-
    tions to Opus Dei, 155
Larraona, Cardinal, 14
Latin America
    Catholic Church's decline, 174
    Catholic sects, 174–75
    Protestant sects, 174, 175
    Tradición, Familia y Propriedad,
        175
    See also Liberation Theology
Lernoux, Penny: on Opus Dei's
    political activity in Chile, 131–32
Liberation Theology, 69, 124–25,
    126, 176
Lismullin Scientific Trust, 152
Lopez Bravo, Gregorio, 135, 148
López Rodó, Laureano, 134, 135,
    136

Magill magazine, 152

Marcinkus, Archbishop Paul, 156

Mateo-Seco, Lucas F., 21, 49–50, 192

    "The Works of Mgr Escrivá de Balaguer . . .", 191

Matesa, *see* Spain

Mercurio, El, Santiago, 144

Moncada, Alberto, 135

Month, The, 3, 153

    "Being Fair to Opus Dei", 4, 5

Mother Jones journal, 132

Mulcahy, Richard, 152

Muzquiz, José Luis, 44

Navarra University, Pamplona, 61–63, 83–84, 148

    banned books, 123

    Mons. Josemaría Escrivá de Balaguer y El Opus Dei, 49–50, 191

    Navarra Bible, 192

Navarro Rubio, Mariano, 135, 136, 148

Navarro-Valls, Joaquin, 141

Nelson, Geoffrey: *Cults, New Religions and Religious Creativity*, 189

Netherhall Educational Association, 149, 167

    property owned by, 150–51, 167

Netherhall House, Hempstead, 64, 68, 113, 151

    anti-promiscuity precautions, 110

    Trust, 151

New Blackfriars journal, 153

New York Times, 122, 137

Newman, Dr. Jeremiah, 153

Nixon, Richard M., 132

Noticias Aliadas, 131

Nueva Diario, Madrid, 138

Observer, 146

Ongania, Gen. Juan Carlos, 132

Onteiro, Marchioness of, 32

Opus Dei, 3–5

    abortive plan to subsidize Vatican, 1970s, 156–57

    allied with dominant classes, 176–77

    apostolates of St. Gabriel, St. Michael, and St. Raphael, 162

    attempt to become "prelatura nullius", 1962, 71

    belief in own perfection, 172

    bishops belonging to, 6

    business activities, 146–59

    characteristics, 9–10, 11, 183, 185

    "circles" of fraternal correction, 113–14, 118

    classes of members, 57–58

    collection of profits from members' professions, 108–9

    confidence of members in Opus Dei's rightness, 126–28

    "confidences" between members and superiors, 112–13, 114, 116–17

    conflict with seminary of Logroño, 1985, 78, 121

    Constitutions of 1950, 5, 8, 50–51, 52–56, 57–58, 60, 105, 107–8, 110–11, 113, 119–20, 121, 122, 126, 136, 145, 154

    Constitutions of Opus Dei, 1982, *see separate entry*

    controlled education in, 121-23

    correct name: "The Priestly Society of the Holy Cross and Opus Dei", 55

    documents, 42

    dress, 110

    DYA Academy, 30, 31, 39

    emphasis on control of media, 141

    founds University of Navarra, 1952 61, 62–63

    governance of women's section, 54, 54n

    hostility to, early 1940s, 39–41

ideal of "family" life, 55
ideology of submission, 118–19
independence of local bishops, 83
infiltration of Spanish universities,
     39
journalistic criticism, 3–4
keeps old form of mass, 68–69
lack of histories of, 21
opposed to Liberation Theology,
     69, 124–25
opposition in Catholic Church
     to, 128–29
"Opus Dei Fifty Years On", 21
ossification after founder's death,
     23
penitential practices, 110–12, 118
political activities, 131–45
power, 6–7
Praxis (book), 105
problems consequent upon leav-
     ing, 168–71
problems of role as "secular insti-
     tute" 69–70
progress: origins in Spain, 3, 13,
     18, 22–23, 28; founder's design
     for, 22–23, 24–25, 30; first res-
     idence, 30, 31; women's sec-
     tion formed, 1930, 32–33;
     organization in 1930s, 31,
     32–33, 34; effect of Spanish
     Civil War on, 35, 37; expan-
     sion post-1938, 37, 39;
     approved as lay "pious union",
     1941, 41-42; obtains own
     priests, 37, 43–45; founds
     Sacerdotal Society of the Holy
     Cross to give title to priests,
     45–46; gains spiritual privileges
     from Vatican, 1945, 48;
     becomes secular institute,
     1947, 49–50, 52, 58–59;
     moves HQ to Rome, 1947,
     51; international expansion,
     1945, 45–51; opened to mar-
ried people, 1947, 51–52; num-
     bers by 1950, 52; full members
     as monks and nuns, 1950,
     55–56; spiritual life, 1950, 56;
     spread to Africa, Peru, and
     Australia, 60–61; takes Roman
     house from Oratorians, 1970s,
     63–64; establishes university
     halls of residence in England,
     64-65; congratulated by Pope
     John Paul II on fiftieth anniver-
     sary, 1978, 72; becomes person-
     al prelature, 1983, 72–76, 77,
     78–79; numbers of priests and
     lay members by 1985, 84
proselytism, *see* Proselytism by
     Opus Dei
"Protestantification", 183–84
question of position as sect or
     cult of Catholic Church,
     173–74, 180–83
question of relations with other
     Catholics, 77–79
relation with local bishops re
     Constitutions, 60
riches, 155
secrecy concerning, 3, 7–8, 59,
     60, 119–21
signs of rank in, 50–51
size, 3, 7, 47, 73
support in Catholic Church,
     127–28
theological traditionalism, 124
"Third Order", 78
weekly confession within order,
     114-15, 116, 118–19
women's role, 109–10
Order of Preachers, *see* Dominicans
Orlandis, José, 47
Osservatore Romano, L', 74, 75, 153
Ottoviani, Cardinal, 62
Oxford, 65
Palazzini, Archbishop (later
     Cardinal), 139, 141

Pannikar, Raimundo, 23–24, 25, 38, 47, 133, 181
on Opus Dei, 24, 25, 172–73
on problems of leaving Opus Dei, 169–70
Park Industrial and Provident Society, 152
Passionists, 82, 112
Pastor, Louis von, 13
Paul VI, Pope, 64, 67, 71–77 *passim*, 81, 84, 123, 129, 138, 156, 170
Ecclesiae Sanctae, 76
Pelagius, 107
Peralta, Tomás de, 15
Peru
Liberation Theology and Opus Dei opposition, 124, 125
Opus Dei influence, 1–2
Prelature of Yauyos, 61
Shining Path terrorists, 2
Sodalitium Vitae sect, 174
Philip Neri, St., 63
Piarists, 16
Pinochet, Gen., 131, 144
Pironio, Cardinal, 128–29
Pius IX, Pope: *Syllabus of Errors, 1864,* 25
Pius XII, Pope, 37, 52, 155
Portillo, Mgr Alvaro del, 21, 30, 44, 45, 47, 48, 49, 74, 75, 110, 119, 141
becomes head of Opus Dei, 1975, 72–73
enquiries to Vatican re revealing Constitution of Opus Dei, 58–59, 60
homily on death of Escrivá, 72
insignia as head of Prelature, 50
Nuper Nuntiatum letter, 86-87
sees popes on making Opus Dei "personal prelature", 72–73
Poveda, Don Pedro, 27–28
Primo de Rivera, Gen., 27, 28

Proselytism by Opus Dei
dealing with parents, 163–66
Easter pilgrimage to Rome as reward, 164
essence, 183
"fishing" in Catholic schools, 162–63
friendship as means of, 162, 172
salvation equated with Opus Dei membership, 172, 184
seeking recruits, 162
youth clubs used for, 163–64

Quechua Indians, Peru, 2

Ratzinger, Cardinal Joseph, 124, 126
Religious sects, 180
Rialp, Opus Dei publishing house, 12, 36
Riberi, Mgr Antonio, 137
Richards, Michael, 64, 65, 149, 151–52, 171
Roche, Dr. John, 5, 108, 152, 153, 166, 171, 172, 199
Rodriguez, Pedro: *Particular Churches and Personal Prelatures,* 77
Rodriguez, Pedro et al. (eds.): *Mons Josemaría Escrivá de Balaguer y el Opus Dei,* 49, 191
Roman Catholic Church
canonization, 11
"clerks regular", 9
Commission on Social Communication, 141
Congregation for Religious and Secular Institutes, 72, 128–29, 170
Congregation for the Causes of Saint, 6, 11, 198
Congregation for the Doctrine of the Faith, 124
friars, 9
incardination system, 82

Index Librorum Prohibitorum, 123
"lay" and "clerical" distinction,
33, 55
Pontifical Academy of Theology,
190
Pontifical Commission for the
Authentic Interpretation of
Canon Law, 191
Provida Mater Ecclesia on secular
institutes, 48–49, 50
religious communities, 9–10
religious orders, 181–82
Sacred Congregation for Bishops,
6, 72, 73, 74, 75, 76, 85
Sacred Congregation for
Religious, 46, 49, 50, 53, 54,
59, 60
Sacred Congregation for the
Clergy, 139, 140, 141
Sacred Congregation of Rites, 34
Sacred Congregation of
Seminaries and Universities,
191
Second Vatican Council, see sepa-
rate entry
Synod of Bishops, 1987, 179
Vatican Bank, see Institute for the
Works of Religion
Vatican's shortage of funds,
1970s, 156–57
Ruiz Jimenez, Joaquin, 134
Ruiz-Mateos, José María, 148–49,
155, 157–58
Opus Dei disowns, 1986, 157-58
Rumasa, see Ruiz-Mateos

Sacerdotal Society of the Holy
Cross, 55, 87, 115, 121, 149,
151, 153
properties in England, 149–50
relation with Opus Dei, 45–46
size, 1946, 47
Sanchez Bella, Fr., 61
Sanchez Ruiz, Fr., 40

Scepter Publishers, Ltd., 12, 152–53
Scepter Bulletin, 153
Second Vatican Council (Vatican
II), 1962-65, 67, 71, 185
changes to standard mass, 68
on personal prelatures, 75–76
Presbyterorum Ordinis, 84, 121–22,
reforms, 67, 124, 125
Segura, Cardinal Pedro, 41
Shaw, Russell, 7, 8, 140, 183
Sindona, Michele, 156
collapse of banks, 156
Smith, Prof. Brian: The Church and
Politics in Chile, 131
Sobrino, John, 174
Society of Jesus, 3, 4, 26, 28, 41,
62, 70, 71, 82, 112, 165, 182,
185
Constitutions, 88
expelled from Spain, 1932, 28
Gregorian University, 63
Razón y Fe journal, 25
Spanish universities, 62
Sodalities of Our Lady, 26, 39, 40
Soldevila, Cardinal, 17–18
Spain
anti-clericalism under Republic,
28
Asamblea Conjunta of bishops,
1971, 137–38, 139, 140, 142,
143
anti-Franco stance, 137
Opus Dei opposition to, 137,
142–44
Vatican document re, 138-40,
141
Banco de Crédito Industrial, 147
Banco Español de Credito, 136
Banco Popular, 135, 136, 157
becomes republic, 1931, 28
Carlism, 193
Cifra news agency, 139
Civil War, 1936-39, 31, 35–36
priests killed, 35

Concordat with Vatican, 137
Conference of Spanish Bishops, 138
Efe news agency, 139
ESFINA finance company, 135
Falange, 146–47, 193
Freemasonry, 40
Institute of Administrative Studies, 134
Matesa scandal, 1969, 147–48, 157
Opus Dei implicated, 148
spread of agnosticism, 26
spread of liberalism, 25–26
Stork, Rev. Richard: "Apologia pro Opere Dei", 127–28
Strathmore College, Nairobi, 61
Studi Cattolici, 144–45
Sunday Times, The, 3

Tapia, María del Carmen, 8, 53, 67, 113, 116, 118, 120, 126, 128, 187, 194
on problems with leaving Opus Dei, 168–69, 171
on Venezuelan contributions to Vatican Bank, 155
Tara Trust, 152
Tarancón, Cardinal Enrique y, 139, 140
Telva magazine, 135
Teresians, 28
Thavis, John, 193
Thomas, Fr. Rolf, 182
Thomas Aquinas, St., 97, 122, 165, 192
Thomas More, St., 11, 12, 128
Time, 144
Times, 165–66
Times Literary Supplement, The: "The Power of the Party: Opus Dei in Spain", 4
Timoney, Seamus, 150
arms sales to Argentina, 150

Opus Dei support, 150
Torreciudad: shrine of Virgin Mary, 196
Torres, Fr. Camilo, 132, 143
Trust House Forte, 151

Ullastres, Alberto, 134, 135
Unification Church (Moonies), 10, 173
University Hostels, Ltd., Dublin, 152

Valls Taberner, Luis, 136, 157
Vargas, Archbishop, 126
Vatican II, see Second Vatican Congress
Vázquez de Prada, Andrés, 17, 18, 27, 28, 29, 31, 34, 35, 36, 39, 40, 43, 45, 51, 53, 60, 62, 64, 65, 69, 190, 194n
El Fundador del Opus Dei, 12
hagiographical approach to life of Escrivá, 12–13, 21–22
Vida Nueva, 6
banned article: "The Transformation of Opus Dei", 74
Videla, Gen. Jorge, 150
Vila Reyes, Juan, 147–48
Villar Palasi, Sr., 134, 147–48
Villot, Cardinal, 140
Vincentians, 22

Warrane College, NSW University, 61
Weber, Max, 183
Wheeler, Mgr Gordon, 65
Wiederkehr, Arthur, 157
Wilson, Dr. Bryan, 180, 182
Wright, Cardinal John, 139, 140
Zorzano Ledesma, Isidoro, 24
biography: God's Engineer, 34
relations with Escrivá, 34
Zulueta, Sir Philip de 151